The Pork Industry:

PROBLEMS AND PROGRESS

The Pork Industry:

PROBLEMS AND PROGRESS

David G. Topel, EDITOR

IOWA STATE UNIVERSITY PRESS, AMES, IOWA

The illustration on the title page, "The Pig and the Duck," is by Danish artist J. T. Lundbye, Sjaelland, Denmark, *ca.* 1843. The original is in the Royal Danish Copper-Plate Collection, Copenhagen. The reproduction was furnished by J. Wismer-Pedersen.

© 1968 The Iowa State University Press
Ames, Iowa, U.S.A. All rights reserved

Composed and printed by
The Iowa State University Press

First edition, 1968

Standard Book Number: 8138-0707-7
Library of Congress Catalog Card Number: 68-9693

Preface

THIS TEXT has been assembled from the proceedings of a national conference which discussed the progress and future of the pork industry with specific reference to pork quality characteristics. Scientists and other leaders of the pork industry reviewed the latest information in several marketing and scientific disciplines.

Grateful acknowledgement is extended to the planning committee consisting of Bernard Ebbing, Frank Crabb, George Ebert, J. Russell Ives, A. L. Erickson, R. R. Konicek, Harold Minderman, L. N. Hazel, R. E. Rust, V. C. Speer, E. J. Stevermer, and Jack Thomas.

Appreciation is directed to the Marketing Division, Iowa State Department of Agriculture, the Iowa Development Commission, and the Center for Agricultural and Economic Development, Iowa State University, for special grants to support this conference. Appreciation for supplemental support is also expressed to the Iowa Farm Bureau and the Iowa Swine Producers Association.

Special thanks are due to the many graduate students and staff members of the Animal Science Department who assisted with the conference and to the Short Course Office staff for their cooperation and interest in planning the conference.

DAVID G. TOPEL
Conference Chairman

Contributors

B. J. AMBROSE, Purchasing Manager, Restaurant and Inn Division, Stouffer Foods Corporation.

FLOYD ANDRE, Dean of Agriculture, Iowa State University.

RICHARD H. BEVIER, Meat Merchandising Manager, Jewel Tea Company.

E. J. BICKNELL, Associate Professor of Veterinary Diagnostic Laboratory, Iowa State University.

ROBERT W. BRAY, Assistant Dean and Director, College of Agriculture, University of Wisconsin.

B. C. BREIDENSTEIN, Manager, Fresh Meat Merchandising, Wilson and Company.

HAROLD F. BREIMYER, Professor of Agricultural Economics, University of Missouri.

E. J. BRISKEY, Professor of Meat and Animal Science, University of Wisconsin.

G. M. BROWNING, Regional Director, North Central Agricultural Experiment Station Directors.

LAUREN L. CHRISTIAN, Associate Professor of Animal Science, Iowa State University.

FRANK CRABB, General Manager, Farmbest.

HAROLD W. DAVEY, Professor, Department of Economics, Iowa State University.

HERRELL DEGRAFF, President, American Meat Institute.

BERNARD EBBING, Director of Hog Procurement, Rath Packing Company.

F. W. H. ELSLEY, Rowett Research Institute, Bucksburn, Aberdeen, Scotland.

A. L. ERICKSON, Vice-President, Oscar Mayer and Company.

FRANK FRAZIER, Executive Vice-President, National Broiler Council.

JOHN R. HARVEY, Associate Editor, *Successful Farming*.

V. W. HAYS, Assistant Director, Agricultural Experiment Station, Iowa State University.

L. N. HAZEL, Professor of Animal Science, Iowa State University.

J. B. HERRICK, Professor, Veterinary Medicine Extension, Iowa State University.

LEE HOUSEWRIGHT, Vice-President, Meat Products Division, Hormel and Company.

PER JONSSON, National Institute of Animal Science, Copenhagen.

M. D. JUDGE, Associate Professor of Animal Science, Purdue University.

R. R. KONICEK, Research Director, Iowa Development Commission.

EARL L. LASLEY, Geneticist, Farmers Hybrid.

JOHN F. LASLEY, Professor of Animal Science, University of Missouri.

R. A. MERKEL, Professor, Department of Animal Science, Michigan State University.

IRVIN T. OMTVEDT, Associate Professor of Animal Science, Oklahoma State University.

ARNOLD A. PAULSEN, Professor of Agricultural Economics, Iowa State University.

PAUL R. ROBBINS, Associate Professor of Agricultural Economics, Purdue University.

ROBERT E. RUST, Associate Professor of Animal Science, Iowa State University.

J. MARVIN SKADBERG, Assistant Professor of Agricultural Economics, Iowa State University.

VAUGHN C. SPEER, Professor of Animal Science, Iowa State University.

JIM STEVENSON, Director of Hog Procurement, Armour Food Division.

W. P. SWITZER, Director of Swine Research, Veterinary Medical Research Institute, Iowa State University.

WARREN TAUBER, Assistant to Vice-President of Marketing, Union Carbide Food Products Division.

DAVID G. TOPEL, Associate Professor of Animal Science, Iowa State University.

DIK TWEDT, Market Research Director, Oscar Mayer and Company.

GIL VANDER KOLK, Director of Meat Operations, Spartan Stores.

H. D. WALLACE, Professor of Animal Science, University of Florida.

M. D. WHITEKER, Associate Professor of Animal Science, University of Kentucky.

J. WISMER-PEDERSEN, Chairman, Meat Research Laboratory, The Royal Veterinary and Agricultural College, Copenhagen.

Contents

ix

Introduction: At the Crossroad

HERRELL DEGRAFF

I DO NOT KNOW whether pork is at a crossroad and must turn right or left or whether it is on a threshold before an open door and need only move into its own very promising future. I prefer the latter view. A crossroad implies a choice, and there may be no choice. An open door implies an opportunity—and I believe the opportunity is a fact. The door is open, and I believe the swine and pork industry can step through it with confidence, because on the other side of the door are potentials of growth and success that can be the romance of the next 20 years in our animal agriculture, as cattle and beef have been the last 20 years. It is this potential that stands before this conference on The Future of Pork. The words and ideas that are expressed here may chart the course that will be followed by the industry.

Pork cuts are widely regarded as having lost favor among American consumers. Even an Assistant Secretary of Agriculture stated not long ago that the loss of demand for pork has been about 2 percent per person per year for several decades. I think this figure is much overstated, but this kind of thinking has done much to create a mental block in the swine and pork industry. An important study of consumer attitudes toward pork now being completed at Iowa State University indicates that pork is consumed by most families and that consumers in the aggregate hold no fundamental aversion to pork. A major finding states that "pork does not appear to face insurmountable obstacles in terms of improving consumer demand."

Hog production is said to require an undue total of skilled labor that is increasingly difficult to obtain. Without doubt this is true on many farms, but it is less true with respect to a new generation of highly competent, specialized swine producers.

Swine production is said to be handicapped by a complex of disease problems that seriously impedes expansion of the industry. Admittedly this is true, but far more so for some producers than for others.

Hog production frequently is said to lag behind other types of live-stock production in the efficiency with which feed is converted into meat. Again, the statement is true, in degree.

But these problems are also challenges. The swine industry has before it more potential for improvement than any other significant enterprise in the total of American agriculture. It is the several aspects of this potential and the means of realizing them that create the "open door," the opportunity, that lies before the pork industry. It is turning this potential into reality that in one way or another challenges each of us who are concerned with the problem.

There is a *new* swine industry in the future of American agriculture. It is based on at least three factors relating to production and probably one relating to consumption.

PRODUCTION FACTORS

The first production factor has to do with basic changes taking place in Midwest agriculture. These are complex and interrelated but can be summarized under the heading "the disappearance of the diversified general midwestern farm." The causes are primarily the adoption of new agronomic and mechanical technology. Hybrid seed corn and other improved seed stock; the rapidly expanded use of commercial fertilizers, herbicides, and pesticides; new high-speed power equipment—all have greatly expanded crop yield per acre and per man and have increased the crop acreage one man or one family can handle. Such factors have resulted in fewer farms, larger farms, and increased specialization in production. The process can be described as the rise of capital-intensive technology that not only encourages specialization but actually forces it. Many farmers in the Midwest have responded by becoming specialized producers of corn and beans. Others, fortunately, have become specialized producers of livestock.

When the 1964 Census of Agriculture appeared, many of us were much disturbed at the sharp drop in the number of farmers who were raising hogs. In Iowa, for example, the number of farms on which hogs were produced declined in the five years from 1959 to 1964 by 21 percent. Over 28,000 farms went out of the hog business in just five years, and there were nearly 34,000 farms on which hogs were either eliminated or reduced in numbers. Over 2.6 million hogs that were raised on these farms in 1959 were *not* raised in 1964. But there is another side to the story. Another 5,600 farms got deeper into the swine business and in 1964 raised 3.3 million more hogs than in 1959. In other words, swine production in Iowa actually increased in this five-year period, but the business rapidly is concentrating in sharply fewer producing units.

These fewer, larger, more specialized swine growers are a new and progressive breed. They are not in production at one time and out at another, depending on their reading of the economic winds. To them swine production is an ongoing business. They may have much money invested in specialized facilities or relatively little. This is still a debated question, with few definitive answers. But they are in the hog business with the intention of staying and the expectation of winning, and they will if their management is right and if some other conditions are met.

The second production factor is the existing technological vacuum in hog production. We noted earlier a belief that the swine industry has great potentials for improvement. These are basically in three areas: (1) breeding efficiency, (2) feed conversion efficiency, and (3) disease control. There are marked differences today on these points between the typical results obtained by the rank and file of producers and the experimental—and also practical—controlled results of leading producers who are out on the growth point of more effective production methods.

This is to say that a significant part of what I have called the technological potential has been realized. Some producers wean more pigs per litter than others; some produce a unit of market hogs with significantly less feed than others; some have been notably more successful in reducing the incidence of swine disease.

But if some of what we called the "potential" is now an achieved fact, it is only a part, and very probably a modest part, of what still can be achieved. It was technological breakthroughs in disease control, in nutrition, and in genetics—and probably in that order—that made possible today's broiler and turkey industries. And then, because there was no aggressively organized, existing poultry industry to pick up and apply the new technological potentials, an integrating industry—in general, the feed manufacturer—moved into the vacuum. This does not have to be true in the swine business. This question rests with the new forward-looking specialized hog raiser. A technological vacuum as great as that which stands before the swine industry will not remain long unfilled, and this is the challenge that faces the swine industry in a large degree.

A third production factor was called to my attention by the recently issued 1966 Summary of Farm Business Records from the University of Illinois. It is reported in this summary that average returns from hog production on Illinois farms have been sharply above break-even returns throughout the last decade. The editors of this summary state: "The hog enterprise has been a very profitable business for the above-average group of hog producers, and a moderately profitable business for average producers." Their analysis of hog enterprise records of the past ten years "indicate there is a reservation profit that exists after all costs of production are paid before managers are willing to enter or continue hog production. Evidently there is a human preference factor that causes hog production to expand less than economic conditions warrant, creating a continuing sizable margin of profit above feed and other costs."

Having studied this summary, I conclude that the degree of comparative profit between hog production and alternative enterprises—as evidenced over a decade of these farm business records—is sufficient to attract increased attention and to cause expansion among the new type of specialized hog producer. Moreover, it is appropriate to note that this so-called "reservation profit" should be added to the unrealized technological potential previously discussed to get the full measure of the circumstances that may attract new producers and new capital into hog production—including possible integrators.

CONSUMER DEMAND

Another area worthy of extended discussion would deal with consumer demand for pork. The consumer demand picture is by no means as dark as the tones in which it is frequently painted. Bacon and spareribs are extremely popular meats. The ham, like the turkey, is an inconvenient unit of purchase for most families; but increasingly the ham, again like the turkey, is being fabricated into various forms, shapes, and sizes that contribute much to better merchandising. Many sausage products in which pork is the major ingredient readily lend themselves to ease of serving and are highly popular in many households.

I am not at all discouraged, rather I am optimistic about the consumer market for pork. I doubt if there is any valid reason why it cannot be moved into consumer markets at something in the magnitude of 60 to 65 pounds per person per year at prices that will maintain a healthy swine industry even with the production techniques now dominant. And as somewhat more can be realized of the swine industry's great potential for production efficiency, the opportunity for market building can be proportionately greater.

So I return to the analogy of an "open door." It is a reality. The swine industry need only step through—aided and indeed carried forward by all who can convert the clearly seen potentials into the actuality of a vigorous, progressive swine and pork business that can and will capture and hold a stronger place in the consumer market.

PART ONE

Marketing and Consumer Acceptance

General Acceptance of Pork

DIK TWEDT

IT IS DIFFICULT to understand why the pork industry—the producer *and* the packer *and* the retailer—pays such small heed to the first law of marketing, which is: "Make what people want to buy; don't try to sell what you happen to make." There have been notable exceptions to this generalization, but the fact that these are *exceptions* to the general rule suggests that there are real reasons why the U.S. per capita consumption of pork has suffered a fairly steady decline since 1879—the earliest year for which I could find reliable consumption estimates. Bannet and Paire's study "Changes in the American National Diet, 1879-1959," published by Stanford University in 1961, estimates that in 1879, per capita pork consumption was about 73 lbs. Compare that figure with the 58 lbs. estimated by the USDA for 1966. With the exception of the drought years of 1935-36, *the 1966 per capita consumption of pork was the lowest in 88 years,* in spite of the fact that the per capita consumption of all meats (at 170 lbs.) was the second highest in our nation's history! It is clear that Americans are eating *more meat* but *less pork.*

What are some of the possible explanations for this unsettling change? It seems to me that the four major areas to which we should direct our attention for a better understanding of the problem are: (1) proliferation of alternatives, (2) increased protein competition, (3) changes in consumer attitude toward obesity, and (4) the image of pork.

PROLIFERATION OF ALTERNATIVES

A century ago shopping for food was different by several orders of magnitude than it is today. A "general store" of that era typically stocked fewer than 60 different products for all consumer needs, including food. It should be remembered, though, that in this early day more than half the consumer dollar was spent for food. In the general store there were few branded items; most of the store's business was in unbranded bulk goods, sold directly from the barrels and boxes in which they were packed by the manufacturers.

The modern supermarket actually supplies a far smaller part of the customer's total needs than did the old general store, but the proliferation of alternatives has been, and continues to be, staggering. In a special presentation on "New Items" made to the Grocery Manufacturers Association last June, Franklin Graf, executive vice-president of the A. C. Nielsen Company, reported that a sampling of 38 chain and supermarket warehouses resulted in a total count of more than 35,000 separately coded sizes, brands, flavors, and types of items. And of this total of 35,000 active items, nearly 6,000 were carried by an average store. During a 12-month period, 7,300 new items were added and 5,500 were discontinued—a net gain of 1,800 items.

Another way of looking at the proliferation of consumer alternatives is to consider the shopping times required for a complete review of all possible purchases. A century ago a customer shopping the entire store, taking five seconds to decide whether or not to buy each available product, would be finished in five minutes. But if she made purchasing decisions at the same rate in today's supermarket, she would not quite get through the task if she were in the store from the time it opened until it closed!

The development of new products to satisfy growing consumer wants is a reflection of the exponential curve of material progress. We live in a world of explosive change. Since the youngest person among you was born, more new products and brands have entered the marketplace than had been offered between the time he or she was born and the birth of Christ. In the words of Loren Eisley, scientist and poet, "Never before has it been literally possible to have been born in one age and die in another."

It is clear that proliferation of food alternatives has been part of the answer for the relative decline in pork consumption. It is equally clear that proliferation of alternatives is not the *entire answer,* since this same time span resulted in doubling the per capita consumption of such commodities as beef and sugar (and sugar has surely been beset with increased competition from noncaloric sweeteners) and more than tripling the per capita consumption of other commodities such as poultry and cheese.

INCREASED PROTEIN COMPETITION

Among red meats, pork's competition with beef has intensified since 1953—the first "crossover year" in which consumers actually ate more beef than pork. Since then, the crossover lines for pork and beef have continued to diverge, with USDA estimates for 1966 showing 79 percent more beef consumed per person than pork.

It is no news that poultry has made astonishing gains as an animal protein source. In absolute pounds consumed by civilians during the last decade, for example, poultry increased 85 percent; breaded shrimp by 120 percent; fish sticks by 53 percent; beef by 47 percent; but pork actually showed a *3 percent loss* during this period when the U.S. population had increased by 19 percent. In its most recent biennial review of 10-year growth patterns in the food industry, *Food Processing & Marketing Magazine* showed substantial increases in 39 of 42 categories of food products, topped by an 822 percent growth in frozen potato products and a 679 percent growth in noncaloric sweeteners (with cane and beet sugar also up by 20 percent). During the past decade, only three of the 42 categories lost ground—pork, with a 3 percent loss, butter (down 11 percent), and citrus fruit used fresh (down 13 percent).

But the threat to pork from increased competition from alternative protein sources is clearly not limited to other animal proteins such as beef and poultry. Within the past two years a technological breakthrough has been achieved in isolated spun soy protein products, and there is every indication that these will play an increasingly important role in the consumer diet within the very near future. With a source of protein that is roughly half the cost of animal protein, and with the ability to provide a very wide range of texture, flavor, and appearance, it seems reasonable to suppose that vegetable proteins will make further inroads into the market for pork products. An interesting recent development is a patented process which combines soy protein with animal protein to yield an entirely new kind of product.

CHANGES IN CONSUMER ATTITUDE TOWARD OBESITY

Almost since the beginnings of recorded history, overweight has been a prestigious sign of affluence. Only the prosperous could *afford* enough food to provide the caloric surplus that results in obesity. And this is still so throughout much of the world. But the United States, as Charles Slater once pointed out, is "the first nation in history to be seriously threatened by mass obesity." It is well within the reach even of those who subsist on public funds to become grossly overweight.

Consumer attitudes toward obesity have, however, undergone a radical change in the last one or two generations. Much of this change has come about through substantial change in educational level. The United States is also the first nation in history in which achieving the level of graduation from high school is typical of the majority of the population. This "crossover," by the way, occurred in 1964, so the changes we are talking about are happening at an increasingly faster rate.

A few years ago I participated in a study of consumer attitudes toward non-nutritive sweetening agents, in the course of which it was revealed that two out of three adults thought that they weighed more than they should. When asked the question, "If you could weigh whatever you wanted to, would you rather weigh *more, less,* or *about the same?*" only one in 20 said "more," about 30 percent said "about the same," and about two-thirds said they would prefer to weigh less.

Regardless of the extent to which people actually *are* overweight—and it is doubtful that two-thirds of the adult population would really qualify as medically obese—it is still a fact of enormous significance that two-thirds of the population consider they are fatter than they would like to be. The ratio of women who considered themselves to weigh too much was even higher than that of men, and it is obvious that women have a disproportionate influence on the choice of foods that are purchased and served.

With proper selection and trimming, pork can be among the leanest of meats. But does the consumer perceive pork to be lean? Just how much of an effort is actually being made by the producer, the packer, the retailer to encourage the consumer to think of pork as a lean meat?

THE IMAGE OF PORK

This last question leads into the fourth and last of the possible reasons why people are eating relatively less pork—the image of pork as a food. Perhaps we should say "images," because it is clear that pork has not one image but several. Although total pork consumption is at a 20-year low on a per capita basis, such pork products as sausage and canned hams have had substantial increases in consumption rate. It would seem to be much more than coincidental that the pork products which have enjoyed the greatest growth are those with the greatest amount of value added by manufacture.

To the extent that people associate "pork" with the pig, there is some reason to believe that its consumer image is less than shining bright. Such phrases as "dirty as a pig," "this place looks like a pigsty," and so forth have conditioned the consumer mind since childhood. Add to this vague fears about diseases such as trichinosis and even hog cholera, and then top it off with publicity about the role of saturated animal fat in arteriosclerosis, and it would be strange indeed if there were no negative ruboff on pork and pork products.

Of all the reasons we have considered as possible explanations for the declining popularity of pork, it seems to me that the availability of alternatives is by far the most important, and the one about which we can do the least, *unless we change the nature of our pork offerings.* The distribution of incomes has been flattened so that the majority of consumers can exercise freer choice in what they buy. In fact it is only within the past decade that, for the first time in any nation's history, "wants" exceed "needs"—in the sense that a higher proportion of consumer income is available for "wants" than for the "needs" of food, shelter, and clothing.

People have been spending more dollars for food, but the *proportion* of disposable income spent for food has been steadily declining—from as high as 58 percent in 1879 to 26 percent in 1947, to 18 percent today. There is little question about the validity of the food manufacturers' message to consumers that "food is a bargain."

But let us look at these same data from a slightly different viewpoint. How many industries, other than the food industry, actually seem to take pride in the fact that their share of the consumer's spendable dollar is *shrinking?* This should be a source of serious concern to all food manufacturers—and particularly to those segments whose share of a shrinking proportion is shrinking at an even faster rate.

If I have been critical of all segments of the pork industry, it is only with the intention of being helpful. I would like to conclude this chapter with nine constructive suggestions—three for each of the three segments of the pork industry.

For the *pork producer,* I would suggest that much greater effort be made to improve the breed through genetic selection and better feeding practices. Secondly, why cannot greater efforts be made to introduce some of the economies of scale to hog production that have made the battery raising of chickens so efficient? And third, it would seem to be well within our technological capacity to eliminate hog diseases—a step which would also be of great help in opening up broader world markets for pork and pork products.

For the *pork packer,* I also have three suggestions. The first is to pay a sufficient premium to really effectively motivate the producer to supply better animals. The second is to accelerate the introduction of convenience foods using pork as a primary or even secondary ingredient. The third, and perhaps hardest to implement without willing cooperation from retailers, is to initiate and consistently meet high standards for the primal cuts now supplied to retailers and to work toward providing even more service through additional processing and packaging.

For the *retailer,* my first suggestion is that he should demand better pork from his suppliers. The second suggestion is a direct corollary of the first—he should be prepared to pay a fair price to those packers who prove that they can and will supply pork of a consistently high quality. Finally, the retailer should do his part in promoting quality pork as one of the most flavorful, delightful sources of protein available to the human palate.

I would like to close with a brief quotation from Charles Lamb. In his "Dissertation Upon Roast Pig," he gives one of the most glowing tributes to pork in all literature.

> Pig, let me speak his praise, is no less provocative of the appetite, than he is satisfactory to the criticalness of the censorious palate. The strong man may batten on him, and the weakling refuseth not his mild juices.
>
> Unlike to mankind's mixed characters, a bundle of virtues and vices, inexplicably intertwisted, and not to be unravelled without hazard, he is—good throughout. No part of him is better or worse than another. He helpeth, as far as his little means extend, all around. He is the least envious of banquets. He is all neighbours' fare.

If we can only get more consumers to thinking about pork and pork products in this way, the future for pork would indeed be bright!

2

Merchandising Characteristics

Retailer's View on Cured and Processed Products

RICHARD S. BEVIER

As THE OLD SERVICE MARKET—with the friendly old butcher with the 16-pound thumb and the 14-ounce scale—passes into history, we find ourselves in a new era of merchandising. In a modern self-service market it is entirely possible that a housewife can complete her entire meat shopping trip without even once talking to a butcher. She shops at her own pace, she makes decisions that defy logic (except to her), and she does the whole thing without any help from us, the retailer. She is independent and she is the complete boss of our operation, even though she may not realize it. If she picks up a chicken instead of a pork roast, regardless of her reasons, we go out and buy more chickens. If she picks up a ham instead of a turkey, regardless of her reasons, we go out and buy more hams. The hard facts of life are that we really do not care *what* she buys, as long as she buys it from *us,* and as long as she comes back to us because of our quality, or our price, or our service, or the combination of all three.

If this is true, she takes on a new importance to industry people.

Pork producers bring to market the kind of meat that sells readily at the best possible prices to packers; packers deliver to retailers the type of pork that meets the individual retailer's specifications; and those specifications come from the retail customers. Over a period of years, each retailer builds up fairly accurate ideas of what his customers want to buy, and they are the basis for his specifications. So, the meat business does not begin on the ranch or on the farm—it begins in a homemaker's kitchen! If she is satisfied with her purchases, we have all done our jobs. If she is unhappy, we hear about it loud and clear, and so does everyone else down the line.

It is impossible to plan any future for the pork industry without knowing the American housewife and including her in those plans. She is our boss, and she is making decisions as she shops that are of vital importance to all of us. Will she buy a picnic ham? or a smoked butt? or a pound of bacon? or will she, instead, purchase one of the 900 other meat items that we place before her? She will spend about six seconds making each individual decision, because she is a walking computer with a complex wiring system. Let us take a look at how she is programmed.

She never heard of the National Provisioner or any of the other marketing sheets around the country, and she could care less, but she does recognize value and will respond immediately to it. And therein lies the first set of challenges to the pork industry. We are faced with the fact that the retailer has no special loyalty to any one part of the industry. A buyer knows that a customer will respond to value, and he goes shopping for values on the open market every week for her. Because he thinks this way, processed pork items are immediately placed in direct competition with chickens from Georgia, turkeys from Minnesota, and cattle from Iowa. Anyone who has been in the meat business for any length of time has quickly found that it is not a "get-rich-quick" way of making a living. The challenge to the industry is one of logistics. Greater efficiency in growing, in slaughtering, in processing, and in warehousing and transportation—all this coupled with volume production— is the only way we can compete with other food industries. We have to be better than they or we *have* no future. The lamb industry and the fresh fish industry have had to face this hard fact of life. As they limit their production each year and let prices rise, the little lady in front of the meat counter digs the hole deeper for them each year.

Let us go back to our boss, the customer. She gets frustrated and angry when she cannot find an item that she has already made up her mind to buy. We can smile at her and offer her all the substitutes in the world, but she will still resent the market man who forgets to order properly. If it was a processed pork item, then our industry suffers for something that wasn't our fault.

Sometimes a late delivery causes the out-of-stock condition, but when we are out of a product, regardless of whose fault it is, each of us has an obligation to each other to go back to our logistics books and try to correct a given situation and see that it does not happen again.

One of the things a woman demands is variety in the things we place

before her, and right here let me compliment the pork industry for what
I think is the outstanding job in the entire meat picture. You have found
more ways to process and package your product than any other group
that I can think of, and you have given us the variety that she demands.
Because of you, we have not felt the need to go to private labels to get
the variety of packaging and quality that we think she wants. In our
entire line of hundreds of items, only five are under private label.

Because of you, we can impress her with attractive counters of a
wide variety of fresh and processsed meat products. Her response and
ours are easy to measure. So far this year, we have sold several million
pounds of processed pork items which we purchased from your industry.
But another hard fact of life about a female customer is that no matter
how good you are, or how hard you work to please her, she still wants to
know "What have you done for me lately?" I pass her question on to
you and ask that you include that question in your plans for the future.

Just as important as variety is freshness, and the customer is really
adamant about it. She is well read on Salmonella; she has heard that
there is some kind of bug in most pork and all of the warning lights go
on in her computer when she sees anything that looks suspicious in one
of your products. She makes one of her six-second decisions and walks
right away from you and from us if she sees anything abnormal in a ham
or a pound of bacon. She feels a deep sense of responsibility to her children to see that they get fresh, wholesome food, and woe be to the store
or the industry that lets her down and makes one of those children sick.
All of us share this responsibility to her.

Rotation of product and checking freshness codes are one way of
facing up to that responsibility, but that is only part of it. For many
years Jewel has prided iteself on its clean, white stores—our number one
commandment, but recently we have appointed a task force to review
everything we are doing in the area of cleanliness and sanitation and to
make recommendations for improvements. And we have found many
things that can be improved. We are not waiting, and you should not
wait for the federal government to force you to clean your own skirts.
Do it now—yourself! This is an obligation we owe the housewives and
ourselves.

There is another obligation that we mutually share. The housewife
probably does not know anything about your end of the business, but
she can spot a fat ham from the far end of the store. And if she has been
burned once or twice by a wasty smoked butt, her radar system will steer
her right around this item. She will give us only one chance to prove
that our sliced cooked ham is as good as that which comes from Poland.
She will trust or mistrust branded bacon items in direct relationship to
her past experience with those brands, and so will the market manager.
He knows that the profit in a case of bacon is not realized until he sells
that last pound. If he keeps staring at three or four packages out of
several cartons which will not move, he quickly decides to stop ordering
the item.

Whether it is picnics or butts or bacon, you do not get three strikes in this game. The fastest way to kill confidence and product turnover is to slip one bad apple in each barrel. The answer is quality control and careful selection. One of the greatest compliments I ever heard paid to an industry was spoken by a little old lady during a recent grand opening of a new store on the south side of Chicago. This woman walked up to the freezer counter and, almost without looking, flipped a hen turkey into her shopping cart. As she walked by me I remarked, "It didn't take you long to make up your mind on that one, did it?" She said, "Sonny, I haven't had a bad turkey in six years—I don't think there are any more bad turkeys." What a great compliment. Someday, when our customers flip picnic hams into their baskets without looking, the pork industry can relax. Plan *not* to relax until then.

As you make your plans for the future, there is another important area in which you can help retail customers, us, and yourselves—that is in educating young housewives. At Jewel we operate a weekly recipe service of which homemakers eagerly take advantage. In addition, in the past year we have carried on a campaign which we call "Ask the Man at Jewel." In this campaign we feature large talking cards which pose various questions such as "How much meat is needed for a serving?" "What are the best cuts of meat?" "How do you carve a bone-in ham?" "How do you broil a dinner ham slice?" These cards are hung directly over the meat counter where customers cannot help but see them. Just in case the meat man behind the counter is not as well versed as he should be, we have printed the complete answers to the questions on the reverse side of the card facing him. It is simple, but effective. Anything you can do to teach more women to use more parts of the whole animal will be appreciated by them and can do nothing but help us. It is a job we have to work hard at before some of the less desirable items become more of a burden on us than they are now. As you make your plans for the future, plan to own more space in each store, but you will have to earn that space yourselves. Make your plans well so that you increase your share of each shopping cart, remembering that the burden is on you because the retailer does not dictate what goes into that shopping cart. Most of all, remember this woman in all of your plans, because she is the beginning and the end of all that we do together.

Retailer's View on Fresh Products

GIL VANDER KOLK

SPARTAN STORES OF MICHIGAN are a retailer owned supply depot, supplying most of the needs to approximately 400 food stores—some small, some large, some excellently operated, some not so well operated. We supply most of the meat needs to about 250 of these stores and ship 1.5 million pounds of meat weekly.

The Spartan stores are vitally concerned with the development of a pork program that will improve the acceptance of pork as a regular menu item and possibly make it a demand item. The stores we serve love to sell pork if it is the kind of pork that meets the desire of Mrs. Consumer. We are aware that much has been done over the years to improve the various characteristics of pork so that it has the potential of coming nearer to meeting those demands and desires, and certainly the search for continued progress should never stop.

My comments will express the view of Spartan retailers and warehouse supervisory personnel on fresh hams, loins, and shoulders, which I will refer to as fresh pork. We will have to assume that it will be the general view of at least some other retailers, whether they be single store or chain store operators.

Spartan retailers view fresh pork as a very desirable product to sell from their display cases. One of the many peculiarities of retailing is that certain products generate more profit than others. Pork is profitable to a retailer. It is easy to handle at store level. It comes in primal cuts, is light in weight, does not have excessive by-products, and is relatively easy to process into consumer cuts. Pork lends itself well to merchandising. There are unlimited ways that it can be offered for sale. There are probably 30 or 40 ways just to merchandise a pork loin and hundreds of ways to promote the various primal cuts. So pork adds variety to the meat display case, and variety generates sales. Pork also has excellent nutritional value, so it is the type of product retailers enjoy selling to their customers.

However, lest you think all is well at retail levels on fresh pork let me hasten to add there are several serious problem areas that have existed for many years and will need attention soon.

Most of you are concerned with the development of the hog to its arrival at the processing plant. Plenty of well-developed hogs must arrive at the processing plants if the processor is going to be in a position to supply the type of pork Mrs. Consumer wants.

The first time retailers actually get to view the fresh pork is when it arrives at their stores. Much of the time they do not like what they see. So regardless of what influence and effect you have on the development of the type of hog that will produce pork acceptable to the consumer, if the packing plant processor, the distributor if there is one, and the retailer do not do their jobs properly, all of your efforts will have been wasted.

The consumer's criteria for pork include the following: (1) leanness, (2) fine texture, (3) freshness, (4) a nice bloom and eye appeal when displayed, (5) well trimmed, and (6) priced so it is a real value. She doesn't know and really doesn't care too much about whose responsibility it is to see that she has the opportunity to buy the kind of pork she wants, but she does know that if she cannot get what she wants, she isn't going to buy.

It is our feeling at Spartan that there is much room for improvement in the operations pork packers or processors perform. In the nine years Spartan has been involved in meat distribution, we have had more complaints, more problems of all kinds, with fresh pork than any other product classification we carry.

The major complaints we hear from our retail meat managers are:
1. Poor trim—too much fat left on primal cuts.
2. Poor cutting standards.
3. Inconsistent sizes in given weight ranges.
4. Too much adjusting of cutting standards to fit particular market conditions.
5. Not properly chilled before cutting and shipping.
6. Product actually dirty.

There has been a tremendous amount of conversation and publicity over the years by various packers about quality standards and rigid control. Most of them have stated they follow the Chicago Board of Trade code of trim. Being relatively new in this business, we asked several companies for copies of the code. So far, no one has turned a copy over to us.

In more recent years we have heard about I.Q. pork, big eye pork, special trim pork, selected pork, meat type pork, premium lean, tender lean, and super trim pork among others.

I believe that every company announcing a special type and trim of pork has done so with good intentions. The theory behind such programs is basically sound, but somewhere along the line, the job just doesn't get done on a consistent basis.

Our experience generally has been: The larger the company, the more inconsistent are quality control and cutting standards. We realize very well that hogs are grown and not manufactured and that there will be some variations in conformation and other variables, but this is no excuse for the poor workmanship that exists in packing companies.

It is not our objective to tell any packing company how to run their business, but we would like to make some suggestions on what might be done to improve the image of pork packers in the view of Spartan retailers and Mrs. Consumer.

I would like to emphasize one point: We have to earn the right to supply our member stores, on the basis of service, quality, and price, the same as a packer or any other distributor.

If I were a pork packer, I would apply some of the same principles used by successful retail store operators.

At Spartan we are continually striving to satisfy our members' needs and desires and at the same time constantly encouraging the members to satisfy their customers' needs and desires.

A large portion of the Spartan advertising budget is spent on television, radio, and newspapers—plugging the theme "Satisfaction is shopping at a Spartan Store." Using this theme we go on to describe what satisfaction is. For example, satisfaction is variety; satisfaction is friendliness; satisfaction is quality products; satisfaction is fair pricing; and satisfaction is lean fresh pork.

We have a number of stores using a large rather startling sign in their meat departments that tells most of the pork story in a few words. "The Leanest Pork in Town."

As mentioned earlier, there has been much written, printed, and spoken about new pork programs involving meat type hogs, special trim, etc. A couple of major packers have come out with full-page ads in trade journals announcing new quality control programs, using so-called meat type hogs. We have made a sincere effort to tie in with several of these programs and paid the premium price for the improved product. I regret to say, however, that there was no consistency in trim, cut, and size selection. There was no complaint on paying the premium price when the product was right.

We realize major packers are processing and shipping millions of pounds of fresh pork annually, so the logical question is: If it's so bad, how can they maintain sales? Our reply would be:

1. Chain headquarters buyers do the buying, and the store managers' complaints have little effect on decisions made at headquarters.

2. They are the only source of supply with large enough quantities for chain operations.

3. Managers have come to accept inconsistent quality as a characteristic of the business.

Spartan is doing the bulk of its pork business with two vendors. One is supplying our so-called special trim pork and another one the so-called regular trim. We have found them to be the most consistent for trim and quality of those we have worked with. With the volume of business we do, it is necessary that we have several vendors.

I would like to quote briefly from an article that appeared recently in the trade journal *Meat*: "During the recent 21st annual meeting of Western States Meat Packers Association, there was a considerable number of questions raised, problems reviewed, even some solutions proposed."

The fabricators and breakers session suggested possible standards for the industries, to encourage more uniform merchandising. Eugene Garrity, Hygrade Food Products Corporation, suggested that a working committee in the association be established to devise uniform standards within the industry. He suggested that standardization of beef cuts, nomenclature, yield, and labor can be developed at the association level.

The reason I quote Mr. Garrity is to point out that they have a similar problem in beef cuts, and if they are smart something will be done about the problem before the government steps in and sets up regulations and controls.

The pork industry is in the same situation. None of us wants more government intervention, but if the matter isn't taken care of soon, I'm afraid they will step in, and we would be inclined to endorse action.

Grading and classifying commodities serves two purposes: (1) It tells the customer, whether at wholesale or retail, what the quality is and (2) it establishes a base from which to work for setting prices.

In regard to pork under present conditions, the cutout varies so much that it is impossible to establish an accurate pricing policy based on cost, and of course all meat retail prices are based on the cutout realized from the primal cuts. For example, if a 70-pound box of pork loins can be cut into 69 or 70 pounds of retail cuts it has much more value than if only 64 or 65 pounds of retail cuts are realized. We believe pork should be so trimmed by the packer that there would be very little if any trimming to be done at store level.

A grading program similar to the dual grading program developed by USDA on beef is a possible way of stabilizing the pork industry. The dual grading of beef is simply the grading of beef first for quality of the meat, with grades of prime, choice, good, standard, etc. Another grading or classifying is for cutability, starting with class one having very high cutability and going down to class five with very low cutability.

It is a known fact that most packers do not like dual grading, mainly because they cannot sell classes four and five at the same price as the higher classes because they aren't a value at the same price. Without dual grading a low cutability choice or good can be shipped out to inexperienced operators and it will be accepted most of the time with few claims for credit. The packer got rid of the product but it wasn't a value. Priced fairly it could be a value.

As we look over the entire line of meats, it is difficult to find other products with as little grading and regulation as pork. All fresh beef, lamb, veal, and poultry are offered with USDA or house grading. All processed products come under certain quality regulations. Pork, however, has no standards for quality or value. The only government regulations are for sanitation and health.

We believe there is a big opportunity to develop better acceptance by both the retailer and the consumer by offering value and satisfaction. Rather than going into detail on how much we do or would be willing to pay for pork, I would prefer stating we are willing to pay whatever the market is for value received. At present we pay approximately 3 cents a pound more for special trim than for regular. There could even be justification for 4 or 5 cents extra if it represented a value.

I mentioned earlier that many of you are more directly concerned with the development of a hog that will better serve Mrs. Consumer's needs. Don't ever stop your search, and at the same time may I suggest you encourage the processor to take advantage of your developments and pass them on to Mrs. Consumer.

Packer's View
on Fresh Products

B. C. BREIDENSTEIN

MERCHANDISING is a term which has a number of different interpretations. Webster defines it as "a comprehensive function including market research, development of new products, coordination of manufacturer and marketing and effective advertising and selling." In contemporary usage, Webster defines it as "buying and selling goods at a profit."

A quality trait can be broadly defined as any characteristic related to value. It is essential that one recognize that such traits may or may not be related to price, depending upon the degree of recognition of their value on the part of the purchaser. The development of desirable quality traits in meat products is usually the result of increased expenditures in animal production and/or marketing, in meat processing including selection, product modifications, and advantageous selling in accord with value. As a result of the necessity for the occurrence of more than one of these prior to the recognition of the monetary value of the improved quality, such monetary recognition of value traits quite frequently lags behind the research or otherwise recognized existence of the trait.

Since this discussion is confined to fresh pork products, the primary value determinants include weight of the cut and its yield of lean, fat, and bone. The primary variables determining value are the relative amounts of lean and fat. After defatting, the percentage of bone is relatively constant as compared to that of either lean or fat except as it may be related to the variations in anatomical reference points used in separating the cuts. There is, of course, considerable variation in this regard as a result of efforts made to increase yields of cuts from a given group of hogs. Weight of the cut is the most apparent criterion related to price. Weight of primal cuts is, of course, related to the final size and to some extent to the shape of the final product offered the consumer. The number of servings in relation to family size and the total package size and cost are unquestionably related to retail rate of movement. Objections of this kind which are related to weight can obviously be easily overcome by separating the primal cuts into parts. This, however, requires additional labor and facilities and reduces the rate of dollar turnover, all of which adds to the cost per unit of weight sold. The traditional price discrimination against heavier weights is undoubtedly related also to the fact that heavier cuts originate from heavier hogs. Heavier hogs are usually both older and fatter.

Variations in lean and fat content are the result of (1) natural variants and (2) the absence of standardized cutting and trimming methods. The magnitude of natural variance can be assessed with some degree of accuracy. Compositional variation resulting from cutting and trimming methods is much less predictable because of the numerous ways in which cutting and trimming specifications may vary. It will probably be worthwhile to explore briefly some of the compositional variations that exist in products cut and trimmed under highly controlled laboratory conditions. The data in Table 2.1 represent unpublished data collected at the University of Illinois and depict some of the sources of variation in ham composition. The hams were selected as having a high cover fat (more than one inch on the untrimmed ham measured opposite the aitch bone) or low cover fat (less than three-fourths inch measured in the same way), either highly marbled (4 or 5 on the Wisconsin scale) or low in marbling (1 or 2 on the Wisconsin scale). A collar length equal to one-third the length of the ham was used with a fat thickness not to exceed one-half inch at any point and beveled to the meat surface at the butt end.

As will be noted, the liveweight of the two groups of hogs was not

TABLE 2.1: Fresh Ham Composition

Animal Description				Percentage of Dissectable Lean		
Marbling	Cover fat	Live-weight	Average carcass backfat thickness, inches	Skinned ham	Skinned, externally defatted, & boned ham	Percentage of fat in dissectable lean
Low	Low	193	1.31	71.2	94.2	5.4
High	High	200	1.71	61.6	86.9	10.1
Mean difference		7	.40	9.6	7.3	4.7

appreciably different but the carcass backfat was quite different. It is of interest to note that more or less "standard trimming" resulted in a skinned ham that still was not particularly standardized in lean content, with the difference between the two groups approaching 10 percent. Dissectable lean expressed as a percentage of externally defatted and boneless ham reveals that apparent variance exists with respect to intermuscular fat, with a difference of 7.3 percent between the two groups. It is apparent from these examples that complete standardization of lean and fat content was not accomplished even though definite effort and care were exercised with regard to processing.

In addition to the inherent variance in composition, wide variations in cutting and trimming methods are prevalent. Yield of green ham from a given description of carcass can be increased by increasing collar length, increasing fat thickness on the skinned ham, and increasing the length of the shank. Since none of these possible variations affects the absolute lean content, it is obvious that lean expressed as a percentage of total weight will be reduced. Ham yields can also be increased at the expense of loin yields by simply cutting further from the aitch bone. There is no evidence to suggest that such a practice has any advance effect on lean yield expressed as a percentage of the resultant ham. Loins and shoulders can be affected in much the same way as hams by cutting and trimming procedures with the same rather obvious results.

The primary problems in the identification and reflection of product values can be clearly inferred from the foregoing discussion. The biological variation in lean, fat, and bone content of carcasses and parts of carcasses represents the potential for the problem. Trimming of cuts represents a means of reducing this variation. "Extra trim" is, however, an expensive process resulting from the labor required and also from the reduced yield.

This discussion has thus far ignored the question of pale, soft, and exudative (PSE) pork. This problem is an example of a situation that has been known to exist for some time. While fact would dispute its potential serious nature, it is a quality problem not yet reflected in price. If one were to ascribe to it a price consideration, the question of magnitude in relation to various degrees of seriousness must be established. The problem of superimposing such a price reflection upon the existing structure is indeed a perplexing and challenging one.

Current buying programs suggest that relatively little attention is being devoted to recognition of variation in composition within weight groupings. There are, of course, notable exceptions. The recent shift in weight ranges of most quotations for loins reflects a recognition of the fact that the makeup of the hog is changing. A highly desirable "meat type" hog simply will not produce a lightweight loin at any reasonable slaughter weight. The same can be said for the hams and shoulders as well.

A statement of buying patterns of the future represents pure conjecture. Such patterns will likewise reflect a further recognition of the need to shift the composition of acceptable weights of cuts to coincide with the changes in the composition of the raw materials (hogs). Sorting of products may provide a means of offering cuts on a value basis within weight groupings. Inherent variants in product composition represent a potential value variance not readily discernible through casual observation.

In conclusion, may I reiterate the contemporary definition of merchandising—"buying and selling of goods at a profit." It therefore behooves us to consider, at least momentarily, the issue of practical reflection of value characteristics in price. Changes in product categorization and/or form including size and shape will result in increased costs. The relevant question is whether or not the value improvement is greater than the cost. In the final analysis, the primary factor determining whether or not a program will be implemented is its profit potential. Such a profit potential may be either short-term or long-term, but it must be present.

Packer's View on Cured and Processed Products

LEE HOUSEWRIGHT

CURING AND PRODUCTION of processed meat items have helped the meat industry, particularly the swine industry, to continue to exist and grow. Since 1947, consumption of pork has declined while consumption of beef has greatly increased. While the consumption of pork has not been as great as the consumption of beef, it has been a very significant source of income for the producer, the processor, and the retailer. As we have already heard, pork and pork items are profitable for the retailer.

Early in the history of the pork industry "salting" or curing of product was really a means of preserving the product or extending its shelf-life. With improved refrigeration, canning processes, and improved packaging, differences in items and form changed the merchandising of much of the pork materials.

A recent review of the marketing of bacon showed that in 1954 about 64 percent of the bacon was sold as packaged sliced bacon, while in 1966 almost 80 percent was sold in this way.

During the past quarter-century, many changes have been made in the curing and processing of pork; and many more changes will occur during the next few years. The consumer wants changes. Continuous improvement is essential in the future if we are to continue to provide acceptable value to the consumer and maintain our position in the competition for the consumer's favor.

We must remember that *pork* as such is not a necessity for survival. It can, because of its nutritional value, fill a need in the diet of man, but we must continue to maintain its value. If it does not sell at retail, we cannot grow.

Eating habits are changing. Meals have changed. Breakfast, once a very substantial family meal with ham and bacon playing a major part, is now almost a thing of the past. Lunch has replaced the noonday dinner of years ago and is not the family meal it once was. The evening meal, supper, was replaced by dinner, and now in many families dinner consists of a series of events as various members of the family come and go. Diets also have taken their toll of meat eaters. Snack foods have taken another group.

However, we know that Mrs. Consumer still wants pork, but she wants a value for her food dollar. She especially likes cured and processed items such as sliced bacon, smoked hams, canned hams, smoked picnics, wieners, bologna, and luncheon meats. These items are often used as feature items by the retailer, and these features affect her buying habits and establish quality and price values for her.

We must continue to improve the quality and consistency of the product. If this requires improved selection and breeding characteristics of hogs and improved environment and feeding, these improvements will have to be accomplished. If it requires improved processing procedures, the packers must accomplish this. Certainly one of the major problems the processors encounter is that of procuring good quality pork (hogs) for our processed pork items—especially for the cured and smoked items.

Not only is the "fat-to-lean" ratio of major importance to the net realization to be obtained from the material from the pork carcasses, but the color and texture of the meat are of extreme importance. In this category, the so-called "pale watery pork" creates a serious problem. This condition causes economic losses in processing, excess purge during curing, greater shrink during smoking, lower protein solubility that affects the emulsions in processed meats, and color variability in finished products. At the consumer level, it can affect cooking rates and yields as well as texture and taste. Apparently research has not yet pinpointed the source of this problem, but it must be solved in the near future as continued improvement in the quality of products is essential.

As a part of the overall program of trying to provide the consumer with convenience products and to increase the profitable use of hams, our company several years ago began to produce a boneless smoked ham that would be uniform in quality, flavor, texture, appearance, and utilization. We felt that removing the skin, bone, and excess fat would give better final value and, consequently, increased acceptance from the consumer. To take the product from the "commodity ham" market and get the extra money necessary to establish and maintain the quality concept required a strong, sound, and continuing merchandising program. We offered a value. We used exacting quality control procedures. Our efforts in the marketing of our Cure 81 ham have proved the concept to be sound.

Unfortunately, not all hams can meet our standards. A principal reason for the nonacceptance is this pale watery condition previously mentioned.

Most of the complaints which Mr. Vander Kolk mentioned on fresh pork have, at times, been made also against the cured products; but we feel that more and more cuts and products from the cuts have been and will be handled in specialized ways to offer greater appeal to the consumer and improved value for her in convenience and quality. As more product is processed this way, a penalty will necessarily be imposed because of off-condition of material, or the acceptable product will bring a premium. Either way the total value to the producer will be affected. Our Cure 81 program has enabled us to utilize not only our own production of acceptable hams but additional supplies within the averages used from other sources. Again, exacting quality control is essential!

One of the more promising fields in new procedures is that of prefrying or precooking. This is more than the so-called "fully cooked" hams and picnics. It involves preparing the products so that they can be made ready for serving in the home or food service outlet with a very minimum of preparation time.

The institutional or food service field offers great potentials for increasing the consumption of pork and pork products, especially portion-controlled servings. In the processed meats, the sales of wieners, bologna, and other luncheon meats and fresh and smoked pork sausage have offered opportunities to utilize vast quantities of pork materials and will continue to show growth in the future. However, all of these continually face the challenge of competition, not only from other meat items but from the "nonmeat" items.

We believe that cured and processed pork items do and can continue to offer value to the consumer and that they play a vital role in providing the nutritional needs and wants of our society.

Restaurateur's View on Fresh and Processed Products

B. J. AMBROSE

OUR COMPANY, Stouffer Foods Corporation, incorporated in 1924, has 46 restaurants and 7 motor inns operating in 21 metropolitian areas. We also process, package, and distribute nationally retail and institutional frozen prepared foods and provide food management service for operations of dining facilities to 53 accounts in 80 locations. This segment of our company is divided into commercial, hospital, school, and vending divisions.

It is our observation that pork as it is viewed today differs from the pork that we served in our restaurants some 20 years ago. Our comments would be that pork today has a toughness, dryness, and stringiness that was neither observed nor noted 20 years ago; as a result, it was determined that a search should be made to find and identify the exact type quality desired by our organization.

By keeping records of characteristics of the product once we determine the "Stouffer Quality" (which is governed by an evaluation of conformation, finish, marbling, texture, distribution of muscling, and surface and seam fat), our supplier would attempt to repeat the selection on a continual basis.

From the standpoint of selecting cuts for Stouffer quality, pork must be judged on the basis of the cut surfaces to determine texture, marbling, firmness, moisture, color, correct trim, and weight. Not all number one hogs produce number one quality meat. For example, a carcass because of excess surface fat could be graded out of the number one category; however, the cuts trimmed to Stouffer's specifications could produce number one quality meat. Several years ago at a Minnesota 4-H Club showing, the carcass that rated number one mathematically on the basis of the pork carcass contest rules rated ninth for meat quality by the judges.

The initial phases of our testing program were conducted on center cut pork loins for roasting. The objective was to specifically determine the quality characteristics and factors that would meet our requirements. This was done by the use of paired loins in which one loin would be the control (present Stouffer quality and specifications) and the second loin would be the variable being checked. A sample from the same hog was shipped to our test kitchen in Cleveland and to the supplier's kitchen in Chicago. The intent was that these loins would be roasted on the same day in both test kitchens using the same cooking directions and then the product would be taste-tested by a regular core of testers.

Our first four tests involved pork loins with (1) heavy amounts of marbling and one-quarter inch fat covering, (2) heavy marbling with three-quarters inch fat, (3) loins void of marbling with three-quarters inch surface fat, and (4) loins void of marbling with one-quarter inch fat. Variables such as carcass weight and sex were held to a minimum. The results from these four tests were not encouraging, so we went further in our search.

We sampled soft and watery loins and loins from the old-fashioned slop-fed hogs; these tests were also discouraging. Loins from peanut-fed hogs were obtained, and when the order was placed with the supplier he wanted to know why we were interested in the product. The supplier was given a brief review of our objectives and testing programs and he commented that they too had found a great deal of quality variations within the peanut-fed hogs. Miss Reba Stagg, Home Economics Director of the National Livestock and Meat Board, gave this appraisal at the eighth annual National Pork Industry Conference in November, 1965, at Purdue University, stating that pork is not predictable in quality traits. "We have sampled pork loins that were frozen and those aged in cryovac two to twelve days in a carefully controlled cooler, but our results were inconclusive and gave us no indications that additional sampling of these two variables was necessary to improve quality traits."

In a trade journal that dates back to 1961, we had noted that scientists at Oregon State University found that injecting hormones into hogs four hours before slaughter helped to overcome toughness by giving meat the ability to retain its moisture and improve its quality.

The University of Missouri has done additional research on the injection of hormones before slaughter; however, we have heard of no industrial application as of now. We had attempted to sample loins from an injected hog, but product was not available. Tests were conducted on cooking methods, cutting yields, drip loss, and evaporation on boned, rolled, and tied fresh hams that had varying degrees of marbling. Hams with four to six ounces of backfat in the channel were evaluated also, but after all the results were tabulated, ham roasts of the current Stouffer quality and specifications were the most desirable.

We visually inspected and sampled pork loins that were wrapped and shipped in clear plastic, polyethylene, and regular parchment paper to determine if these elements had any adverse effect on the eating quality of the pork loins. No significant difference was noted; thus, there was no change in the wrapping material that had been in use.

Heavier type loins were tested for a short period of time in one of our Cleveland restaurants, but we found the end product dry and chewy.

Dr. Agnes Frances Carlin, Professor of Food and Nutrition at Iowa State University, issued a report, "Relation of Oven Temperature and Final Temperature to Quality Pork Loin Roasts." We experimented with the lower temperatures but found, as did Dr. Carlin, that neither the degree of doneness nor oven temperature used affected the flavor or tenderness.

We had our supplier obtain samples of fresh hams and pork loins from Canada in order for us to see if there was any difference in flavor and tenderness, but here again, the product was chewy and dry although the flavor was good.

Our cooking procedures and recipes were evaluated to determine if our methods of preparation needed to be altered. We found our present instructions to be the most acceptable.

Up to this point, the results obtained from the observations have not given us any definite direction. We are now testing in Cleveland pork from hogs which have been exposed to controlled feeding and environment, but we have not yet received enough fresh pork from this type of feeding to give an appraisal.

We are all aware of the factors which have contributed to the decrease in the demand for pork. There are many reasons—an unfavorable health image, competition from the poultry industry because of uniformity in quality, and the quality advances and greater emphasis and improvements in beef breeding. Industry-wide, if more searching were done, many more reasons could be listed.

We at Stouffer's do not list fresh pork as frequently as we have in the past because of lack of reliable uniformity and consistency in quality. In 1958, for example, fresh pork constituted 10.7 percent of our total yearly meat usage. There has been a steady decline each year, and in 1966 the figure was 5.2 percent of our usage. This is a reduction of 5.5 percent in a period of eight years. The processed pork category, which includes items such as smoked and canned hams and bacon, has increased from 13.9 percent in 1958 to 17.7 percent in 1966. This is an excellent example of the packing industry exercising controls to produce a product to satisfy the demands of the consumer.

What quality control techniques have been investigated and quickly utilized by the swine producers to insure that we, the purchasing agents, and our guests will receive tender, flavorful, fresh pork with every purchase? The entire pork industry must understand our needs and desires and the factors which we consider to be important if they wish to share in the market and reverse the downward trend in consumer acceptance.

Fresh pork today is leaner than it was in the past because the industry out of necessity had to find new ways to produce animals that yielded more lean edible meat in relation to waste and low value materials, but has the hog industry penalized themselves with this development? How much research has been done by the industry to find out why restaurant operators such as Stouffer's have not listed fresh pork on their menus? We are waiting for our first request for this type of information.

I have given you the steps we have taken so far and the efforts involved on the part of many people to try and improve the quality of fresh pork which we serve in our restaurants. We are naturally discouraged with the results of these tests because we lack a positive and direct course of thought or action. It appears we have exhausted every practical aspect available to us today to improve fresh pork.

I need not remind you that the pork industry has many, many problems. I have made you aware of one which we consider to be very important—quality. The problems cannot be solved in a hurry, but those in the industry must now unite, pool information, and work together to recapture the market they have lost.

PART TWO

Future Roles in Supplying Protein Requirements

3

Relationships of Supply, Demand, and Price

HAROLD F. BREIMYER

THE FUTURE economic position of pork will be determined less by overall supply and requirement forces as such than by the future pattern of international trade, both commercial and concessionary, as it is shaped by the policies of individual countries acting unilaterally and by actions of regional trade associations such as the European Common Market and Latin American Free Trade Association.

NEEDS VS. DEMANDS, AID VS. TRADE

There is a difference between physical needs and economic demand. Only if wherewithal in the form of buying power be present can need be translated into demand, and this is the principle to which we in this conference should hearken. That economic capacity to enter into trade varies widely and that concessionary trade has become a major factor should be self-evident. I propose that the following ideas also can be regarded as essentially self-evident. If so, we can accept them a priori:

1. That pork ranks high among preferred sources of protein in nearly all parts of the world other than those where it is subject to religious or other dietary restriction. Indeed, in a great many nations including much of continental Europe and the British Isles, unlike the United States, pork is not regarded as lower caste than beef.

2. That demand for pork within individual nations thus will increase as the financial capacity to buy it increases, and that this will generate an increase in world demand to the extent that trade channels are open (in an economic sense).[1] This principle is believed valid irrespective of whether nonmeat sources of protein make some modest inroads on demand for meat.

---

[1] In an FAO report, demand elasticity for pork is estimated at 0.0 in the United States and Canada, around 0.3 to 0.4 as an average for most countries of Europe (but 0.7 in the Netherlands and Yugoslavia), 1.2 in Japan, and 0.5 in several countries of Latin America. "Produits Agricoles—Projections Pour 1975 et 1985, Annexe Statistique," CCP 66/5, Add. 1, FAO, Rome, May, 1966, p. 28.

3. That production capability will not be a limiting factor. My premise is that world capacity to produce feedstuffs is great, and that even in the event the feed supply should begin to prove inadequate the hog can out-compete the cow for it, particularly the beef cow. The bovine, not the hog, is more vulnerable to tightness of feed supply, for the double reason that cattle convert feed to meat with lower efficiency than do hogs and that a beef cow produces only 0.9 of a calf per year whereas a sow will raise 14 pigs.

4. That the United States is an efficient producer of hogs and of feedstuffs for hogs. We enjoy an advantage worldwide in producing corn, the basic feed for hogs. Whether we are superior in converting the corn into hogs is a moot issue, but we probably are basically no less efficient than other countries in this respect.

In this simple prospectus I do not intend to overlook such matters as the need to tailor product to the specifications of the market and the hurdles in the form of sanitary barriers to international trade in pork. With regard to the former, no voice has been more persistent than mine in calling for adoption of tight quality standards in selling both pork and live hogs. And insofar as the United States may lag behind other countries in efficiency in pork production, the difference lies mainly in quality control. Several countries put us to shame in this respect.

With regard to sanitary barriers to trade, they have elements both of genuine disease control and of disguised trade restrictionism. The genuine half of the issue can be dealt with only by taking steps to eliminate the disease danger. The second half puts sanitary barriers as the clumsiest among the many trade-limiting devices in use throughout the world—devices such as quotas, tariff duties, gate prices, and the like.

In human affairs it is easier to deal with the physical than the institutional. That is to say it is easier to manage hogs than people. Problems in controlling quality of pork and making it disease-free are simple compared with those in facilitating international trade in pork. For this reason I choose to couch most of my remarks in the latter terms.

If we may assume that diets of much of the world's population are deficient in protein and that pork as a source of protein is highly acceptable if not preferred, we lead directly to the paradox that those who need it most are least able to buy it. Next we engage the issue of commercial trade vs. concessionary grants and sales (as sales for local currency). About 15 years ago the Eisenhower Administration publicized the phrase "Trade not Aid." Like most such phrases, it was literally false but symbolically sound. To the extent that nations lacking an adequate food supply are able to earn foreign exchange through their own exports, they have less need for concessionary food aid. The inverse is pointedly true. Insofar as those nations are not able to expand exports, a difficult dilemma is posed to all the wealthier nations of the world, and particularly the food surplus ones: Are they willing, as a matter of warm humanitarianism or cold national self-interest, to finance the sending of protein food to peoples who need it but cannot buy it?

TABLE 3.1: Production of Pork, Selected Countries, Selected Years (million pounds)

Country	Average 1934–38	Average 1946–50	Average 1956–60	1965	1966
Canada	621	956	980	1,029	1,027
U.S.A.	7,337	10,612	11,135	11,140	11,337
Germany	n.a.	1,530	3,347	4,262	4,176
France	1,494	1,389	2,465	3,025	2,739
Italy	650	577	834	985	936
Netherlands	548	293	816	1,083	1,111
Denmark	725	520	1,157	1,539	1,530
U.K.	1,012	465	1,481	2,055	1,947
Spain	n.a.	n.a.	532	565	680
Greece	40	35	51	79	87
Japan	n.a.	n.a.	325	898	1,245
U.S.S.R.	3,459	n.a.	5,360	6,780	7,280
Argentina	225	320	409	432	556
Brazil	369	520	1,041	1,314	1,323
Colombia	n.a.	n.a.	110	116	n.a.

Source: *Agricultural Statistics,* 1951 and 1952, USDA; and "World Meat Production Record Set," USDA, FAS, FLM 5–67, June, 1967, p. 5.

The United States has provided food to needy peoples abroad on many occasions over many years. For almost 15 years it has engaged in a program under P.L. 480, variously known as Food for Peace and Food for Freedom. Most of the foods supplied have been carbohydrate rather than protein; the protein that has been included has been mainly that of milk or of specially prepared foods of primarily cereal base.

Our program of concessionary grants and sales under P.L. 480 came about partly because we were embarrassed by excessive stocks of farm products in storage. Among the several reasons given for adopting the program was the prospect that P.L. 480 sales would themselves be market-developing. Some success in this regard can be claimed, as in Spain and Taiwan. These two one-time concessionary markets are now commercial.

EMINENT OPINION

So our argument is brought back to the nagging question introduced at the beginning of this chapter: Will nations of the world engage in foreign trade policies that will facilitate expansion of commercial trade in so important a protein food as pork, or will countries such as the United States face a persistent conscience test as to whether they will make protein foods available to peoples that need it but lack foreign exchange with which to buy it?

At the recent International Conference of Agricultural Economists eminent authorities virtually forced the delegates to consider such a problem. Professor Borrie of the Australian National University warned that world population growth shows little sign of slowing up very much very soon. Sir Frederick Bawden, distinguished director of the

TABLE 3.2:   Consumption of Pork per Capita, Selected Countries, Selected Years (pounds, carcass weight basis)

Countries	Average 1956–60	1964	1965
Canada	51	52	49
U.S.A.	64	65	59
Germany	64	74	74
France	48	61	61
Italy	20	20	21
Netherlands	47	52	61
Denmark	83	79	75
U.K.	43	61	65
Spain	18	25	n.a.
Greece	7	11	11
Japan	4	7	8
U.S.S.R.	26	20	n.a.
Argentina	18	17	21
Brazil	16	16	16
Colombia	8	7	7

Source: "World Meat Consumption," USDA, FAS, FLM 11–66, Nov., 1966, p. 4.

Rothamsted Experiment Station in England, gave assurance that the *physical* capacity for meeting food needs is adequate. "The amount of food needed by the year 2000 could almost certainly be met by applying methods already understood to the area of land now used to raise crops or stock . . ."[2]

It was Dr. Thorkil Kristensen, Secretary-General of the OECD, who figuratively twisted the tails of delegates, especially those from the more developed nations.[3] He made them squirm when he said that if the densely populated, less developed nations are to have the kinds of diets we so glibly say they ought to have, the developed nations must adopt one of two kinds of policies. As one choice, they must make it easier for the poorer nations to become larger exporters, so that they can earn the foreign exchange with which to buy good food in ample quantity. This means that wealthy nations must refrain from subsidizing their own exports of farm products that compete with the farm exports of poor nations (which cannot afford to subsidize); and further that they must themselves buy industrial goods from those same underdeveloped nations. The other choice, obviously, is for the richer nations to continue to give food to the poorer ones.

About 80 economists from the United States were present at the session. All squirmed, for it is obvious that the United States subsidizes the export of several farm products, either directly or indirectly. Further, although the U.S. record in reducing tariff rates on industrial products is a good one, we fall short of welcoming all the industrial products that

[2] F. C. Bawden, "Trends and Prospects From the Standpoint of Natural Scientists," *Intern. J. of Agrarian Affairs*, May, 1967, 2:128.

[3] Thorkil Kristensen, "The Approaches and Findings of Economists," *Intern. J. of Agrarian Affairs*, May, 1967, 2:130–56.

TABLE 3.3:   Level of per Capita Demand for Pork, Selected Regions, Selected Years, and Projections for 1975 and 1985 (kilograms per year)

Region	1962	1965	Projected 1975[a] I	II	Projected 1985[a] I	IV
World Total	8.5	8.7	9.1	9.7	9.3	10.7
North America	26.5	26.5	26.5	26.5	26.5	26.5
Western Europe	15.6	16.1	17.0	17.6	17.5	18.8
Germany	30.9	31.8	34.0	34.9	35.6	37.3
France	26.0	26.7	28.4	29.1	29.6	31.0
Italy	6.9	7.5	8.8	9.5	10.0	11.7
Netherlands	18.5	18.8	20.1	20.7	21.4	22.7
Northern Europe	16.1	16.4	17.3	17.8	18.2	19.2
Denmark	37.8	38.1	38.9	39.3	39.6	40.1
U.K.[b]	9.3	9.5	10.3	10.8	11.1	12.2
Southern Europe	4.7	5.0	5.6	6.0	5.9	6.5
Japan	2.2	2.8	4.0	4.5	4.7	6.1
U.S.S.R.	12.9	13.6	15.5	16.2	17.3	18.8
Latin America	5.5	5.6	5.8	6.1	6.0	6.8
Africa	0.4	0.4	0.4	0.5	0.5	0.6
South Asia	0.1	0.1	0.1	0.1	0.1	0.1

Source: "Produits Agricoles—Projections Pour 1975 et 1985, Annexe Statistique," FAO, CCP 66/5, Add. 1, May, 1966.
[a] Alternatives for low and high incomes.
[b] Possibly incomplete, excluding bacon.

underdeveloped nations may want to send us. And we definitely harm some of those nations by imposing rules such as that most of the sugar sent to the United States must be sent in raw.

I do not need to remind you of how quickly various economic interests in the United States clamor for protection against imports whenever they run into an economic bind. Of course, not all the squirming was done by U.S. delegates. European delegates were entirely aware of the increasingly restrictionist policy on agricultural trade (with third countries) being adopted by the six countries of the European Common Market. Indeed, there are a number of signs that international trade, after having been progressively liberalized for about 30 years, is now moving toward more restriction—often by subtle devices rather than by the traditional tariff.

SIGNIFICANCE TO THE UNITED STATES

So far as commerical demand for pork by U.S. consumers is concerned, clearly our own population growth will bolster markets significantly only if the downward trend in consumption per person can be halted or reversed. Whether the United States can hope to increase its commercial exports of pork to developed nations is also an uncertainty. Most projections show that those nations have a growing demand for pork and a growing deficit. Before we get too excited about possible prospects we must remember that (1) most of those nations have an advanced agriculture and can expand their own hog production, at a cost that is not exorbitant; and (2) it is those nations that have been rather quick to restrict trade, and they sometimes choose to import corn rather than pork. Also, sanitary restrictions often impede pork exports to those commerical foreign markets.

It seems likely that any expansion in commerical exports would be of certain individual pork products. The United States is a high-income consumer of pork, and we tend to consume the higher valued products and export those of lower value. This pattern might well continue, for our consumers' preferences for the various cuts of pork do not correspond exactly with the anatomy of the hog.

As for exports to underdeveloped nations, my remarks above apply. From a nutritional standpoint those nations ought to constitute a huge potential market for pork. Yet they are far short, generally, of being able to buy protein foods in the commerical market.

This brings me back to my main point. Nutritionally, the world needs for protein food are tremendous. If underdeveloped nations are to generate the buying power so as to fill those needs commercially, they must advance industrially, and their export markets for their own farm and industrial products must not be blocked by the protectionist actions of the more developed countries. But the trend seems to be toward more restrictions on international trade rather than fewer, and in particular toward regional preferential trading arrangements. The prolonged negotiation required for any change in trade policy is itself a way to obstruct liberalization of trade. It can amount to foot dragging on a massive scale.

Otherwise, the crucial issue becomes the willingness of developed nations to supply protein foods on a concessionary basis. This too divides into two parts: (1) Will the governments and the citizenry of those nations support such a policy? (2) Will animal proteins such as meat be chosen or will only vegetable proteins be supplied?

4

Efficiency of Grain Conversion

ARNOLD A. PAULSEN and
ROBERT HARMEL

GRAIN CONVERSION TO PORK

THE PORK INDUSTRY of the world is associated with the world's grain industry. Pork results largely from the conversion of grain. Hogs can eat a great many things, but by and large, they must eat grain.

The largest number of hogs in the United States is in the Corn Belt near grain production. The pigs of Europe in Denmark, Germany, and Poland are located near barley production. The hogs of Mainland China are in the grain-growing area. Brazil's rather large number of pigs is in her grain belt also.

There are some obvious exceptions to the association of pigs with grain. Argentina and Uruguay have large volumes of grain but few hogs. India, Indonesia, and Pakistan have large quantities of grain but few pigs. So, although pigs are present in large quanties *only* where grain is grown, not all grain-growing areas have large quantities of pigs. The lack of association is generally explained by the absence or presence of people. In the River Plate countries of Latin America, grain is plentiful and people are relatively scarce, and the effort to harvest grain and convert it to pork is not interesting. In Asia people are plentiful and, although much grain is produced, it is consumed directly by people because they outcompete animals, including pigs, for the use of scarce grain.

The nations of the world follow roughly a pattern with respect to association of grain and pigs. The association can be found more easily if we correct for the people as a factor. If we plot per capita grain availability against pigs per capita we find to some extent that if more grain is available per capita, more pigs per capita will be present (Fig. 4.1). Some countries in the lower right of the figure do not fit the pattern well. If we ignore these the association is rather good. Some countries with semi-arid grain areas have a substantial share of total

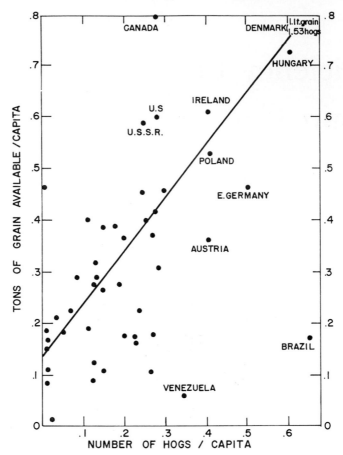

FIG. 4.1.   Relationship between grain and pigs, selected countries.

grain in the form of hard wheat and have fewer pigs than might be expected (Canada, United States, U.S.S.R., and Turkey). Other countries in a cool humid area with root crops available have more pigs per capita than might be expected. The countries to the far right in the figure seem to be explained also by the availability of other feeds. Besides Brazil and Venezuela they are Colombia, Peru, and Chile with potatoes in the mountains; New Zealand and Switzerland with large dairy industries; and Togoland and Congo in Africa who apparently support their rather small numbers of pigs on nongrain crops.

Looking at the world as an economist I see another pattern in the process of grain conversion to pork. The process is associated with the "rich." Higher densities of pigs per capita are found in countries with higher incomes per capita. To use grain production capacity to provide meat is a luxury. The luxury of pork can be afforded also by the "rich" in poor countries. Money has the command over resources, and if the rich desire to eat pork, the markets will allocate some scarce grain to pork production even in a hungry country.

Grain conversion to pork, of course, reduces the volume of calories. A serving of 500 calories from pork may require 10 potential servings of cornmeal mush to be used in the process. The value of the pork serving, of course, may be 30 times the value of one serving of cornmeal mush. Therein lies the economic basis of the U.S. pork industry. The reason for existence of the pork industry is to increase the value of feed grain about three times by making tasty pork out of it.

MUSCLE AND WORLD PROTEIN REQUIREMENTS

Of the animal protein currently consumed, the bulk of it is from beef, milk, and poultry rather than from pork. Little Denmark produces, consumes, and exports a great deal of pork; yet only 20 percent of her animal protein is from pork (Fig. 4.2).

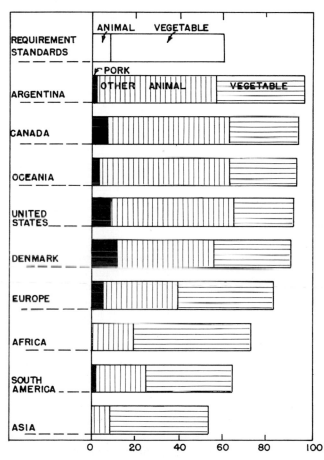

FIG. 4.2. Grams of protein per capita per day by source for selected countries and regions.

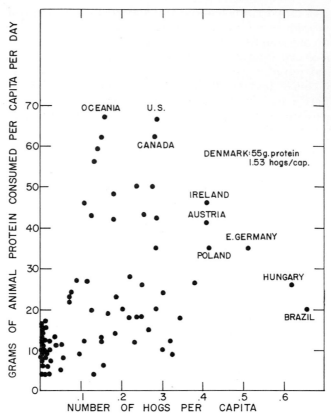

FIG. 4.3. Relationship between animal protein per capita
and number of hogs per capita.

As one might expect, there is no definite association between the
density of pigs and the total amount of animal protein per capita.
Some countries with relatively few pigs have adequate levels of animal
protein consumed per person. Some countries can have rather large
numbers of pigs and still not consume very much animal protein per
capita (Fig. 4.7). As one moves from the lower right to the upper left
of Figure 4.3, probably two main changes take place: (1) The de-
pendence upon pork as a main source of animal protein is reduced, and
(2) the efficiency of the nation's pork industry improves. Since these
two factors are not required to move at the same time, Denmark—where
pork production is probably quite efficient—lies to the right of the United
States and Canada.

Low use of pork as a source of animal protein is obvious for much
of the world as we see the density of hogs relative to people in Table 4.1.

In the world, trade is possible. By the process of trade, one country
can gain the benefit (product) of another country's resources and efficiency in exchange for a product of its own resources and efficiency. Some

TABLE 4.1: **Density of Hogs Relative to People**

Region	Hogs per Capita	Population
		(millions)
South America	.47	159
Eastern Europe	.40	122
North America	.25	287
U.S.S.R.	.24	230
Western Europe	.22	323
Oceania	.18	14
Asia	.09	1,681
Africa	.04	140
WORLD	.16	2,956

countries in the world are more efficient in pork production and some countries import pork and others export it. It seems interesting to look at the association in the world between consumption of animal protein from pork and the density of hogs per capita (Fig. 4.4). The United States is nearly self-sufficient with respect to pork and rather efficient in production. Thus, if we draw a line from the dot for the United States to the origin, we should have those countries less efficient or exporting or both to the right and those importing pork or more efficient to the left of the line.

Some of the world is extremely well provided with meat, while about half of the world has less than the estimated minimum daily requirement of animal protein (Fig. 4.5). Since in these countries of low average meat consumption there are some people who consume meat at the level of U.S. citizens, other people in poorly fed countries are very deficient in protein, receiving virtually none at all. How large is the animal protein deficit? Obviously not large relative to the excess of animal protein consumed by the countries with enough animal protein. Economically, of course, the animal protein deficit countries could not bid away from the rest of the world enough meat to raise diets to the minimum. They do not have the "effective demand" to buy that quantity of meat.

Looked at another way, the protein deficit in Indonesia, Africa, India, and Mainland China is equal in size to two complete U.S. pig crops.

EFFICIENCY IN THE FUTURE

Efficiency in the future for the world pork industry will probably come from several sources—supplemented or balanced rations, disease and pest control, and better animals. The technology for this efficiency is probably already known. Efficiency is not, however, now present in the bulk of the world's pig-raising areas. Feed that is not fit for human consumption is often given to pigs in the Mediterranean countries, in Latin America, and in Asia. Too often that food is also not fit for the

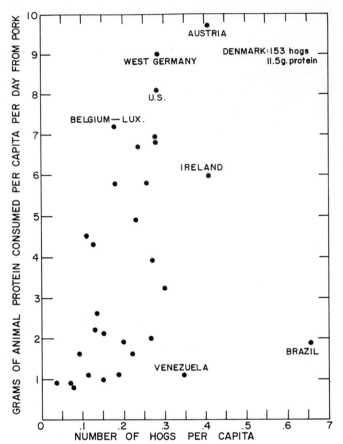

FIG. 4.4.   Relationship between hogs per capita and grams of protein from pork per capita.

pig, although the "waste" does need disposal and the use of it is not competitive with other uses as is the use of grain. Much assistance is needed to teach farmers of the world how to supplement pig rations made up partly of waste and by-products.

The current control of pests and disease is poor in most of the regions of pork production. Probably most of the world's pork comes from reasonably healthy hogs, but a great share of the areas and producers that have pigs have disease and pest problems. Losses from animal diseases in some developing countries without animal health programs are over 40 percent.[1]

Improved animals are much needed for future pork efficiency in the poor, low-meat countries. Much better animals are now available in advanced countries or could be selected from current local stock. In

[1] Report of the President's Panel on World Food Supply, 2:275, 1967.

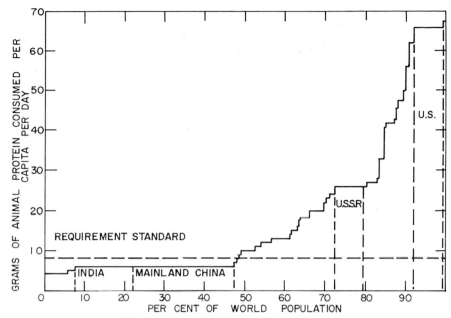

FIG. 4.5. Animal protein and world population.

my opinion, the effort to improve pork needs to concentrate on feed and health rather than on breeding.

The future for exports of U.S. pork to meet the protein requirements of poor underfed countries is not very bright. It is not only almost physically impossible to deliver pork to poor Asians but it is too costly to satisfy U.S. humanitarian inclinations.

The U.S. pork industry may get the opportunity to meet the high-income demand for pork in Asia, Latin America, and Africa, but we must, of course, compete with Denmark and Poland. Europe will probably import grain rather than pork to meet its growing high-income demand.

REFERENCES

Newspaper Enterprise Association, Inc., The World Almanac Division, *The World Almanac, 1967.*

U.N. Department of Economics and Social Affairs, Statistics Office, *Statistical Yearbook, 1966, 1967.*

U.N. FAO, *The World Meat Economy,* U.N. FAO Commodity, Bull. Series No. 40, 1965.

U.N. FAO, *U.N. FAO Commodity Review, 1965.*

U.N. FAO, *The State of Food and Agriculture, 1966.*

U.N. FAO, Statistics Division, *Production Yearbook, 1961, Production Yearbook, 1962, Production Yearbook, 1963, Production Yearbook, 1964, Production Yearbook, 1965.*

U.N. FAO, Statistics Division, *Trade Yearbook, 1961, Trade Yearbook, 1962,*

Trade Yearbook, 1963, Trade Yearbook, 1964, Trade Yearbook, 1965, Trade Yearbook, 1966.

U.N. FAO, Statistics Division, *Food Balance Sheets, 1960–62.*

USDA, ERS, *A Graphic Summary of World Agriculture, 1958,* USDA Misc. Publ. No. 705, 1964.

USDA, ERS, in cooperation with FAS, *The World Food Budget, 1962 and 1966,* USDA, Foreign Agricultural Economics, Rept. No. 4, 1967.

USDA, ERS, *World Food Needs,* USDA Inf. Bull. No. 261, 1962.

USDA, FAS, *World Agricultural Production and Trade,* USDA Stat. Rept. for 1963, 1964, 1965, 1966, and 1967.

5

Nonmeat Food Products

Development and Marketing

JOHN R. HARVEY

WE ARE LIVING in an age of substitutes and synthetics. For years, substitutes and synthetics have been moving in on the dairy industry. Oleomargarine, the butter look-alike, is the prime example. Now there are many imitations such as the coffee whiteners—the nondairy products that compete with cream. It is hard to think of a single dairy product that does not have an imitation or substitute. At the moment imitation milk is being sold in certain western states. This "filled milk" uses vegetable oil to replace butterfat and sells for about 10 cents a half-gallon less than genuine milk.

Substitutes have moved into the meat picture, too. Meatless meats that simulate pork are now on the market. There are products that look like ham, sausage, and bacon chips. Many of these products are made from soybeans. Wheat is another protein source, and yeast extracts and other nonanimal proteins are also used.

The process is secret and complicated, but briefly this is what happens. Soybean protein is processed and spun into fine, silklike threads. These threads are combined into a ropelike tow that is white, tasteless, and fibrous. In a sense, this is the "raw meat." These protein filaments are combined, textured, and treated with synthetic colors and flavors and with fat, amino acids, minerals, and vitamins. The final product looks— even cooks—like real meat. It also chews, smells, and tastes like meat— some trained testers have been fooled. This man-made "meat" can be adjusted for many characteristics such as tenderness, amounts and kinds of fat or amino acids, and quantity of cholesterol. Also the shape, color, and flavor of textured soybean protein can be varied. It can be shaped into slices, flakes, cubes, or irregular granules. Colors and flavors simulate those of bacon, beef, and chicken. Just about any meat, fruit, nut, or vegetable can be duplicated—in fact an entire five-course banquet can be served with substitutes and synthetics.

Worthington Foods of Worthington, Ohio, manufactures and markets a long list of meatless meats that resemble everything from beef to scallops. Their "ham" is called "Wham," and when properly prepared it is mighty close to the real thing. Wham has a fat content only one-third that of regular ham. Meatless meats can contain as high as 30 percent protein—average in most meat is 13–22 percent. These engineered foods can contain as little as 1 percent vegetable fat compared to an average 9 percent animal fat in meat.

In some parts of the country meatless meats can be found on supermarket shelves, in other places only at health food stores. Most of these new foods rate high in both taste and appearance.

The line of meatlike foods available besides ham and sausage includes frankfurters, fried chicken, roasts and steaks, meat loaf, chipped beef, luncheon loaves, and other popular meat cuts. Also available are cubes, strips, and granules of simulated ham, chicken, and beef. These are the principal protein ingredients in soups, chili mix, baby foods, potpies, casseroles, and ham and chicken salad mixes. There is "instant" meatless meat loaf that comes in a can—you just add water to the mix and bake.

Meatless meat manufacturers point out that spun soybean protein foods have no bones, skin, or excess fat so there is no waste and no shrinkage. The pork sausage-like product fries without any loss in size or weight—the real stuff shrinks 30–40 percent.

Another advantage: each serving duplicates the last in weight, size, shape, and food value. Also storage life of mock meat is longer. Frozen, canned, and dehydrated forms will keep indefinitely. Thawing and refreezing of frozen forms have no adverse effect on food value or texture. Once frozen spun soybean protein food is thawed, it will keep for ten days to two weeks under refrigeration.

One of the disadvantages of meatless meats is the high cost. The ham substitute sells for about 69 cents for an 8-ounce package. Also if the food product is not properly prepared, the taste is terrible.

TVP, Texgran, Supro 610, and BacOs are all members of a family of new foods with tremendous potential and a common parent: the soybean. The versatility of these products is almost unbelievable. TVP stand for "textured vegetable protein" and was developed by the Archer Daniels Midland Company. This product can be used as the "meat" in soups, patties, gravies, pizzas, camper food, ground meat dishes, health foods, and many others. TVP comes in chunk, granular, or strip form. It contains no waste and less than 1 percent fat—none of it animal fat. Since it is dehydrated, it keeps indefinitely without refrigeration.

Texgran is a similar product made from soybeans and developed by Swift & Co. It comes in all sizes, colors, and flavors. Most popular is a bacon-like crumble which is run through a smokehouse to give a natural, characteristic flavor and aroma. It is all usable—there is no shrinkage and it is uniform in quality. This new protein food sells to food manufacturers for 80 cents a pound. At present it is primarily a convenience food for hotels, restaurants, and institutions and has not been introduced on the consumer market.

Ralston Purina's Supro 610 is a new soybean protein powder that will be used by food manufacturers to enrich existing food and as a main ingredient in new foods. These might include meal-in-a-glass breakfasts, dry soup mixes, dietetic foods, and instant high-protein beverages.

If you have eaten Skippy peanut butter containing "Smoky Crisps" then you have already been introduced to a bacon substitute developed by General Mills. General Mills' BacOs look and taste like fried bacon bits and serve the institutional trade as garnish for salads, casseroles, and other dishes.

There are other companies besides those already named working to create new foods—some of them "meat analogues"—from the magic soybean. These include Central Soya, Crest Products, Loma Linda Foods, General Foods, and others. USDA and university scientists are also pushing research on foods from soybeans. One example is at the University of Illinois which received a $70,000 grant from USDA to study the composition and nutritional properties of soybean foods.

Low-cost, high-protein foods for the developing countries are the goal of a joint research project by USDA and Howard University in Washington, D.C. The new foods consist of main dishes, soups, beverages, and desserts and are developed from soybeans, cottonseed, and peanut flours. Home economics students from Africa and Asia form student taste-test panels, advise researchers on how these new foods would be received at home, and recommend seasonings enjoyed by their people. Nutritionally, these new foods could replace meat, milk, eggs, and other animal proteins in short supply in many countries.

In addition to the use of various grains, there is some "way out" food research under way, such as making food from fuel. Gulf Oil scientists are turning petroleum into soups, cereals, and cookies. A French laboratory has converted refined kerosene and diesel fuel into synthetic foods that look and taste like meat and fish. Food yeasts are being grown on city wastes. Mushrooms grown on packinghouse waste can simulate ground beef. Protein rich algae are under study too. Nobody is saying we will be eating petroleum protein soon, or sprinkling deep sea algae powder on our corn flakes, but some far-out food research does hold out hope for the hungry in underdeveloped lands.

The National Livestock and Meat Board reports that Americans will have consumed about 33.5 billion pounds of beef, veal, pork, and lamb in 1967—more than twice as much as any other country in total consumption. (However, it is estimated that 50 million Americans do not eat meat some or all of the time because of religious belief, health restrictions, or personal preference.) The United States, with roughly 6 percent of the world's land area and 6 percent of the world's population, is producing and consuming nearly 30 percent of the world's supply of beef, pork, lamb, and veal. (This is three times as much beef and veal and nearly twice as much pork as is produced in Russia.) In 1966 each American ate 170.5 pounds of red meat: 104 was beef; 58 was pork; 4.5 was veal; 4 was lamb and mutton. Besides this we averaged 36 pounds of chicken and 10.6 pounds of fish. (We Americans spend $89 billion a year for food, yet this is only about 18 percent of our disposable income.) The question many people ask is: Can we continue to afford to raise meat animals when they are such inefficient converters of vegetable protein to meat? Besides, these animals compete directly with man for basic foods such as the soybean. Some look at the world population explosion and say *no*. Some say the earth's population is growing at a rate of 2 percent per year and the food supply at the rate of 1 percent. A world population clock at Chicago's Museum of Science and Industry clicks at more than 7,000 per minute.

The late Damon V. Catron, former Head of the Food Science and Nutrition Department at the University of Missouri, pointed out that animal proteins may become more of a dietary luxury in the future for these five reasons: (1) World population will double in about 35 years. (2) Animals compete directly with man for much of his food protein coming from plants. (3) Animals are inefficient nitrogen converters from plant protein. (4) Animal production requires another production step involving additional inputs, risks, and time. (5) Income levels may not permit the purchase of animal proteins in many countries of the world. But he thought Americans would continue to consume large amounts of meat, milk, and eggs.

Cornell economist Kenneth Robinson feels there will be continued displacement of one type of commodity by another—such as substitution of beef or poultry for pork—rather than large-scale substitution of synthetic products for those of agricultural origin or vegetable for animal protein. Laws contribute to maintaining the status quo. An example of this is the length of time it took states to legalize the sale of colored margarine.

Naturally, not all the experts agree on the future of meat substitutes, but most agree on this much: (1) More soybean products will be used as thickening and binding agents and as substitutes or extenders for meat in frankfurters, chili, meat loaf, and others. (2) Meatless meats from spun soybean fiber will continue to satisfy those who for religious, health, or other reasons eat no meat. (3) Hospitals, restaurants, and the institutional trade—always on the lookout for products easy to prepare, nutritious, convenient, and with little waste—will increase their use of meatlike substitutes. (4) There is a promising future for edible soybean protein products as a group of new foods not resembling or approximating foods we have known in the past. (5) New foods that are priced right, have eye appeal and effective promotion, and provide family satisfaction will penetrate the retail market. (6) High-protein powders, flours, or meal hold the most promise for overpopulated, undernourished nations—not synthetic meat products. (7) Soybeans will continue to gain in importance. (8) Pork chops and beef steak—the real ones—will still make the meal for years to come.

Use in Processed Meat Products

WARREN TAUBER

THE USE OF NONMEAT PROTEINS in processed meat items is often the result of economic pressure. This practice is frequently encountered where meat is scarce and nonmeat protein sources are readily available.

It can readily be seen that adequate functional uses will upgrade both the meat product and the added nonmeat protein if requirements of improved texture, handling, and acceptable shelf-life can be obtained by the judicious use of nonmeat protein materials.

Many of the nonmeat proteins used in processed meat items are residues from cereals and soybeans or are items such as skim milk or egg proteins. In some instances the protein is concentrated or isolated from the specific source, i.e., soy protein and casein. Protein fibers have been prepared from soy protein, and the fibrous structure has been used to simulate meat products with some modest degree of success. The fibers at present are quite expensive relative to the isolated protein or to the concentrate and meal.

The U.S. Department of Agriculture permits up to 3.5 percent of milk powder or certain cereals in comminuted sausage, but it is not permissible to use additives of this type in fresh sausage. However, in England fresh sausage may contain 25 to 50 percent of cereal based on the moistened weight of cereal. The English type sausage frequently has limited acceptance in the United States because of the cereal flavor and textures, and conversely the U.S. all-meat sausage is often considered tough or rubbery by the British.

Where nonmeat protein materials are to be used with processed meat items, it is important to establish the following factors for acceptance: (1) good water absorption, (2) emulsification of fat, (3) reasonable price, (4) neutral or desirable flavor, (5) ease in handling and storing, (6) little labor in preparing for use, and (7) suitable color. The nonmeat protein material rarely meets all of these requirements for sausage products, although some of the binders meet some of these factors to a very high degree.

On inspection of processed meat products, we can separate specific groups whereby functional requirements are needed.

1. Fresh sausage types where it is desirable to extend the meat to produce economical products.

2. Processed products where legal limits have been established for binders or extenders and we produce items to meet certain economic demands.

3. Sausage products with offal contents that need an additional binding material so that a desirable texture is maintained. This may include loaves and puddings such as scrapple, souse, and panhaus.

4. Products such as English or Canadian sausage where binders or extenders in excess of our normal legal additions are used.

5. Boneless meat products, such as boneless ham, where the formed and molded shape is retained by heating the meat mass and by binding the chunks or layers of muscle with a small amount of suitable proteinaceous material such as gluten, egg white, or gelatin. Egg white has proven to be a superior material for binding of meat surfaces, and a patent application has been filed recently for this usage.

The use of soybean meal up to levels of 30 percent of the total sausage solids has been successful. In the mild flavored products that are popular today, some soy flavor is detected in the finished product. Some texture changes resulted in sausages containing soybean meal after ten days or so of storage. The sausage product became soft and mushy. The beany flavor of sausage containing soybean meal may be corrected by the use of spice at a level somewhat higher than the level of today's bland product. The texture changes may be corrected by formulation changes in which an increase in heat-coagulable protein should be helpful. The animal proteins are usually heat-coagulable, whereas vegetable proteins do not heat-coagulate readily.

At the present time the use of nonmeat proteins in processed meats is best where the vegetable sources are used as extenders for more economical products. The functional use of nonmeat protein material is restricted to a few specific applications. The future may well be in the area of extenders and for preparing low-cost, adequate nutrition.

The isolation of protein and reshaping the protein into fibers for food is interesting but adds an additional cost to the product.

Considerable additional work is needed in the area of flavor reduction, in masking of flavor, in improving texture, and possibly in the developing of practical handling techniques for the improved use of vegetable proteins in processed meat products.

PART THREE

Nutritional Influences on High-Quality Production

6

Prenatal and Postnatal Effects on Subsequent Performance and Carcass Quality

F. W. H. ELSLEY

A COMPREHENSIVE STUDY of the effects of nutrition upon the growth of the pig is outside the scope of any single chapter. With this in mind, this chapter is restricted to a discussion of a few of the principles which control the relationship between the development of the growing pig and the dietary energy intake of the dam and of the pig itself in the earlier stages of growth. No attempt is made to discuss either the inter-relationship of individual nutrients or the effects of varying mineral and vitamin intakes upon the growth of the pig.

GROWTH AND DEVELOPMENT

The growth processes of mammals can be considered from two aspects: (1) the rate of increase of the body mass, usually referred to as *growth* and described by changes in liveweight, and (2) the alterations in the form of animals which result from changes in the rate of increase of individual components of the body, described as *development*.

The improvements made by Sir John Hammond at Cambridge in the 1930's in the technique of serial slaughter gave rise to a number of experiments in which the development of the pig was examined either by dissection of the body into component tissues (McMeekan, 1940a, b, and c; Cuthbertson and Pomeroy, 1962) or by examination of the chemical composition of the whole body (Cuthbertson and Hosie, 1963; Elsley, 1964). The nutritional implication of these studies can best be understood if the growth and development of the components of the body are

TABLE 6.1: Comparison of Chemical Analyses of Newborn Pigs

	No.	Wt. kg.	Protein gm.	Protein % D.M.[a]	Ash gm.	Ash % D.M.	Fat gm.	Fat % D.M.	Nitrogen-Free Extract, %
Manners and McCrea (1953)	3	1.45	174	69.0	60	24.0	18	7.1	—
Berge and Indrebo (1953)	6	1.12	135	68.9	47	24.4	13	6.6	10
Mitchell *et al.* (1931)	23	1.30	132	69.8	44	23.5	12.6	6.6	15
Spray and Widdowson (1950)	16	1.46	165	71.1	51	22.0	16	7.0	—
Elsley	400	1.03	113	69.0	36	22.1	14	8.8	14

[a] D.M. = Weight of protein + ash + fat

considered in two separate categories, that is essential tissues and storage depots.

For the purposes of this chapter, essential tissues (ET) include bone; muscle; internal organs; circulatory, nervous, digestive, and reproductive systems; other components of the body such as skin; and that part of the fat which is a necessary component of those tissues already mentioned. Storage depots (SD) include nonessential lipids, super-mineralization of bone tissue, and localized accumulations of carbohydrate such as liver glycogen. Although this division of the components of the body is not ideal from some points of view, it has value in elucidating the principles of the relationship between nutrition and growth.

Essential Tissues

The growth rate of the essential tissues is of the greatest significance to those engaged in the production of meat. This is because of the direct relationship between the growth rate of essential tissues and the growth of lean meat. The rate of gain of the essential tissues is largely dependent on the environment, and in particular on the intake of nutrients by the pigs and on the balance of the individual nutrients in the diet. Under optimal environmental conditions, the rate of gain will largely be determined by the genetic potential of the pigs and by their sex. The rate of gain of the essential tissues, although differing between groups of pigs, usually follows the same general pattern (Fig. 6.1).

The developmental changes which occur in the relative proportions of the components of the essential tissues and in the composition of the individual tissues during the growth of the pig from its embryonic to its mature form have received close attention since Dr. Hammond indicated

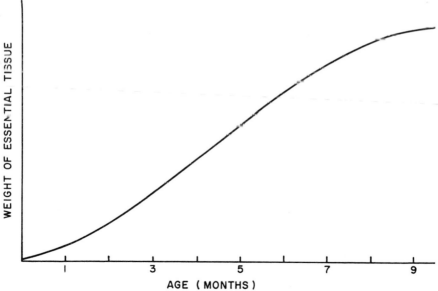

FIG. 6.1.   Growth of essential tissue of pigs fed ad libitum.

their nature and importance. It is now well known that the various tissues attain their maximum rate of gain at different stages relative to the overall growth of the essential tissues. For example nervous tissue, or to a lesser extent bone tissue, can be termed early-maturing while muscle tissue which attains its maximum rate of gain at a later stage is termed later-maturing. Similarly, maturity rankings can be given to each of the component bones of the skeleton, to individual muscles, and to parts of the body. Thus the head and the limbs are early-maturing while the abdomen, in particular the loin region, is late-maturing.

These changes are necessary to maintain the functional integrity of the body with increasing size and to provide maximal functional efficiency with changes in the environment. Thus the appendicular skeleton and its associated muscles exhibit similar development at the stage in which rapid mobility of the piglet becomes important for its survival. Huxley (1932) demonstrated that these apparently complex changes could be explained by a very simple mathematical expression. He showed that, within a species or a genotype, the weight of a particular tissue or part of the body was largely determined by the total weight of the animal. Huxley found that if y is the same size of the organ or part of the body under study, x is the size of the whole body, and b is the growth coefficient of the part of the body, then $y = ax^b$ gave a useful quantitative description of differential growth. In particular b could be used to compare quantitatively the relative maturity of different tissues or parts of the body.

Storage Depots

The only storage depot of major practical importance is the non-essential lipid. Analyses of the carcasses of pigs killed serially over a wide range in liveweight have clearly shown that the proportion of the fat content of the body increases as liveweight increases (McMeekan, 1940 a, b, and c; Cuthbertson and Pomeroy, 1962; Hörnicke, 1962). None of these authors has drawn a distinction between the essential and non-essential fractions of the total fat, and it is necessary in this chapter to consider the fat content of the body as a whole. Since most of the fat in the body is likely to be in the nonessential category, fat deposition can be considered to be largely independent of the growth of the essential tissue. The proportion of fat deposited at any stage of growth is therefore not dependent on the fact that fat is a late-maturing tissue but is dependent on the nutritional status of the animal. This was demonstrated graphically by Fowler (1967 b).

Fowler plotted the cumulative intake of metabolizable energy (total feed energy less energy of urine and feces) consumed by pigs fed ad libitum during growth from weaning to 260 lb. liveweight (Fig. 6.2). If the energy lost as heat is subtracted from the metabolizable energy, the energy remaining (and therefore available for tissue deposition) was termed by Fowler *productive energy*. The amount of fat deposited will then be determined by the amount of productive energy in excess of that used for the growth of the essential tissues. It also follows that a

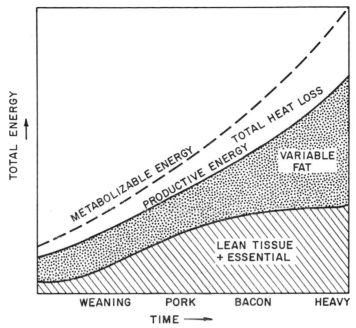

Fig. 6.2. Partition of metabolizable energy in the growing pig on unrestricted feeding (Fowler, 1967).

surplus of productive energy could occur during any stage of growth, either due to an excessively high energy intake or a temporary reduction of the growth of the essential tissue.

From this brief review of the growth and development of the pig, the objectives of the nutritionist in establishing nutrient requirements for pigs can be listed.

1. It is essential to define the conditions which allow the maximum rate of gain of the essential tissue to be achieved.

2. It is necessary to investigate to what extent the balance between the growth of the components of the essential tissue can be disturbed by nutritional means, and in particular to determine if the lean content or the distribution of the lean tissue can be altered at any particular stage of growth.

3. The utilization of nutrients to produce tissues which do not directly or indirectly increase the lean content of the carcass is undesirable. The utilization of energy in the production of storage fat must be reduced as far as possible, particularly since the energy content of fat is much higher than that of the essential tissue.

EFFECT OF NUTRITION ON PRENATAL GROWTH

The growth and development of the fetal pig has received considerable attention since Dr. Mitchell and his co-workers conducted the first comprehensive study at Illinois (Mitchell *et al.*, 1931). Their results have been substantiated and expanded by De Villiers *et al.* (1958),

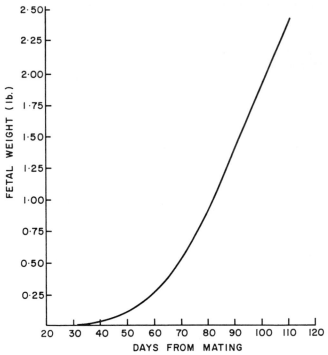

FIG. 6.3. Growth of fetal pigs (Elsley and MacPherson, 1967).

Pomeroy (1960), Ullrey *et al.* (1965) and Elsley *et al.* (1966). Although these studies were conducted with pigs of different genetic origin and maintained in greatly differing environments, the results show very little variation in the pattern of fetal development. The pattern of fetal growth which emerges from these studies is shown in Figures 6.3 and 6.4. The rate of deposition of the individual nutrients increases during pregnancy, but even at the end of the pregnancy period the absolute amounts of nutrients deposited represent only a small proportion of the total daily feed intake of the sow. The composition of the pigs at birth obtained in a series of experiments is given in Table 6.1. This shows that at birth the pig consists almost entirely of essential tissues and contains virtually no fat. The fat and carbohydrate content of the newly born pigs probably reflects the requirement of the neonatal pig for energy during the period when its ability to maintain thermostasis is inadequate rather than a store of excess energy.

Growth

The relation between feed intake of the pregnant sow and the growth of the fetal pigs has been studied by a number of British and American research workers. The lack of agreement between many of their results may reflect inadequacies in either the number of animals used or the

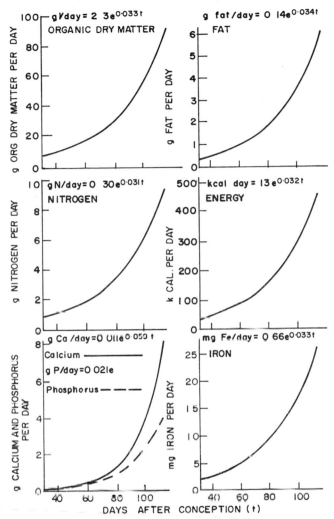

FIG. 6.4. Increase in nutrient deposition during pregnancy (Mouutgaard, 1962).

standardization of animals before the imposition of the experimental treatments rather than a variation in the biological response to changes in feed intakes.

We have conducted a series of experiments at the Rowett Institute during the last six years in which some of the effects of both feed intake and energy intake of the pregnant sow on the weight of the pigs at birth have been studied. In all these experiments the daily intakes of protein, minerals, and vitamins have been in agreement with the standards published by the National Research Council of America (N.R.C., 1964) and by the Agricultural Research Council of Great Britain (A.R.C., 1967). Results of the experiments were combined to determine the overall re-

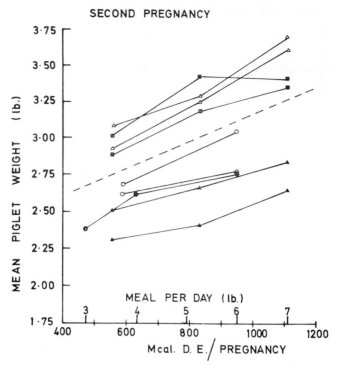

FIG. 6.5. Relation between energy intake and birth weight
(Elsley, 1967).

lationship between intake of energy by the sow and the mean weight of
the pigs at birth. An example of the results is given in Figure 6.5 and
is based on the results from 280 sows during the second reproductive
cycle. These results indicate that under our conditions there is a linear
relationship between the digestible energy consumed by the sow during
pregnancy and the mean birth weight. However, large changes in feed
intake are required before the birth weight is markedly affected; for
example, an increase in feed intake from 3.5 to 7 lb. only increases mean
birth weight by 0.4 lb. Most of the additional feed intake is used in
increasing the extra-uterine body mass of the sow apart from the changes
in the reproductive tract and its contents. It can be demonstrated that
the net gain of the sow (that is the increase in maternal tissue over the
pregnancy period excluding the products of conception) is linearly related to the feed intake of the sow during pregnancy (Fig. 6.6). If increases in feed intake are used in order to produce heavier pigs at birth,
this would inevitably lead to increased gain in the weight of the sow.

Development

A number of studies have been made of the effect of nutrition on the
growth of the pig, but comparatively few workers have examined the
effect of variation in feed intake of the sow on the development and

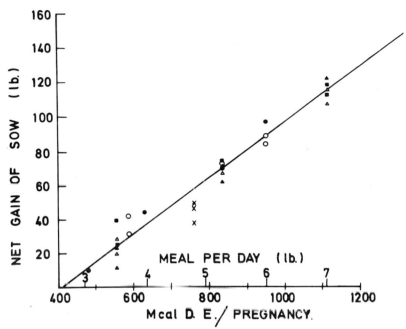

FIG. 6.6. Relation between energy intake and net gain of
sow during pregnancy (Elsley, 1967).

composition of the pigs at birth. Livingston (1962) reported that the
muscle fiber thickness of certain muscles of the newborn pig was apparently depressed by low concentrations of protein in the sow's diet. However, in studies involving chemical analysis of 600 newborn pigs, we
found no significant effect on the composition of pigs at birth from
sows given intakes of feed which ranged between 3.5 and 6 lb. of feed
per day, or from protein concentrations ranging from 11 to 18 percent
crude protein; (Elsley *et al.*, 1965, 1966). Neither Livingston (1959) nor
Livingstone *et al.* (1966) could find any evidence that the protein intake
of the pregnant sow had any effect on the growth and development of
the progeny from birth to slaughter at 200 lb. liveweight.

From the evidence discussed in this chapter, it appears that the
major effect of nutrition during pregnancy is on the weight of the pigs
at birth. There is no evidence that the composition of the pigs will be
affected by nutrition of the sow within the extremes of nutritional re-
gimes normally encountered under practical conditions.

EFFECT OF NUTRITION ON POSTNATAL GROWTH

While it is extremely difficult to affect the growth and development
of the fetal pig, it is well known that after birth the growth and the composition of the pig can be controlled by nutritional means. In European

markets in which the fat content of a pig can cause a 20 percent variation in the price received by the farmer, considerable emphasis has been given to those factors controlling both growth and carcass composition.

The choice of the optimum feeding pattern for growing pigs from birth to slaughter has been influenced by the results of an experiment conducted by Dr. McMeekan at Cambridge in the 1930's. Despite the small number of animals involved, the experiment has had a worldwide influence on the attitude of nutritionists to methods of feeding pigs. It is because of the profound influence that this experiment has had upon our subsequent thinking that it is important to examine its results in the perspective of later experiments.

McMeekan (1940 a, b, and c) reared pigs according to four prede-termined growth rates by controlling their feed intake (Fig. 6.7). The treatments were termed High-High, High-Low, Low-High and Low-Low, indicating the level of feed intake from birth to 16 weeks of age and from 16 weeks until slaughter at 200 lb. liveweight.

The main results of McMeekan's experiment are given in Table 6.2. This table demonstrates that the treatments greatly influenced the fat contents of the carcasses at 200 lb. and apparently altered both the muscle to bone ratio and the proportion of the higher-priced to lower-priced joints in the carcasses. The results obtained by McMeekan with pigs were combined by Palsson (1955) with results from similar studies with sheep and cattle to produce a complex hypothesis for explaining the relationship between nutrition and carcass composition. Palsson made no distinction between essential and storage tissues but classified the tissues and parts of the body by defining their maturity. Palsson's conclusions can be briefly summarized as follows:

1. Early-maturing tissues or parts of the body are less affected by reductions in feed intake than late-maturing components of the body.

2. The stage of growth at which restriction occurs is important, since the development of any tissue or part of the body can be relatively more retarded by a restriction of feed intake during the stage when that component is increasing most rapidly.

TABLE 6.2: **Effect of Plane of Nutrition Upon Composition of the Carcasses of Pigs Killed at 200 Lb. Liveweight (After McMeekan, 1940 a, b, and c)**

| | Weights of tissues relative to H-H = 100 | | | | | | | Treatment Differences in Adjusted Weight | |
| | | Unadjusted Means | | | Adjusted[a] Means | | | | |
Treatment	H-H	LL	HL	LH	LL	HL	LH	SE	Sig.
	(lb.)								
Total bone	15.8	111	105	89	97	96	96	2.1	NS
Total muscle	58.1	120	114	91	101	101	101	0.5	NS
Subcutaneous fat	40.5	66	87	117	53	75	131	7.1	...

[a] Adjusted by Elsley et al. (1964) so that the weight of total bone and muscle in the carcasses were comparable.

If this hypothesis is correct, it has certain practical implications. It would suggest that the level of feeding at any stage will have its effect on subsequent periods of growth and upon the eventual composition of the carcass at slaughter. It also implies that regulating feed intake is a powerful tool for manipulating the proportions of the components of the body. For example the method of feeding can influence the proportion of bone in the carcass and affect the proportion of higher-priced parts of the carcass.

This hypothesis has been generally accepted, although Wallace (1948) and subsequently Wilson (1954), Fowler (1959), and Elsley *et al.* (1964) questioned the interpretation placed on the results. All these authors pointed out that the feed intakes had greatly affected the fat content of the carcasses. The pigs were killed at similar liveweights, but the differences in fat content resulted in differences in the content of essential tissue in the carcasses. Elsley *et al.* (1964) demonstrated by re-analysis of McMeekan's data that once the difference in the weight of fat-free carcass between the treatments had been removed, no major differences in the composition or the proportions of the fat-free body could be attributed to the nutritional treatments. Fowler (1967 b), in a more detailed analysis of the same data, did in fact show that some modification of the balance of the components of the essential tissue was possible under conditions of extreme nutritional stress. These changes were not, however, dependent on the maturity of the tissues, as suggested by Palsson, but were consistent with the functional modifications of the body to counter specific circumstances. Such changes, although of academic interest, had little practical significance.

From this evidence an alternative view of the interrelationship between nutrition and growth can be stated in a simpler form: The restriction of feed intake causes a more or less uniform retardation of development except insofar as fat tissue is concerned. If this simple statement is accepted, there are no advantages to be gained in attempts to alter by nutritional means the balance of the components forming the essential tissue.

PRACTICAL IMPLICATIONS

The potential growth rate of the essential tissues in the young pig is high, but the maximum rate of gain will not be achieved until the pig is weaned unless milk production of the sow or consumption of supplementary feed is also high. Under British conditions suckled pigs receiving no creep feed attain weights of approximately 28 lb. liveweight by the time weaning occurs at 56 days of age (BOCM, 1960; Lodge and McDonald, 1959). The milk yield of the sow can be increased by increasing feed intake in lactation and the fat concentration of the milk by feeding generously in pregnancy, but this increase in milk production is usually only sufficient to marginally increase pig weight. The greatest increase in weaning weight for suckled pigs can be attained if creep consumption is increased (Lodge *et al.*, 1959).

The choice of the optimum rate of gain during the early stages of

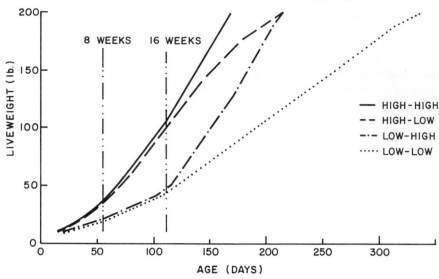

Fig. 6.7. Liveweight changes of pigs (McMeekan, 1940 a, b, c).

growth has aroused considerable controversy in Europe. In the 1950's great emphasis was given in Great Britain to the production of heavy weaners at 56 days of age, while in Denmark emphasis was given to lower growth rates. Rate of gain was considered important since, according to Palsson (1955), high growth rate in the early stages should favor the growth of early-maturing tissues such as bone and muscle. Boaz and Elsley (1962) controlled the growth rate of suckled pigs so that the pigs weighed 30, 40, or 50 lb. at 56 days of age. The pigs were then fed under standard conditions to 200 lb. liveweight. The growth rate of the pigs to 56 days of age had no major effect on the subsequent growth of the pigs or on the composition of the bacon carcasses. Pigs which were lighter at 56 days of age were older at slaughter merely because they reached 50 lb. later than the heavier weaners. Under our conditions excessive fat deposition did not occur in suckled pigs which reached 50 lb. liveweight, and high growth rates in the early stages were desirable since they reduced age at slaughter.

The introduction of systems of weaning pigs before 8 weeks of age, for example at 10 lb. liveweight, made consistent high growth rates possible at a much earlier stage. This system of rearing involves differences in, for example, total energy intake and diet composition, and these may have a considerable effect on growth and development. Lucas *et al.* (1959) found that pigs weaned at 10 lb. liveweight and given feed ad libitum up to 50 lb. liveweight subsequently grew 8 percent more slowly and utilized feed 9 percent less efficiently than sow-reared pigs also weighing 50 lb. at 8 weeks of age. Elsley (1963 b), who killed pigs at 8 weeks of age, found that the early-weaned pigs contained more fat and less bone and muscle than sow-reared pigs of the same weight. This suggests that at our present state of knowledge early-weaned pigs cannot be reared at their maximum liveweight gain without at the same time depositing extra storage fat. This was demonstrated by Lucas *et al.* (1959), Elsley (1963 a), and Fowler (1964), who all found that reductions in growth rate up to 50 lb. liveweight for early-weaned pigs resulted in more efficient utilization of feed and led to a reduction in the fat content of the carcasses of the pigs when killed at 200 lb. liveweight.

It has been suggested that checks in the growth rate of pigs which occur at weaning or when pigs are kept in unfavorable environments can have an effect on the subsequent growth of the pig and upon carcass composition. The deliberate introduction of a 3-week growth check at weaning at 10 days of age (Lucas *et al.*, 1964), the imposition of weight stasis for 3 weeks at 50, 100, or 150 lb. liveweight (Lucas *et al.*, 1961 a) or for 5 weeks at 50 or 100 lb. liveweight (Lucas *et al.*, 1964) had no effect on carcass composition at 200 lb. liveweight and little effect on the growth rate subsequent to the check. Fowler (1967) has recently reported that variations in the feed intake which reduce or increase feed intake by 12 percent on a weekly or fortnightly cycle have no effect on the overall growth rate or on measures of carcass composition, as long as total feed over the experimental period remains unchanged. These results all support the view that the growth of the essential tissue is merely accelerated or decelerated, and as long as excessive fat deposition is not induced the growth and carcass composition of the pigs are unchanged.

The period of growth in which level of feed intake has its most dynamic effect is from about 50 lb. to slaughter. It is in this period that the intake of dietary energy can exceed that required for growth of the essential tissue and thus cause excessive fat deposition. It is for this reason that the feed intake of a large proportion of pigs produced in western Europe is reduced, either from 50 lb. liveweight or, more commonly, from 100 lb. liveweight. A restriction of feed intake to below appetite generally reduces total fat content but also reduces daily liveweight gain. The effects of such reductions in feed intake on feed conversion efficiency are not consistent, because the efficiency with which feed is utilized is dependent on both the caloric density of the tissue deposited and the requirements for maintenance. A reduction in feed intake decreases fat deposition and therefore the caloric content of the gain. However, this effect is frequently offset by the increase in the maintenance cost of each unit of tissue deposited, resulting from extension of the growing period. The relationship between percentage of daily feed restriction and daily gain and thickness of the backfat has been studied by a number of workers, such as Vanschoubroek *et al.* (1967), using data from Europe and America (Figs. 6.8 and 6.9). These average responses to changes in feed intake are of use when general policy decisions are being taken, but they have little practical use to the individual farmer. This is because the potential rate of gain of essential tissue is largely under genetic control, and the individual response to changes in feed intake from farm to farm may vary greatly even under standard feeding conditions. It is hoped that geneticists will undertake highly intensive breeding programs to raise

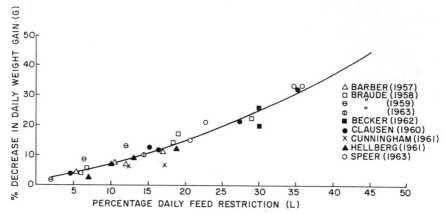

Fig. 6.8. Effect of feed restriction on daily weight gain.
$G = 1.9600 + 0.3715L + 0.0133L.^2$

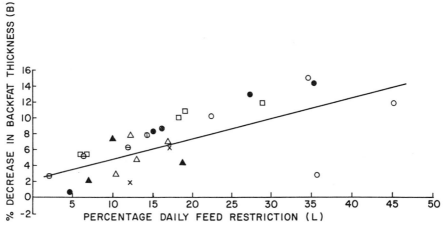

Fig. 6.9. Effect of feed restriction on backfat thickness.
(Key to symbols is given in Fig. 6.8.) $B = 2.3740 + 0.2515L.$

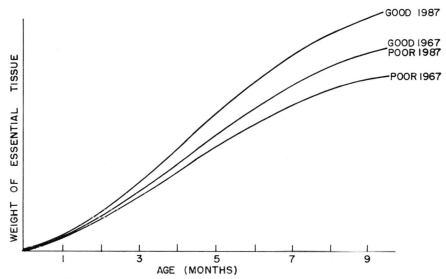

FIG. 6.10. Growth of essential tissue of pigs fed ad libitum.

the potential essential tissue growth rate. This is not equivalent to breeding programs which select pigs which can be fed ad libitum and still produce an acceptable quality of carcass; such a program may have a tendency to select pigs with low appetites rather than high lean tissue growth
rates. If the genetic potential for lean tissue growth is increased, the position may be as shown in Figure 6.10. Under such conditions, feeding
systems based on high intakes or ad libitum feeding could produce carcasses with a low fat content.

REFERENCES

Berge, S., and Indrebø, T. 1953. *Meldinger Norg. Landbrukshoegskole.* 34:481.
Boaz, T. G., and Elsley, F. W. H. 1962. *Animal Prod.* 4:13.
Cuthbertson, A., and Hosie, K. E. 1963. *Animal Prod.* 5:220 (Abstr.).
Cuthbertson, A., and Pomeroy, R. W. 1962. *J. Agr. Sci.* 59:215.
De Villiers, V., Sørensen, P. H., Jakobsen, P. E., and Moustgaard, J. 1958. K.
    vet.-og Landbohøgsk. Inst. Sterilitetsforsk. Arsberetn. p. 139.
Elsley, F. W. H. 1963a. *J. Agr. Sci.* 61:299.
———. 1963b. *J. Agr. Sci.* 61:243.
———. 1964. *Ann. Zootech.* 13:75.
Elsley, F. W. H., Anderson, D. M., and MacPherson, R. M. 1965. *Proc. Nutr.
    Soc.* Vol. 24.
Elsley, F. W. H., McDonald, I., and Fowler, V. R. 1964. *Animal Prod.* 6:141.
Elsley, F. W. H., McDonald, I., and MacPherson, R. M. 1966. *Animal Prod.*
    8:353.
Fowler, V. R. 1959. Thesis, University of Reading, Berkshire, England.
———. 1964. Ph.D. Thesis, University of Leeds, Leeds, England.
———. 1967a. *Animal Prod.* 9:272 (Abstr.).
———. 1967b. Nottingham University Easter School, "Growth and Development
    of Mammals," Butterworths Scientific Publications, London. In press.

Hörnicke, H. 1962. Z. Tierphysiol. Tierernähr. Futtermittelk. 17:28.
Huxley, J. 1932. *Problems of Relative Growth,* London: Methuen.
Livingston, D. M. S. 1959. Ph.D. Thesis, University of Aberdeen, Scotland.
———. 1962. *Animal Prod.* 4:296.
Livingstone, R. M., MacPherson, R. M., Elsley, F. W. H., Lucas, I. A. M., and
    Lodge, G. A. 1966. *Animal Prod.* 8:337.
Lodge, G. A., and McDonald, I. 1959. *Animal Prod.* 1:139.
Lucas, I. A. M., Calder, A. F. C., and Smith, H. 1959. *J. Agr. Sci.* 53:125.
Lucas, I. A. M., Livingstone, R. M., and McDonald, I. 1961. Proc. 8th Int.
    Congr. Anim. Prod., Hamburg, General Reports, 209.
———. 1964. Proc. 6th Int. Congr. Nutr., Edinburgh, 568.
McMeekan, C. P. 1940a. *J. Agr. Sci.* 30:276.
———. 1940b. *J. Agr. Sci.* 30:387.
———. 1940c. *J. Agr. Sci.* 30:511.
Manners, M. J., and McCrea, M. R. 1963. *Brit. J. Nutr.* 17:495.
Mitchell, H. H., Carroll, W. E., Hamilton, T. S., and Hunt, G. E. 1931. Bull.
    Ill. Agr. Exp. Sta. 375.
Moustgaard, J. 1962. "Foetal Nutrition in the Pig." In *Proceedings, Nutrition
    of Pigs and Poultry Conference.* Butterworths Scientific Publications, Lon-
    don, pp. 189–206.
N.A.S./N.R.C. Pub. No. 1192. "Nutrient Requirements of Domestic Animals.
    II. Nutrient Requirements of Swine."
Palsson, H. 1955. "Progress in the Physiology of Farm Animals," pp. 430–543.
    J. Hammond (ed.), Butterworths Scientific Publications, London.
Pomeroy, R. W. 1960. *J. Agr. Sci.* 54:31.
Spray, C. M., and Widdowson, E. M. 1950. *Brit. J. Nutr.* 4:332.
Ullrey, D. E., Sprague, J. I., Becker, D. E., and Miller, E. R. 1965. *J. Animal
    Sci.* 24:711.
Vanschoubroek, F., De Wilde, R., and Lampo, Ph. 1967. *Animal Prod.* 9:67.
Wallace, L. R. 1948. *J. Agr. Sci.* 38:93.
Wilson, P. N. 1954. *J. Agr. Sci.* 42:369.

Nutritional and Management Effects on Performance and Carcass Measurements

V. W. HAYS

It has been stated that pork carcass quality is about 5 percent dependent on genetics, 10 percent dependent on nutrition, and 85 percent dependent on management, and that it is easy to turn a good pig into a poor carcass and a relatively poor pig into a reasonable carcass by the appropriate management systems. There is little comfort in such estimates; the only positive element from a nutritionist's viewpoint is that nutrition was credited with having as much influence on carcass quality as breeding. Practically speaking, such estimates are quite correct in that the management represents the artful combining of the proper environmental conditions, including diet, to make the most of the limited genetic potential available at the time. Such management does not, however, result in permanent improvement in genetic material or nutrition programs.

Rapidity of gain in pigs and carcass characteristics are genetically controlled, but each may be markedly influenced by the balance of nutrients and the rationing of the diet. Any essential nutrient may directly or indirectly affect carcass measurements through its influence on rate or pattern of growth. Nutritional deficiencies which result in extended and marked reduction in growth rate, followed by ad libitum intake of an adequate diet, may result in excessive fat deposition, hence a high ratio of fat to lean in the carcass. Extended stunting of growth by disease or adverse environmental conditions other than nutrition may have similar effects. The most common and readily demonstrated effects of nutrition on carcass characteristics relate to energy intake, protein (amino acid) intake, and protein to energy ratio in the diet.

The related effects of protein and energy are not simple. Excess protein may be utilized almost as efficiently as carbohydrates for energy pur-

67

TABLE 7.1: **Effects of Diet Restriction and Protein Intake on Energy and Protein Utilization**

Protein Level Feeding Level	Low Low	High Low	Low High
Trial 1			
Feed intake/day, gm.	1600	1600	2450
N intake/day, gm.	31.2	53.1	47.8
Dig. energy/day, cal.	4836	4698	7311
N retention/day, gm.	10.3	14.3	16.6
N retention, %	33.0	26.9	34.4
Trial 2			
Feed intake/day, gm.	1630	1640	3220
Daily gain, gm.	284	243	755
Feed/gain	5.82	6.95	4.40
Loin eye area, sq. in.	4.33	4.24	4.14
Carcass protein, %	15.2	15.6	14.6
Carcass fat, %	38.4	37.7	40.0

Source: Cunningham *et al.*, 1962.

poses. This is apparent from the metabolizable energy values of feedstuffs as reported by Diggs *et al.* (1965) and the rates of gain on high-protein diets as reported by Wagner *et al.* (1963). The high-protein ingredient soybean meal is similar in energy content to high-carbohydrate feedstuffs such as corn (3.72 vs. 3.77 metabolizable kilocalories per gm.). If adequate energy in the form of carbohydrates or fat is not provided, the pig will utilize protein for energy purposes at the expense of tissue synthesis. These interrelationships are exemplified by studies of Cunningham *et al.* (1962) as summarized in Table 7.1. The low level of feeding (1600 gm/day) of the low-protein diet was not adequate in protein or energy for maximum protein retention; at this level of intake, protein was used for energy purposes. Additional protein resulted in some increase in total protein deposition, but the reduction in percentage retained and the response to the similar intake of protein in combination with a higher level of energy confirms that energy level was inadequate for maximum retention and that protein was being used for energy purposes.

ENERGY LEVEL

The effects of energy intake on performance and carcass measurements may be illustrated by varying the total feed intake (restricted feeding vs. self-feeding) or by varying the energy density of the diet (by substituting fat for carbohydrates or carbohydrates for fibrous materials). Either method of varying energy intake is effective in influencing carcass measurements, but one is able to exercise more control over energy intake by restricted feeding than by varying the energy density of the diet.

An example of the effects of moderate restriction is presented in Table 7.2. Food restriction resulted in a reduction in rate of gain and backfat thickness and an increase in size of loin eye. As has been reported by other researchers (Becker *et al.*, 1962; Braude *et al.*, 1958; Ellis and Zeller, 1931), moderate restriction resulted in a small but significant improvement in efficiency of food conversion. Note that restricting to scale

TABLE 7.2: **Effects of Food Restriction on Performance and Carcass Characteristics**

	Treatment		
To 120 lb. 120 lb. to 200 lb.	Ad Lib. Ad Lib.	Ad Lib. 6.5 lb/day	To Scale[a] To Scale[a]
Average daily gain, lb.	1.49	1.41	1.24
Feed/gain	3.92	3.86	3.81
Average backfat, cm.	3.92	3.71	3.50
Depth of eye muscle, cm.	4.41	4.52	4.43
Width of eye muscle, cm.	7.51	7.51	7.64

Source: Brande *et al.*, 1958.
[a] 2.0 lb/day for pigs weighing 32 to 36 lb. and 0.1 lb. additional for each 3.0 increase in weight to a maximum of 6.5 lb/day.

resulted in a 17 percent reduction in rate of gain but only in 11 percent reduction in backfat thickness. Similar results from the reports of Greer *et al.* (1965) are presented in Table 7.3.

It is well established, as exemplified in these two tables, that restricting the feed intake during the finishing stage will result in a higher ratio of lean to fat in the carcass. The magnitude of the reduction in fat deposition is dependent on the degree of restriction and the length of time the restriction is imposed. As illustrated by the data in Tables 7.2 and 7.3, a restriction sufficient to result in a rather marked reduction in rate of gain is required to appreciably decrease backfat thickness or increase the proportion of lean cuts in the carcass.

To limit fat synthesis, the diets should be formulated so as to limit only the energy intake, and energy should not be limited to less than that required for maximum lean tissue synthesis. Limiting the intake of other nutrients will result in reduced synthesis of lean tissue. Limiting the intake of a low-protein diet may have little or no effect on the ratio of fat to lean in the carcass.

Axelsson and Erikson (1953), Whatley *et al.* (1951), Coey and Robinson (1954), Crampton *et al.* (1954), Bohman *et al.* (1955), Handlin *et al.*

TABLE 7.3: **Effect of Restricting Corn Base Diets on Performance and Carcass Characteristics**

Trial 1			
Feed intake, kg/day	3.15	2.44	2.06
Avg. daily gain, kg.	0.77	0.61	0.51
Feed/gain	4.09	4.00	4.04
Ham and Loin, % of carcass	35.9	38.0	38.4
Backfat, cm.	3.78	3.40	3.22
Fat in *l. dorsi*, % of D.M.	20.7	14.3	15.3
Trial 2			
Feed intake, kg/day	2.61	2.11	1.80
Avg. daily gain, kg.	0.70	0.55	0.45
Feed/gain	3.73	3.84	4.00
Ham and Loin, % of carcass	37.1	38.6	39.4
Backfat, cm.	3.73	3.61	3.28
Fat in *l. dorsi*, % of D.M.	16.4	13.0	11.4

Source: Green *et al.*, 1965.

TABLE 7.4: Effect of Limited Feeding and High-Fiber Diets on Performance and Carcass Characteristics

Level of protein, %	18–14	18–14	22–18	14–11	13–12	16–12
TDN	76	76	76	76	62[a]	62[b]
Level of feeding	100	70	100	100	100	100
Avg. daily gain, lb.	1.42	1.16	1.44	1.45	12.8	0.88
Feed/gain	3.85	3.67	3.84	4.01	5.58	6.98
Backfat, in.	1.69	1.64	1.72	1.77	1.58	1.17
Lean cuts, %	46.0	48.6	47.8	45.5	47.9	51.9
Fat in *l. dorsi*, % of D.M.	15.1	9.6	11.4	15.4	9.9	10.9

Source: Merkel *et al.*, 1958a,b.
[a] Diet diluted with 30% corncobs.
[b] Diet diluted with 53% alfalfa hay.

(1961), and others have reported on the effects of limiting energy intake by adding fibrous feeds to the diet. Such effects may be illustrated by the studies of Merkel *et al.* (1958 a,b) in which ground corncobs or alfalfa meal was used to dilute the energy content of the diet (Table 7.4). A 30 percent level of ground corncobs resulted in a 6.7 percent reduction in backfat thickness and a 9.9 percent reduction in rate of gain. Similar effects may be noted from substituting low-energy ingredients such as barley for corn, as illustrated in Table 7.5.

Pigs fed diets high in fiber will consume more total feed to partially offset the effects of added fiber (Table 7.4). As a result, it takes a rather large difference in fiber content to appreciably influence the carcass measurements. As in the case of limited feeding, the rate of gain must be markedly reduced before backfat thickness is significantly decreased. In either case, limited feeding or diluting the diet with fiber, the improvement in carcass value is seldom sufficient to offset the added production costs. This is particularly true of diluting the diet with fiber, as the cost of adding fibrous feeds to diets frequently approaches that of adding commonly used high-energy ingredients such as corn or grain sorghums.

Altering the energy intake by adding fat to the diet has the reverse effect of adding fiber. Whereas the pig markedly increases food intake to compensate for energy dilution, there is a reduction in food intake when fat is added to the diet. However, those pigs receiving diets with added fat normally consume more energy per day than do similar pigs fed diets without added fat, since their reduced intake is not of such magnitude as

TABLE 7.5: Effect of Substituting Corn and Barley on Performance and Carcass Characteristics

Grain	Corn	Barley	½ Corn ½ Barley
Avg. daily gain, lb.	1.87	1.55	1.80
Feed/gain	3.37	4.48	3.77
Backfat, in.	1.47	1.27	1.40
Loin cuts, % of carcass	46.7	48.3	47.2
Loin eye area, sq. in.	3.91	4.26	4.04

Source: Handlin *et al.*, 1961.

TABLE 7.6: **Effects of Energy and Protein Content of Diet on Performance and Carcass Characteristics**

Energy level, production	950 kcal/lb			1170 kcal/lb		
Protein level, %	25	19	13	25	19	13
Avg. daily gain, lb.	1.42	1.55	1.63	1.53	1.63	1.77
Feed/gain	3.23	3.33	3.41	2.63	2.56	2.72
Lean cuts, % of carcass	53.8	54.2	52.8	52.8	52.3	51.3
Backfat, in.	1.24	1.25	1.30	1.36	1.42	1.47
Fat in *l. dorsi*, % of D.M.	7.9	9.2	12.6	10.4	12.2	16.9

Source: Wagner *et al.*, 1963.

to offset the increase in caloric density of the diet. The effects of increasing the energy concentration of the diet by adding fat are illustrated in Tables 7.6 and 7.7. Within the same protein level, 10 percent added fat resulted in a 10–15 percent increase in backfat thickness and a 30–35 percent increase in intramuscular fat. An increase in energy intake resulting from adding fat to the diet, substituting fat or carbohydrates for fiber, or increasing the daily allowance of feed results in a fatter carcass as measured by yield of lean cuts, external fat covering, and intramuscular fat content.

PROTEIN LEVEL AND PROTEIN QUALITY

The pig is dependent on an adequate supply of the essential amino acids for growth and development. One cannot force the pig to synthesize tissue proteins beyond his genetic potential by feeding excessive protein, but one can readily reduce the rate of tissue synthesis by allowing inadequate protein. Inadequate total protein or a deficiency of any one of the essential amino acids will reduce growth rate and tissue protein synthesis. Table 7.8 illustrates the effects of inadequate protein on performance and carcass characteristics. A reduction in protein level sufficient to reduce growth rate 10 percent resulted in a 9 percent increase in backfat thickness and more than 75 percent increase in intramuscular fat in the loin eye. Similar illustrations of the effects of dietary protein on carcass characteristics may be noted from the data presented in Tables 7.6 and 7.7.

Dietary protein levels and energy levels have a much greater influence on intramuscular fat deposition than on backfat thickness, percent

TABLE 7.7: **Effects of Energy and Protein Content of Diet on Performance and Carcass Characteristics**

Energy level, metabolizable	1310 kcal/lb			1640 kcal/lb		
Protein level, %	25	19	13	25	19	13
Avg. daily gain, lb.	1.14	1.29	1.30	1.30	1.46	1.39
Feed/gain	4.12	4.05	4.03	3.08	3.11	3.08
Lean cuts, % of carcass	58.5	57.3	56.8	56.4	55.8	54.3
Backfat, in.	1.00	1.04	1.10	1.16	1.26	1.34
Fat in *s. ventralis*, % of D.M.	16.6	18.3	20.3	18.0	19.2	22.2

Source: Wagner *et al.*, 1963.

TABLE 7.8: Effect of Dietary Protein on Performance and Carcass Characteristics

	Protein Level, Percent	
3 to 7 weeks	20	16
7 weeks to 110 lb.[a]	17	13
110 to 200 lb.	14	10
Avg. daily gain, lb.	1.57	1.42
Feed/gain	3.30	3.57
Backfat, in.	1.58	1.72
Lean cuts, % of carcass	51.6	49.2
Fat in *l. dorsi*, % of D.M.[b]	12.4	22.2

Source: Seymour *et al.*, 1964.

[a] Protein level change at 125 lb. in one of three experiments.

[b] Data available for Exp. 3 only, other data average for 3 experiments.

of lean cuts, or performance characteristics. Note Table 7.9 in which the fat in the *longissimus dorsi* of pigs finished on 12 percent protein averaged 16.3 percent, whereas that of pigs finished on 16 percent protein averaged only 9.3 percent. This represents a 75 percent difference in intramuscular fat and only a 5 percent difference in backfat thickness (3.58 vs. 3.76 cm.) or a 4.2 percent difference in rate of gain (663 vs. 635 gm/ day).

Even greater differences in intramuscular fat may be demonstrated by varying both the energy and protein levels. Pigs fed high-energy–low-protein diets (Table 7.6) had twice the amount of fat in the *longissimus dorsi* as did pigs fed low-energy–high-protein diets (16.9 percent vs. 7.9 percent).

The data available to date indicate that the level of fat in the *longissimus dorsi* muscle is only slightly correlated (0.1) with the amount of backfat as illustrated by the summarization in Table 7.10 of the correlation coefficients between these two parameters. Limited data would suggest that the fat content of other muscles may be more highly correlated with backfat thickness. In one experiment, Wagner (1964) observed

TABLE 7.9: Effect of Protein Level on Performance and Carcass Characteristics

	Protein Level[a]	
Item	16%	12%
No. of pigs	64	64
Avg. daily gain, lb.	1.46	1.40
Feed/gain	3.46	3.62
Backfat, in.	1.41	1.48
Ham and Loin, % of carcass	38.74	37.88
Fat in *l. dorsi*	9.32	16.32

Source: Wagner, 1964.

[a] Pigs fed 20% protein from weaning at 10.6 lb. to 50 lb. body wt.

TABLE 7.10: Correlation of Carcass Backfat Thickness and Intramuscular Fat in *Longissimus Dorsi*

Exp. No.	No. of Pigs	r
1	108	0.18
2	144	0.24
3	96	0.11
4	30	0.07
5	75	0.07
6	30	—0.09
7	72	—0.02
8	72	0.12
9	72	0.18
10	64	0.14
11	64	—0.06
Total	827	Average 0.09

Source: Wagner, 1964.

a correlation of 0.47 between the fat content of the *serratus ventralis* and backfat thickness. Duniec *et al.* (1961) have also reported a low phenotype correlation (0.2) between the fat in the *longissimus dorsi* and the fatty tissue in the pork carcass. They further estimated the genetic correlation of these two parameters to be of the order of 0.1 and estimated the heritability of tissue fat to be similar to that of backfat thickness and of the order of 0.5 to 0.7.

The low genetic correlation between backfat thickness and intramuscular fat suggests that we can continue to select for reduced waste fat but still maintain adequate intramuscular fat for good eating quality. The marked influence of diet on intramuscular fat should also allow for continued emphasis on genetic selection for reduced waste fat with the alternative of regulating intramuscular fat by dietary means.

CHEMICAL RELATIONSHIP OF DIETARY AND BODY FAT

The chemical composition of dietary fat markedly affects the composition of pork carcass fat. The pig converts excess carbohydrates to saturated or monounsaturated fatty acids of 16 or 18 carbon chains. The polyunsaturated fatty acids in the carcass are primarily of dietary origin. It appears that the pig preferentially utilizes carbohydrates to meet the energy needs of metabolism and that the dietary fatty acids are stored in the tissue. Dahl (1958, 1960) has observed that one can recover a high percentage of the total linoleic acid consumed by the pig. Because of the apparent preferential deposition of dietary fatty acids, relatively low levels of fat in the diet will markedly influence fatty acid composition of tissue fats. This is well illustrated by the work of Dahl as summarized in Tables 7.11 and 7.12. The fat present in barley or in oats will exert a measurable effect on the linoleic acid content of carcass fat. Our data with corn and barley diets also illustrate retention of a high proportion of the dietary linoleic acid (Table 7.3). Even though barley is very low in fat and contains less than 0.3 percent linoleic acid, if the pig is fed barley

TABLE 7.11: Effect of Diet on Composition of Fat in Pork Carcasses

	Barley[a]	Oats[b]	Barley + Potatoes
Backfat			
Iodine value	57.7	67.2	57.8
Linoleic acid, %	7.0	15.6	6.5
Leaf fat			
Iodine value	49.0	56.8	48.2
Linoleic acid, %	6.5	13.2	5.6

Source: Dahl, 1958.
[a] Barley—1.7% fat, iodine value = 120.
[b] Oats—5.5% fat, iodine value = 106.

to market weight, the fat in the carcass contains appreciably higher levels of linoleic acid (Tables 7.3 and 7.12). Oats are both higher in linoleic acid and lower in digestible carbohydrates and lead to a carcass markedly higher in linoleic acid, a combined result of the deposition of dietary fatty acids and the reduced synthesis of saturated fatty acids from carbohydrates. Such responses illustrate how readily one may influence the composition of pork fat by dietary variations.

Lean meat synthesis by pigs is genetically controlled, and the feeding of excessive nutrients will not permit exceeding the genetic potential. However, to approach the genetic limits for tissue protein synthesis, environmental conditions, including nutritive intake and balance, must be ideal. We have made considerable progress in recent years in reducing the fatness of our pigs as measured by backfat thickness or yield of lean cuts. But why has it taken so long to come such a little way with a characteristic for which we apparently have hardly begun to exploit the genetic variability and one which we estimate as having a heritability coefficient of about 50 percent (Craft, 1958)?

I think it is mainly because we have not tested the pigs under the environmental conditions which will permit them to express their full

TABLE 7.12: Effect of Diet on Composition of Fat in Pork Carcasses

	Potato Flour[a]	Barley[b]	Oats[c] + Barley
Backfat			
Iodine value	57.7	57.5	57.7
Linoleic acid, %	2.0	7.5	9.8
Leaf fat			
Iodine value	48.8	47.1	49.2
Linoleic acid, %	1.4	6.3	8.8

Source: Dahl, 1960.
[a] Potato flour diet—0.3% fat, 0.02% linoleic acid, iodine value = 104.
[b] Barley—1.9% fat, 0.13% linoleic acid, iodine value = 123.
[c] Oats—5.0% fat, 0.42% linoleic acid, iodine value = 114.

genetic potential. There is little doubt that we can sort the poor ones from the good ones, whether we have a well-balanced diet fed ad libitum or not. It is doubtful, however, that we can continue to make rapid progress unless we strive to maintain excellent environmental conditions.

The diet has a marked influence on the ratio of fat to lean in the carcass and particularly on the level of intramuscular fat. Also the composition of the fat is highly dependent on the diet. Exploitation of these nutritional principles, combined with continued genetic improvement, will lead to pork products of desirable and uniform quality.

REFERENCES

Axelsson, J., and Erikson, S. 1953. The optimum crude fiber level in rations of growing pigs, *J. Animal Sci.* 12:881.

Becker, D. E., Jensen, A. H., and Breidenstein, B. C. 1962. Limited feeding for finishing pigs, Ill. Agr. Exp. Sta. Mimeo. A.S.-571.

Bohman, V. R., Hunter, J. E., and McCormick, J. 1955. The effect of graded levels of alfalfa and aureomycin upon growing-fattening swine, *J. Animal Sci.* 14:499.

Braude, R., Townsend, M. J., Harrington, G., and Rowell, J. G. 1958. A large-scale test of the effects of food restriction on the performance of fattening pigs. *J. Agr. Sci.* 51:208.

Coey, W. E., and Robinson, K. L. 1954. Some effects of dietary crude fiber on live weight gains and carcass conformation of pigs, *J. Agr. Sci.* 45:41.

Craft, W. A. 1958. Fifty years of progress in swine breeding, *J. Animal Sci.* 17:960.

Crampton, E. W., Ashton, G. C., and Lloyd, L. E. 1954. Improvement of bacon carcass quality by the introduction of fiberous feeds into the hog's finishing ration, *J. Anim Sci.* 13:327.

Cunningham, H. M., Friend, D. W., and Nicholson, J. W. G. 1962. Efficiency of conversion of protein, energy and carbon in pigs restricted late in the fattening period, *Can. J. Animal Sci.* 42:176.

Dahl, O. 1958. Influence of the basal diet on the quality of pig fat, *Acta Agr. Scand.* 8:106.

———. 1960. Influence of the basal diet on the quality of pig fat, *Acta Agr. Scand.* 10:33.

Diggs, B. G., Becker, D. E., Jensen, A. H., and Norton, H. W. 1965. Energy value of various feeds for the young pig, *J. Animal Sci.* 24:555.

Duniec, H., Kielanowski, J., and Osińska, Z. 1961. Heritability of chemical fat content in the loin muscle of baconers, *Animal Prod.* 3:195.

Ellis, N. R., and Zeller, J. H. 1931. Utilization of feed by swine as affected by the level of intake, *Am. Soc. Animal Prod.* p. 270.

Greer, S. A. N., Hays, V. W., Speer, V. C., McCall, J. T., and Hammond, E. G. 1965. Effects of level of corn and barley-base diets on performance and body composition of swine, *J. Animal Sci.* 24:1008.

Handlin, D. L., Ables, J. R., Kropf, D. H., and Wheeler, R. F. 1961. The effects of finishing rations on growth rate, feed efficiency and carcass characteristics of swine, S. Car. Agr. Exp. Sta. Bull. 491.

Merkel, R. A., Bray, R. W., Grummer, R. H., Phillips, P. H., and Bohstedt, G. 1958a. The influence of limited feeding, using high fiber rations, upon growth and carcass characteristics of swine. I. Effects upon feed-lot performance, *J. Animal Sci.* 17:3.

Merkel, R. A., Bray, R. W., Grummer, R. H., Phillips, P. H., and Bohstedt, G. 1958b. The influence of limited feeding, using high fiber rations, upon growth and carcass characteristics of swine. II. Effects upon carcass characteristics, *J. Animal Sci.* 17:13.

Seymour, E. W., Speer, V. C., Hays, V. W., Mangold, D. W., and Hazen, T. E. 1964. Effects of dietary protein level and environmental temperature on performance and carcass quality of growing-finishing swine. *J. Animal Sci.* 23:375.

Wagner, G. R. 1964. Carcass composition and growth performance of swine as influenced by nutrition. Ph.D. Thesis, Iowa State Univ., Ames.

Wagner, G. R., Clark, A. J., Hays, V. W., and Speer, V. C. 1963. Effect of protein-energy relationships on the performance and carcass quality of growing swine. *J. Animal Sci.* 22:202.

Whatley, J. A., Jr., Gard, D. I., Whiteman, J. V., and Hillier, J. C. 1951. Influence of breeding and energy content of the ration on pork carcasses. *J. Animal Sci.* 10:1030.

8

Nutritional and Management Effects on Muscle Characteristics and Quality

H. D. WALLACE

Most of us have marveled at the tremendous improvement which has taken place in our hogs during recent years. Today our hogs are leaner, heavier muscled animals capable of producing very desirable pork products. Paralleling this progress in swine breeding and selection has been a great advance in swine nutrition knowledge. Unfortunately, we have not concerned ourselves very much with the relationship of the two or, more specifically, the special nutritional needs of the meatier hog. A pig can attain his maximum genetic potential for carcass excellence only if fed and managed properly. It is really quite surprising what poor feeding will do to a hog carcass. Feeding practices in this country have not been giving the meaty, heavy muscled pig a fair shake. For years we have been developing feeding formulae for least-cost performance with almost complete disregard for the end product. Pounds of live hog produced has been the overriding consideration and still remains too much so. There is great need for improvement in our pork products, and it is my contention that better feeding and management can play a tremendous role in this improvement.

About eight years ago we at Florida University started to take a serious look at this problem. It seemed that recommendations for dietary protein levels in particular had reached a point inconsistent with quality pork production. The swine industry was involved in an all-out effort to improve the leanness of our hogs through selection while at the same time was following feeding practices which pushed these good hogs back toward the fat kind. So our main interest has been to demonstrate and

The author gratefully acknowledges the contributions of Dr. A. Z. Palmer, Dr. J. W. Carpenter, Dr. G. E. Combs, and the several graduate students of the Animal Science Dept., Florida University, who participated in the research herein reported.

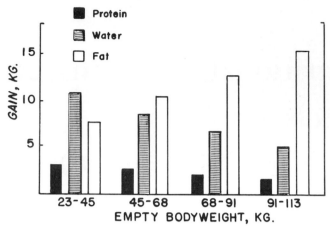

FIG. 8.1.   Body composition change of pigs during growth-finishing period.

emphasize what has been happening and to accumulate data which should be helpful in correcting the situation.

Figure 8.1 shows body composition changes during the growing-finishing period. As pigs move toward market weight the proportions of protein and water in the gains decrease while the proportion of fat increases. The gains between 23 and 45 kg. are represented by 3.2 kg. of protein, 10.9 kg. water, and 7.7 kg. of fat; whereas gains between 91 and 113 kg. are represented by only 1.8 kg. protein, 5.0 kg. water, and 15.5 kg. fat. Of course, these values would vary from animal to animal and would be quite different for an extremely meaty hog. The tendency to fatten during the finishing period is normal and desirable, but it is most important that maximum lean deposition be encouraged or permitted during this period.

In Figure 8.2 the lean-fat relationship is further illustrated by data obtained at our station. Percent lean cuts decreases as slaughter weight increases. Percent fat trim increases as slaughter weight increases. The lightweight hogs (68 and 82 kg.) produced more lean meat per unit of weight and made more efficient gains per unit of feed consumed. Since other production and processing costs come into play here, one cannot justify feeding pigs to only 68 kg. However, too often good hog prices and/or cheap corn entice producers to feed hogs to extremely heavy weights. This is a practice which should be vigorously discouraged. If producers were paid according to the true value of most such hogs, the practice would become unpopular and the swine industry as a whole would greatly benefit. There is a need in this area for the producer to change to a philosophy of producing hogs of proper weight. Certainly the industry should not continue to happily absorb this wasteful production.

The data and comments from here on are based on Florida experiments involving typical corn-soybean meal diets. The pigs used have

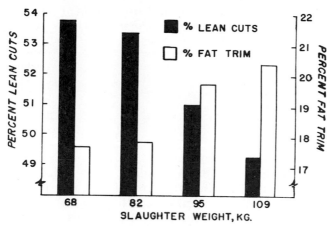

Fig. 8.2. Lean-fat relationship as influenced by body weight.

been three-way crossbred pigs: 50 percent Hampshire, 25 percent Duroc, and 25 percent Landrace. These pigs would be considered good meat type hogs but would not qualify as outstanding in muscling and meat characteristics.

The next point which I wish to emphasize concerns the relative performance of barrows and gilts as shown in Table 8.1. For this table and other tables to follow, statistically significant differences are described in the usual manner (** = P < .01) (* = P < .05). Most of us are familiar with the fact that barrows gain somewhat faster and finish markedly fatter at a given weight than gilts. Gilts gain more efficiently and produce longer, leaner, and more heavily muscled carcasses. I show these data only because they are pertinent to later discussion, and I wanted to emphasize this normal sex difference. I would also point out that many of these animals were fed on experiment only through the finishing period, thus accounting for the rather poor feed conversion values shown in the table.

The data shown in Table 8.2 show the chemical analyses of samples

TABLE 8.1: **Comparison of Feedlot Performance and Carcass Characteristics of Barrows and Gilts**

	Barrows	Gilts
No. of animals	317	311
Daily gain, lb.	1.62**	1.53
Feed/gain, lb.	3.66	3.44**
Dressing percent	70.55	70.78
Carcass length, in.	29.66	29.89**
Backfat thickness, in.	1.32	1.23**
Percent four lean cuts	51.23	52.59**
Loin eye area, sq. in.	3.57	3.89**

TABLE 8.2: Fat and Moisture Content of the *Longissimus Dorsi* Muscle as Influenced by Sex

	Barrows	Gilts
No. of animals	100	100
Fat, percent	7.55**	5.89
Moisture, percent	70.76**	72.06

taken from the loin eye muscle. The values indicate clearly that pork chops from barrows can be expected to contain more internal fat, less moisture, and of course less total protein. These differences are great enough that we should consider them relative to diet formulation and feeding practices. There is no reason to believe that the dietary requirements of barrows and gilts are the same. In fact, after the animals reach 100 lb. liveweight or thereabouts, there is every reason to believe that requirements are quite different. The data in Table 8.3 suggest that there is indeed a difference in requirement relative to dietary protein. The values in parentheses indicate the dietary protein levels fed. Pigs were started on test at about 50 lb. liveweight. When they reached 100 lb., dietary protein levels were reduced or held constant as indicated. If we look at the data for the animals fed 17 percent throughout the experiment we find just about what we would expect for adequately nourished pigs. Barrows have gained faster but the gilts yielded leaner carcasses. The marbling scores are an estimate of the amount of internal fat present in the loin eye muscle. The scale used runs from 0–33 with 0 = void and 33 = extremely abundant. The values shown here for pigs fed 17 percent protein indicate a normal marbling picture with the barrows exhibiting more marbling. The next set of values for the 17–15 percent protein sequence are almost identical to those above indicating that a reduction of protein level to 15 percent during the finishing period had no effect on performance or carcass. The third set of values wherein the pigs were fed 13 percent protein throughout gave a different result. Gilts were adversely affected as seen by the daily gains. Also, in terms of lean cutout the carcasses were downgraded so that they were no leaner than those from barrows. Barrows on the other hand maintained a normal growth rate and yielded about the same lean cutout as barrows on the

TABLE 8.3: Influence of Sex on Dietary Protein Requirement

		Daily Gain	Lean Cuts	Marbling Score
		(lb.)	*(percent)*	
Gilts	(17–17)	1.65	52.1	13.8
Barrows	(17–17)	1.75	50.7	16.7
Gilts	(17–15)	1.59	52.2	12.3
Barrows	(17–15)	1.67	50.9	17.6
Gilts	(13–13)	1.49	50.9	13.6
Barrows	(13–13)	1.69	51.0	23.0
Gilts	(13–11)	1.36	48.8	17.0
Barrows	(13–11)	1.50	48.9	22.6

TABLE 8.4: Sex, Dietary Protein Level, and Feed Restriction Interrelationships

		Daily Gain	Lean Cuts
		(lb.)	*(percent)*
Gilts	(17, Full)	1.78	51.17
Barrows	(17, Full)	2.00	49.89
Gilts	(11, Full)	1.60	48.71
Barrows	(11, Full)	1.73	48.26
Gilts	(17, Restr.)	1.35	53.02
Barrows	(17, Restr.)	1.20	52.24
Gilts	(11, Restr.)	1.13	50.67
Barrows	(11, Restr.)	1.15	51.44

higher protein levels. It is of interest to note, however, the rather marked increase in marbling of the barrow carcasses, a typical observation when pigs are borderline or short on protein, particularly during early growth. Finally we see that neither sex was adequately nourished for either optimum gain or optimum lean cutout when a 13–11 percent sequence of protein was employed.

In Table 8.4 additional data are presented which illustrate sex, protein level, and feed restriction interrelationships. These pigs were on test from 100 lb. liveweight to a slaughter weight of 210 lb. The first comparison of barrows and gilts full fed a 17 percent diet indicates the same differences previously mentioned. For the second comparison in which barrows and gilts were full fed on an 11 percent diet it is seen that gains are slowed for both sexes and carcass leanness is also reduced for both. In the third comparison when a 17 percent diet was fed on a restricted basis the gilts seem to have fared somewhat better in terms of gains. This suggests again that protein is somewhat more critical relative to energy for gilts. Carcass leanness was improved markedly for both sexes due to feed restriction. When an 11 percent diet was fed on a restricted basis gains were slowed for both sexes, but the low protein again appeared to have a more adverse effect on gilt carcasses than on barrow carcasses.

Table 8.5 summarizes our experience with one method of limited

TABLE 8.5: Influence of Feed Restriction on Feedlot Performance, Carcass Measurements, Carcass Firmness, and Chop Tenderness

	Restricted	Full
No. of pigs	156	156
Daily gain, lb.	1.32	1.82**
Feed/lb. gain	3.85	3.55**
Backfat thickness, in.	1.12**	1.26
Loin eye area, sq. in.	3.92**	3.76
Percent lean cuts	53.74**	51.66
Carcass firmness score	2.40	1.99**
Chop tenderness	8.36	7.73*

feeding in which animals were restricted continuously at 5 lb. of total feed per head per day from 100 lb. body weight to slaughter. Restricted pigs gained much more slowly and required an average of 18 days longer to reach the finished weight. The restricted pigs also required considerably more feed per unit of gain; carcasses were not as firm as those from full-fed pigs, and cooked chops were measureably less tender. Carcasses were much leaner as shown by the carcass measurements. However, we have not been very excited about this method of feed restriction, mainly because of the adverse effect on feed conversion. Certainly a depression in feed conversion cannot be tolerated along with the longer feeding period required. This method of course is just one approach to feed restriction; others may be more feasible.

Table 8.6 summarizes some of our work on dietary protein level as it relates to performance and carcass quality. This has been our most

TABLE 8.6: **Influence of Dietary Protein Level on Feed-lot Performance and Carcass Measurements**

	17–15 Percent	13–11 Percent
No. of pigs	124	124
Daily gain, lb.	1.71**	1.47
Feed/lb. gain	3.16**	3.57
Backfat thickness, in.	1.28**	1.39
Loin eye area, sq. in.	3.75**	3.31
Percent lean cuts	52.25**	49.38
Marbling score	12.40**	18.16
Feed cost/pig	$15.07	$15.87

interesting area of study. Pigs fed the higher protein level gained much faster, requiring two weeks less time to reach slaughter weight. Gains were much more efficient and all carcass measurements indicated vastly superior carcasses. The marbling scores are of particular interest. Low-protein pigs yielded much fatter carcasses in general, but increased fatty infiltration into muscle tissue was especially noticeable. The added feed cost of $0.80 per hog for the low-protein pigs is a significant feature of the study. The question arises as to whether intermediate protein levels would be adequate. We have determined that levels higher than the 17–15 percent sequence are not necessary. We have also observed that a 15–13 percent sequence is adequate for barrows but at least 16–14 percent is needed for optimum performance of gilts.

Fat and moisture determinations for loin eye muscle samples are presented in Table 8.7. It is evident that the fat present in the pork

TABLE 8.7: **Fat and Moisture Content of the *Longissimus Dorsi* Muscle as Influenced by Dietary Protein Level**

	17–15 Percent	13–11 Percent
No. of pigs	100	100
Fat, percent	4.81**	8.63
Moisture, percent	72.33**	70.49

chop eye is much greater for the low-protein pigs. Although the protein values are not given here, there is no question but that protein content of the loin eye muscle from the high-protein pigs is considerably higher, approximately 2 percent.

In Table 8.8 the influence of protein level and sex on tenderness of baked chops is presented. In this test a trained taste panel chewed samples of the lean tissue and scored tenderness according to a code from 1–9: 1 = too tough to be edible, 5 = average tenderness, and 9 = mushy. It can be seen that the chops in general were above average in tenderness.

TABLE 8.8: **Influence of Protein Level and Sex on Tenderness of Baked Chops**

	17–15 Percent	13–11 Percent	Average
Barrows	6.18	6.85	6.51
Gilts	6.17	6.43	6.30
Average	6.18	6.64**	

Chops from barrows were more tender than chops from gilts, and chops from pigs fed the low-protein diet were markedly more tender than chops from pigs fed adequate protein. Tenderness in pork has not been a very important consideration since animals are normally quite young when slaughtered and differences in tenderness do not approach those seen in beef. However, it is well to appreciate that factors such as sex, feed restriction, and level of dietary protein intake can influence tenderness.

Table 8.9 illustrates the effect of cooking method on chop tenderness.

TABLE 8.9: **Influence of Method of Cooking on Tenderness of Chops as Measured by the Warner-Bratzler Shear**

		17–15 Percent	13–11 Percent	Average
Barrows	(baked)	6.01	5.11	5.56
	(fried)	7.61	7.15	7.38
Gilts	(baked)	6.04	5.80	5.92
	(fried)	7.98	7.74	7.86
Average	(baked)	6.03	5.45	
	(fried)	7.80	7.45	

In this case tenderness was determined by a mechanical shear, and the greater tenderness is indicated by the lower value. The data substantiate the previous data obtained by the panel method and illustrate that a fried pork chop is not as tender as a baked pork chop.

In reality the low-protein diets are deficient in one or more amino acids, and in Table 8.10 this effect is illustrated. The amino acids lysine, methionine, and tryptophan were all added to the diet of one group of pigs. The added amino acid levels were such as to provide total levels comparable to those provided by a 17 percent protein diet. It is evident that the amino acid supplementation exerted a tremendous effect on these pigs. Rate and efficiency of gain were improved, and all carcass cri-

TABLE 8.10: **Influence of Supplementing a Low-Protein Diet (13–11 Percent) With Amino Acids (Lysine, Methionine, and Tryptophan) on Feedlot Performance and Carcass Measurements**

	Without Amino Acids	With Amino Acids
No. of pigs	22	22
Daily gain, lb.	1.36	1.44
Feed/gain	3.76	3.36
Backfat thickness, in.	1.41	1.26**
Loin eye area, sq. in.	3.24	3.74**
Percent lean cuts	49.20	52.69**
Marbling score	17.48	8.83**
Percent protein in loin eye muscle	20.15	22.27**

teria indicated that at least one of these amino acids was a limiting factor for the production of lean well-muscled carcasses.

Recently there has been considerable interest in the feeding of a combination of stilbestrol and testosterone to pigs during the finishing period. Hopefully this might improve swine performance and produce a leaner carcass. The effect of supplementing the diet with this hormone combination is shown in Table 8.11. This test involved 48 individually fed pigs which were on the test from 45 kg. liveweight to 93 kg. Feed intake and consequently rate of gain were decreased significantly by hormone feeding. Feed conversion was not improved. Carcasses were somewhat leaner, but there was no indication that muscle development was improved, as seen by the loin eye area measurements. Two protein levels were also involved in this study. A 14–12 percent sequence was compared to a 12–10 percent sequence, and the data are summarized in Table 8.12. The higher protein level produced faster and much more efficient gains and influenced carcass leanness more favorably than did the hormone supplementation.

In this study a significant interaction of protein level and hormone supplementation was observed relative to feed conversion. In the presence of adequate protein the hormone was helpful but with the lower

TABLE 8.11: **Influence of Feeding a Combination of Stilbestrol and Testosterone on Feedlot Performance and Carcass Measurements**

	Without Hormones	With Hormones
No. of pigs	24	24
Daily feed, lb.	6.82**	6.08
Daily gain, lb.	2.03**	1.79
Feed/gain	3.38	3.40
Backfat thickness, in.	1.41	1.33*
Carcass length, in.	30.90	31.20
Loin eye area, sq. in.	3.62	3.61
Percent lean cuts	48.65	49.27
Marbling score	14.6	15.1

TABLE 8.12:   Influence of Dietary Protein Level on Feedlot Performance and Carcass Measurements

	14–12 Percent	12–10 Percent
No. of pigs	24	24
Daily feed, lb.	6.39	6.50
Daily gain, lb.	1.96	1.87
Feed/gain	3.28**	3.50
Backfat thickness, in.	1.38	1.35
Carcass length, in.	30.96	31.13
Loin eye area, sq. in.	3.73*	3.51
Percent lean cuts	49.36	48.55
Marbling score	14.8	15.1

protein level it was not. The most disheartening observation in this work has been the undesirable odor and flavor imparted to the meat as a result of hormone supplementation. At the time the carcasses were cut, blade loin roasts were taken from each animal and frozen and later used for odor and flavor studies. The roasts were individually cooked in covered Pyrex ovenware according to prescribed methods and scored by an eight-member trained panel. Degree of odor and flavor were the factors considered. Results are summarized in Table 8.13. The roasts were scored from 1 through 4, with 1 = none and 4 — strong. The (+) and (—) indicate with and without hormone treatment. The hormone effect was clearcut as all differences shown are significant. Irrespective of protein level or sex, the hormone treatment caused an undesirable aroma and flavor in the pork. It is particularly interesting to note that the gilts were affected just as much as the barrows. It is also interesting to note that untreated pigs showed average scores slightly over 1, indicating that undesirable odors and flavors were present in some of these pigs. Subsequent testing at our station is tending to confirm these results. Other stations that have been working with this product apparently have not encountered this problem to the extent that we have. This I cannot explain, but I feel very strongly that we cannot afford to add another quality problem to the many that already exist. This undesirable odor and flavor is not masked by the seasoning in sausage or by smoke curing processes. Preliminary checking of meat from two additional feeding trials indicates that the off flavor and odor are indeed real.

TABLE 8.13:   Influence of Hormone Feeding on Aroma and Flavor of Pork Roasts

Items		Aroma Score	Flavor Score
12–10	(+)	1.81	1.60
12–10	(—)	1.09	1.05
14–12	(+)	1.85	1.73
14–12	(—)	1.10	1.09
Barrows	(+)	1.87	1.66
Barrows	(—)	1.07	1.07
Gilts	(+)	1.79	1.67
Gilts	(—)	1.13	1.06

Our greatest opportunity for the improvement of pork products, at least from a feeding standpoint, lies in providing diets more adequate in protein. It is true that pigs will seemingly do well on finishing diets containing 10, 11, or 12 percent protein, but it is clear that meaty hogs—the kind we are trying to produce today—need more. Not only do they need more for best gains and efficiency of feed conversion but they need more to produce the quality of carcasses which they are inherently capable of producing. It is foolhardy to think that we cannot afford to feed our hogs more protein. We cannot afford not to, because the whole proposition ultimately relates to the most efficient production of edible meat. A diet skimpy in protein, as many of our finishing diets are, will not permit efficient production of lean pork. A further refinement of our feeding methods would call for a separation of barrows and gilts during the finishing period, with a 2 percent higher dietary protein allowance for the gilts.

REFERENCES

Crum, R. C., Jr., Wallace, H. D., Palmer, A. Z., Carpenter, J. W., and Combs, G. E. 1964. The influence of protein level on feedlot performance and carcass characteristics of barrows and gilts, Fla. Animal Sci. Mimeo. Series AN65-3.

Wallace, H. D., Britt, L. A., Carpenter, J. W., Palmer, A. Z., and Combs, G. E. 1966. Effects of dietary protein levels and amino acid supplementation on the feedlot performance and carcass characteristics of growing-finishing swine, Fla. Animal Sci. Mimeo. Series AN67-3.

Wallace, H. D., McCabe, G. E., Palmer, A. Z., Koger, M., Carpenter, J. W., and Combs, G. E. 1960. The influence of slaughter weight on economy of production and carcass value of swine, Fla. Animal Sci. Mimeo. Series No. 60-12.

Wallace, H. D., Palmer, A. Z., Carpenter, J. W., Britt, L. A., Warnick, A. C., and Combs, G. E. 1967. Influence of protein level and hormone supplementation during the finishing period on feedlot performance, carcass characteristics and pork acceptability, Fla. Animal Sci. Mimeo. Series AN67-10.

Wallace, H. D., Palmer, A. Z., Carpenter, J. W., and Combs, G. E. 1965. A study of the relationship of feed restriction and dietary protein level in finishing hogs, Fla. Animal Sci. Mimeo. Series AN65-9.

———. 1966. Feed restriction of swine during the finishing period, Fla. Agr. Exp. Sta. Bull. 706.

Wallace, H. D., Palmer, A. Z., Carpenter, J. W., Taki, Ghazi, and Combs, G. E. 1964. The influence of protein level on feedlot performance and carcass characteristics of barrows and gilts, Fla. Animal Sci. Mimeo. Series AN64-16.

Wallace, H. D., Palmer, M. E., Palmer, A. Z., Carpenter, J. W., and Combs, G. E. 1963. The influence of protein level on feedlot performance and carcass characteristics of barrows and gilts, Fla. Animal Sci. Mimeo. Series AN 64-7.

PART FOUR

Disease Problems

9

Health Maintenance
in the 1970's

J. B. HERRICK

HEALTH is one facet in the production of any type of livestock that creates constant demands for disease-preventing procedures. Disease and all of its manifestations are always present, waiting to take their toll of the efficiency of livestock production. Disease control or health maintenance must be set up as a preventative measure instead of merely waiting till sickness strikes and then relying on treatments. Death does not present the biggest loss; lowered feed efficiency and extra time and labor caused by disease produce far greater losses.

In looking at swine production in the future, there are several factors to consider in evaluating the importance of minimal disease levels in swine herds:

1. Production costs are going to necessitate cost accounting which will vividly point out the voids in a swine production program. Consequently, health measures now considered unrealistic will be necessary. Programs will be needed to prevent disease instead of merely trying to treat it. This will lead to minimal disease level herds. Previously unknown sanitary procedures will need to be implemented. Labor in most cases will be the limiting factor.

2. Feed additives and therapeutic, biological, and chemotherapeutic agents are going to be scrutinized more carefully in the future, with emphasis placed upon residues found in meat. Possibly prescriptions and other restrictions will change present usage.

3. Economics pertaining to the confinement method of raising swine will create problems heretofore seldom encountered. Education relative to these specific problems will receive top priority. Disease manifestations other than those now recognized will appear to be paramount. Waste disposal in its present form will be antiquated.

4. Available diagnostic services must precede all health programs. The link between prevention or cure and loss is adequate diagnostic services. It is fortunate that hog cholera is being eradicated in that with

its eradication, other disease manifestations previously masked are being presented to the diagnostician. The veterinarian and his laboratory will serve as a link in identifying these problems on the spot. Herd history, technique in obtaining tissues, and on-the-spot reliable diagnosis will be necessary.

5. Swine production will become more exacting. Units of 1,000 or more going to market in less than four months; 2 to 3 more pigs marketed per sow; closed herds (closed to animals and man); and other such production procedures will need to be implemented. Environmentally controlled buildings specifically designed for different phases of the life cycle of the hog will be commonplace, and units where life cycle production is manisfested may be obsolete. Specialization in hog production may possibly exist whereby one producer specializes in production of pigs up to 5 weeks of age, another takes them to 8 weeks of age, and another to market weight.

SANITATION

A concept of sanitation must exist in swine production where minimal disease only is tolerated.

1. Seed stock of minimal disease status—SPF (as known today)—will be only one facet of this evaluation. Confinement with sanitation now makes erysipelas and roundworm infestation controllable.

2. Closed herds will exist and management practices will prevail where outside swine will not enter a swine production unit. Seed stock will be isolated from the rearing and finishing unit. Sows will be retained for a minimum of five to eight litters, depending on productivity. This will allow for greater disease resistance than is thought to be possessed by gilts. Methods of stimulating antibody production for disease resistance are now being researched. Specific units will have specific caretakers or require a complete change of uniforms prior to entry. Artificial insemination, estrus synchronization, and a completely renovated program outlined to market 10 pigs per litter instead of 7 to 8 must be implemented to make the enterprise economical.

3. Sterilized feed may become a reality. At most, testing feed for contamination will be an important part of the program. Laboratory aid on such a procedure will be mandatory.

SPECIALIZATION

Swine production will become a specialization. In reality, only a few producers will have management ability to handle such a program. A key link in this entire program will be a herd health program, prearranged cooperatively by the producer and his veterinarian and designed to prevent disease instead of relying on treatments. This will involve:

1. A program outlined on paper with specifics for an entire life cycle approach. The responsibility of both the veterinarian and the producers will be delineated.

2. Diagnostic facilities for immediate postmortems and testing. Confinement in the form of hospital facilities will be a must.

3. A surgical-like concept of sanitation for the entire swine pro-

duction unit. Implementation of surgical cleanliness for sanitation will be enacted and supervised by a verterinarian. Complete change of clothes will be necessary for all those who enter such facilities.

4. The veterinarian as a regular employee. In most cases, the veterinarian will be on a retainer fee based on so much per pig marketed. Regardless of fee, the veterinarian will be used to prevent disease instead of treating the sick. Periodic (in some cases daily) inspections will be made of the herd.

5. Allocation of costs of production for herd health maintenance.

SWINE HERD HEALTH PROGRAM

Original Stock

Swine bred for vigor and physical soundness are able to resist most diseases and parasites better than weaker animals. Replacement stock or swine purchased to start a new herd should be purchased from a reputable breeder who follows an effective disease prevention program and who produces swine free from genetic defects that might impair their health or vigor. Homegrown replacements should be selected only after a careful analysis of health and performance records and a critical evaluation of individual animals. Occasionally it may be necessary to introduce new bloodlines which are capable of increasing the disease resistance of the herd. This may be done through artificial insemination.

Large units may have their own isolated seed stock herd as part of their program.

Environment

A healthy environment is a clean environment. Cleanliness and sanitation are basic to animal health.

Cleaning and Washing. A clean surface can be obtained only by using liberal amounts of hot water, approved cleaning agents, and elbow grease.

1. Scrape, sweep, and shovel out all dirt, bedding, cobwebs, and manure.

2. For routine cleaning scrub all surfaces except aluminum with a solution made by adding 1 lb. of lye to 20 gal. of boiling water. When cleaning up after a serious disease outbreak, use a stronger solution such as 1 lb. of lye to 5 or 10 gal. of water. The lye solution is used primarily as a cleansing agent and not as a disinfecting agent. Since lye is irritating to the skin, wear protective clothing and rubber gloves when working with it. Do not use lye solutions on aluminum surfaces because of its corrosive action. A steam cleaner with a detergent or a high-pressure hot water cleaner with a detergent may be used.

3. Rinse all surfaces well with clear water.

4. Inspect after cleaning to be sure all dirt has been removed. Check all corners, cracks, and crevices. If any dirt is found, repeat the washing and rinsing process until all surfaces are clean.

Disinfecting. Only a clean surface can be disinfected. Any dirt that remains after cleaning will neutralize the disinfectant or prevent it from coming into contact with the germs. Disinfectants work best on warm surfaces.

With a high-pressure system or a brush apply one of the many disinfectants available. Two of the commonly used effective disinfectants are:

1. Compound solution of cresol (saponated solution of cresol). Mix 1 pt. of this solution with 4 gal. of water to make approximately a 3% solution.

2. Sodium orthophenylphenate. Mix 1 lb. with 12 gal. of water. Sodium orthophenylphenate is readily soluble in water, has no objectionable odor, and remains stable in the presence of organic matter. If the temperature of the building is below 60° F. the solution should be heated to 120° F. as this disinfectant is not effective at low temperatures.

REGARDLESS OF DISINFECTANT USED, ALWAYS READ THE LABEL AND FOLLOW DIRECTIONS!

The entire farrowing house and all equipment should be cleaned and disinfected at one time and left vacant for a minimum of two weeks before the farrowing season starts. If farrowing pens and equipment must be used more than once during a farrowing season, clean and disinfect between each use and leave vacant for as long as possible. A two-week vacant period is desirable.

Nutrition

Even though the proper ration is provided, it is not uncommon for small pigs to be pushed back from the feeders by larger pigs, and as a result they may suffer from nutritional deficiencies. This can be remedied to a great extent by sorting pigs according to size and by providing adequate feeder space.

Hogs with certain diseases such as virus pneumonia, diarrhea, or internal or external parasites may be supplied excellent rations but become nutritionally deficient because of poor appetites or poor absorption of the nutrients. These underlying diseases must be prevented before the ration can be effective. Adoption of a good health program will result in healthy animals and assure maximum feed utilization and conversion.

Exposure to Disease-Producing Organisms

Most diseases are introduced into a herd by newly purchased animals, but diseases may also be introduced mechanically by contaminated trucks and equipment, on dirty footwear, by stray animals and birds, and in feed or feed containers.

Exposure to disease-producing organisms can be minimized by adhering to the following rules.

New Purchases

1. Buy only animals known to be healthy directly from a reputable breeder or sale.

2. Investigate the health status of the seller's herd thoroughly.

3. Buy only swine that have been properly immunized against the diseases peculiar to your herd. Obtain dates of immunization and type of products used.

4. Purchase new stock at least 30 to 60 days before intended use. Isolate all new purchases for 30 to 60 days before adding to the herd. During this time the new stock should be examined for various diseases such as brucellosis, leptospirosis, tuberculosis, mange, lice, and internal parasites. During the isolation period any necessary vaccination or treatment should be administered. Some newly purchased animals may be disease "carriers" yet remain healthy during the isolation period. Precautions should be taken to avoid the introduction of a disease by this route. The presence of a carrier may be detected by placing homegrown pigs with the new stock during the entire isolation period. If a carrier animal is present the homegrown animals, in most cases, will show signs of the disease before the end of the isolation period and thereby warn the owner of possible dangers to the breeding herd. Thorough postmortems then can be conducted on the homegrown pigs, searching for signs of disease.

Mechanical Transmission of Diseases by Man

1. Do not allow any visitors in any swine unit.

2. Establish a working routine. Take care of the youngest animals first and proceed up the age scale, attending the adults and sick animals last.

3. Before entering the farrowing house put on clean coveralls and thoroughly clean and disinfect footwear. Have a pan of disinfectant at the entrance to the farrowing house for scrubbing boots. Change disinfectant daily. Compound solution of cresol, sodium orthophenylphenate, or other disinfectants may be used in the footbath. When purchasing a disinfectant for use in footbaths, read the label and make certain it is satisfactory for that purpose.

4. Curtail direct traffic between the farm and auction markets, sales, shows, and other farms.

5. Always wash and disinfect hands thoroughly before going from one group of hogs to another.

Disease Transmission by Stray Animals and Birds

1. Keep all dogs, cats, and wild animals out of hog pens and housing units.

2. Keep pigeons and other birds out of hog houses.

Disease Transmision by Vehicles, Equipment, and Feed Containers

1. Keep all commercial trucks out of hog-raising areas unless previously disinfected.

2. Make sure feed bags and other feed containers are not contaminated with dirt or manure. Do not allow hogs to come into contact with feed containers.

3. Clean and disinfect self-feeders, troughs, waterers, and other equipment before moving them from one unit to another.

4. Disinfect the beds of trucks before and after transporting hogs.

Disease Transmission From Neighboring Farms

1. Fence off streams which flow through hog farms upstream. Do not allow hogs access to these waters.

2. Do not keep hogs in lots adjacent to a neighbor's hog lot.

3. Maintain strong, hog-tight fences to keep hogs in their pens and to keep stray hogs out.

Detection and Identification of Diseases

Have all breeding stock tested annually for brucellosis, leptospirosis, and tuberculosis. Carefully observe all hogs daily for symptoms of disease. Be alert for such signs as poor appetite, diarrhea or constipation, lameness, rapid or labored breathing, skin lesions, swellings, and nervous system disturbances. Isolate sick hogs at the first sign of a disease and call a veterinarian. An early, accurate diagnosis will minimize the chances of a serious disease becoming widespread in the herd. Have any necessary laboratory work done before starting medication. Medicines frequently mask symptoms and make it difficult to isolate the causative organisms.

Treatment and Control

Each particular disease must be handled in a specific manner. There is no effective "one-shot" treatment that will cure all diseases. When drugs are indicated they must be selected wisely and used correctly. In some diseases the best approach may be to sell out, clean up, and start over. Obviously, in order to determine the correct treatment procedures an accurate diagnosis must be made. Your veterinarian, as a result of his training and experience, is the one person in your community who is best qualified to make a diagnosis and recommend the most effective and economical treatment. Rely on his ability and make an all-out effort to follow his recommendations.

Records

Accurate production records are useful when selecting breeding stock and evaluating management and feeding practices. To be complete the records should include the following information on the health status of the herd:

1. Vaccination—dates and products used.
2. Internal parasite treatment—dates and products used.
3. External parasite treatment—dates and products used.
4. Brucellosis, leptospirosis, and tuberculosis tests—dates and results.
5. Disease record—dates, diagnosis, treatment, and results.

Accurate records cannot be maintained without a system of identification that makes it possible to know each animal. To avoid inaccuracies all data should be recorded as it occurs.

The check list shown in Figure 9.1 is an example of a health record that has been used effectively.

Litter Number_____Dam_____Sire _____

Date Farrowed_____Number in Litter_____

Birth Weight_____Breed_____

Before Farrowing:

_____Fecal Exam-Results_____External Parasite Exam-Results _____

_____Sow Wormed-Date_____Product _____

_____External Parasite Treatment-Date_____Product _____

_____Farrowing Pen Cleaned-Date _____Disinfectant Used_____

_____Sow Scrubbed and Penned-Date _____

At Farrowing:

_____Iodine Treatment of Navel_____Needle Teeth Clipped_____Ears Notched _____

After Farrowing:

_____Iron Treatment-Date_____Product_____

_____Iron Treatment-Date_____Product_____

_____Iron Treatment-Date_____Product_____

_____Castration-Date_____

_____Vaccination (Hog Cholera)-Date_____   Product _____

_____Other Vaccination-Date_____Product_____

_____Weaning-Date _____Weaning Weight_____

_____External Parasite Treatment-Date_____Product_____

_____Brucellosis, Leptospirosis, and Tuberculosis Test-Date_____

Worming Schedule (Determined by results of fecal exam)

_____wks.-Date_____Results of fecal exam_____Product _____
_____wks.-Date_____Results of fecal exam_____Product _____
_____wks.-Date_____Results of fecal exam_____Product _____
Later—Date _____Results of fecal exam_____Product _____

Disease Record:

_____Isolate Sick Animals_____Autopsy Dead Pigs, then Bury or Incinerate

_____Secure an Accurate Diagnosis_____By Veterinarian_____By Lab

Date _____   _____   _____

Diagnosis _____   _____   _____

No. Sick _____   _____   _____

FIG. 9.1. Check list for swine health program.

HERD HEALTH CALENDAR

WHAT	WHEN
Check sow for internal and external parasites. Treat if necessary.	2 to 4 weeks before farrowing.
Clean and disinfect farrowing pen and equipment.	2 or more weeks before use.
Scrub sow—especially udder, teats, and flanks.	Immediately before moving into farrowing pen (at least 3 days before farrowing).
Apply iodine to stump of navel cord.	At birth.
Clip needle teeth.	At birth.
Notch ears.	At birth.
Administer iron.	2 days.

Note: Oral iron—repeat every 3 days.
Injectable iron—repeat in 7 to 10 days.

WHAT	WHEN
Castrate boar pigs.	1 to 2 weeks.
Vaccinate—hog cholera.	5 weeks—MLV and serum.
Vaccinate—erysipelas.	10 to 14 days after hog cholera vaccination.
Vaccinate—leptospirosis.	10 weeks.
Have fecal samples checked for internal parasites. Treat if indicated.	5 weeks, 10 weeks, 12 weeks, and later as needed.
Test all breeding stock over 6 months of age for brucellosis, leptospirosis, and tuberculosis.	Sows—after farrowing, but at least 3 weeks before breeding. Boars—every 6 months.
Revaccinate—leptospirosis and erysipelas.	Sows—5 weeks after breeding. Boars—every 6 months.
Revaccinate—hog cholera.	Sows and boars—every 2 years. (When a killed vaccine is used, revaccinate annually.) Do not vaccinate sows 3 weeks before breeding or during gestation.
Examine all breeding stock for external parasites. Treat if necessary.	Just before breeding.
Buy replacement stock from healthy herds. Isolate all new stock for 30 to 60 days.	Whenever new stock is purchased.

10

Outlook of Disease Problems and Role of Disease Research

W. P. SWITZER

IT IS MY BELIEF that swine housing will evolve into two distinct patterns: (1) least labor confinement systems and (2) least capital rearing systems. The disease pressures and problems under these two systems will be different.

The least labor confinement system may be defined as intense confinement housing with nearly complete automation. On the other hand, the least capital rearing system will utilize the cheapest suitable land available, with all natural terrain features used for low-cost housing, feeding, and sanitation. There are limited geographical sites available where this type of operation is indicated, but where such terrain is available, it often is considered as just poor quality land of little value instead of being recognized for what it is—namely a poor man's $100,000 confinement rearing house. A young man with an intense interest in swine production but very limited capital is probably better off to start with such a system instead of the more up-to-date, high-cost confinement housing.

The disease problems and pressures delineated under these two divergent systems may be divided into seven groups: (1) leg and joint problems, (2) housing vices, (3) respiratory diseases, (4) diarrheas, (5) parasites, (6) reproductive failures, and (7) acute septicemic diseases.

LEG AND JOINT PROBLEMS

Pigs in intense confinement are usually housed on concrete, steel, or oak surfaces which impose an intense stress on the hoof and pastern. Therefore, it is important to have pigs with a fast-growing hoof and with short pasterns with proper angulation. The legs must be straight.

A line of pigs with proper hoof growth for confinement will often develop excessively long toes on pasture. The converse is also true, namely lines of pigs with good short toes on pasture will often be excessively sore-footed in confinement.

Most confinement systems provide no bedded area for the pigs.

When the pigs are at rest, the surfaces of the metacarpal and metatarsal regions bear a considerable amount of weight. Minor projections or tuberosities may become traumatized and result in callus formation, bursitis, or synovitis (inflammation of bursa or of tendon sheaths). These become puffy and very sore. When this happens, the growth of the animal is usually retarded. Therefore, the conformation of the several minor projections on the leg bones becomes very important in the ability of a line of pigs to successfully adapt to intense confinement. These same minor conformation differences are of little consequence to pasture-raised swine.

It may take a few generations of selection to adapt the foot and leg conformation of a particular line of swine to the transition from pasture to intense confinement.

I have grouped infectious arthritis of swine into four classes for ease of discussion, namely erysipelas, streptococcal, mycoplasmal, and miscellaneous.

Erysipelas Arthritis

It is my estimation and limited observation that erysipelas arthritis in swine is reduced by intense confinement. This is probably due to removal from contact with the organism in the soil. Even though the exact role of soil in the spread of this disease is still not clearly defined, contaminated soil associated with climatic factors probably plays an important role in pasture outbreaks.

Streptococcal Arthritis

Streptococcal arthritis is relatively common in young pigs and also occurs in older swine. Little factual information is available on this common arthritis. There is casual acceptance of the fact that it usually results from the organism gaining entrance through the navel, though there is little if any research to support this contention and considerable field evidence to indicate otherwise. It has not been established how the organism survives between groups of young pigs. If records are kept, it will often emerge that certain sows or groups of sows on a farm will have this problem in their litters at a high frequency while other groups of sows will go through the same farrowing house with no problems. It would seem that the dam is the primary reservoir for the transmission of this condition and that determination of where this reservoir exists in the dam will enable the detection and either elimination or treatment of these individuals so as to break the transmission cycle. When this becomes possible, the tendency for this problem to build to major proportions in some confinement systems should be eliminated.

Mycoplasmal Arthritis

Mycoplasmal arthritis (PPLO) is of major concern in pigs from 75 lb. to market weight. There are many basic facts about the transmission of this disease that are not known, but it appears that the incidence of arthritis in intense confinement and on pasture can be very high in some herds. It does not appear that breaking contact with the soil eliminates this disease. Our present concept is that the nasal carrier state probably facilitates spread of the disease. It is not expecting miracles to believe that at some future time therapy may become available that will clear the nasal carriers or that vaccines will be developed that will prevent the arthritis.

Miscellaneous Causes of Arthritis

There are several other causes of infectious arthritis in swine. These include staphylococcus, coliform organisms, corynebacteria, and others. It seems that the incidence of these is often higher in nursery-reared pigs than in pasture-reared pigs.

HOUSING VICES

The principal "social vice" in confinement swine is cannibalism. This usually assumes the form of tail biting. It may occur on rare occasions in pasture-reared swine but usually is a problem associated with confinement. Some producers tend initially to regard tail biting as just an annoying disfiguration until they realize the retarding effect the endurated and abscessed tail stumps have on growth rate. Many different preventative methods have been used, ranging from putting playthings in the pens to surgical amputation of the tail at an early age. These procedures help but they do not come to grips with the basic problem, which is the ability of the line of swine being reared to adapt to the psychological stresses associated with confinement housing. The best solution is to use any of the approaches that will temporarily improve the problem while selecting replacement stock that has a disposition and temperament better suited to confinement rearing.

RESPIRATORY DISEASES

With the exception of lungworm infection, nearly all of the respiratory diseases of swine are expected to be intensified by confinement rearing because of ready air-borne transmission in the crowded and moist environment of confinement houses. Therefore, use of breeding stock as free of pneumonia and rhinitis as possible is of prime importance.

Bordetella bronchiseptica rhinitis is the principal cause of turbinate atrophy in this region. Initially this organism in swine was extremely susceptible to treatment with sulfonamides. In recent years, the use of some type of sulfonamide-antibiotic additive in pig creep has become very common. The incidence of bordetella rhinitis has dropped to about half of what it was, but a high percentage of the infections are now resistant to the sulfonamides. Therefore it appears that this current control measure will become of limited usefulness and that additional measures must be developed. These may take the form of additional drugs suitable for the elimination of the organism from the nasal cavity, or it may be possible to develop a suitable vaccine even though the natural disease is not self-limiting. This latter technique of control would be the most desirable and does have some preliminary research findings to support hopes for its eventual accomplishment.

The common and widespread pneumonia of swine appears to be due to a mycoplasma. The causative organism can be grown in the laboratory, and work is under way to evaluate treatments, serologic tests, and vaccination for its control. Again there are preliminary experimental data to suggest that immunization and treatment may be possible at some future time. One major hurdle that must be surmounted is the notion that if a pig is not gasping for breath, it does not have pneumonia. Most of the lesions due to this infection involve only a percentage of the total lung area. The pig breathes normally and is considered by the producer to be normal. Producers need to be educated to the fact that normal appearing pigs may have pneumonia, and they should start looking at the lungs of their pigs.

DIARRHEAS

There are certain diarrheal diseases of swine that are spectacular and dreaded by all knowledgeable swine producers, for example T.G.E. Other diarrheal diseases are so common they are accepted with indifference by swine raisers. An example of this is the so-called coliform diarrhea in baby pigs. The total economic loss to the swine industry caused by this latter disease syndrome is several times that caused by T.G.E. We are only now beginning to see research into the cause and prevention of this complex. This is a very important problem to any producer undertaking intensive use of farrowing and nursery facilities. It also occurs in pasture-reared pigs but at a reduced frequency. Knowledge about this disease complex must be gained so that it can be controlled, or many intense confinement farrowing and nursery installations are doomed to bankruptcy.

The second "doomsday diarrheal disease" for confinement growing-finishing units is vibrionic dysentery. Once this disease becomes established in a large confinement building and has developed drug resistance to the various available therapeutic agents, the producer is faced with the almost impossible task of depopulating the building and adequately disinfecting it. Some liquid manure disposal systems are such that they almost defy adequate cleaning and disinfection. There is no financially acceptable solution for eradication of this disease from some of our present confinement buildings. This disease must be investigated intensely in a crash program. At the present time, I know of no group even working on this problem.

PARASITES

Most of the common parasite eggs of swine are not infectious for pigs until they have had a few days to ripen or to undergo developmental stages outside the pig in the soil or in earthworms. Therefore, we expect that confinement systems will reduce the internal parasite problems in pigs. It should be expected that lungworms would be completely eliminated by a complete confinement system. This does not always happen, perhaps due to occasional earthworms migrating into the confinement house or to occasional infectious stages being reached outside the earthworm.

The incidence of ascarids in pigs in adequately cleaned confinement houses is very low. However, it is possible for ascarid eggs to go through the necessary development to become infectious in a few days on concrete. Therefore, some housing systems are better than others in the control of roundworms. Confinement-reared swine almost always have fewer round-worms than pasture-reared swine.

It is very likely that chemotherapeutic feed additives will be developed to kill the roundworm larva as soon as it hatches in the intestine before it has a chance to do any damage. Such compounds will negate the advantages of confinement systems in roundworm control.

A very bright spot in the future improvement of the image of pork is a recently developed technique for the detection of trichina parasites in pork carcasses at the packing plant. Dr. W. J. Zimmerman has developed an inexpensive yet relatively accurate procedure for doing this. If this finds widespread use in the packing plants, we may look forward to the day when restaurants ask you how you want your pork chop cooked.

REPRODUCTIVE FAILURES

The problem of reproductive failure in breeding stock housed in complete confinement is sporadic. There are some herds that seem to have little trouble while other herds have severe and persistent losses. Often the breeding herds not having problems are actually housed in small lots and not in intense confinement. There will have to be a great deal of information accumulated before satisfactory intense confinement of breeding herds can be accomplished. It is my opinion that effects of psychic stresses and low-level nutritional deficiencies on the reproductive cycle in swine probably account for many of these failures and that infectious disease is of relatively minor importance. This type of problem may be encountered at a low incidence in some pasture herds.

SEPTICEMIC DISEASES

Acute septicemic diseases can occur in both pasture- and confinement-reared swine. There are several different generalized diseases in swine, but those considered here are hog cholera, acute erysipelas, and acute salmonellosis.

The control of exposure that housing gives should reduce the chances of exposure to hog cholera, provided adequate management is utilized. Hopefully the hog cholera eradication program will progress to the point that this disease is completely eliminated in this country.

Acute swine erysipelas should occur at a much reduced frequency in confinement-reared swine due to elimination of contact with potential soil reservoirs of the organism.

Acute salmonellosis may occur in confinement-reared swine. The close proximity and relatively heavy fecal contamination facilitates the spread of this disease once it is introduced by contaminated feed, carrier swine, rodents, or other vectors. This disease can be expected to constitute a continuing source of trouble once a confinement house becomes seeded down with the organisms.

PART FIVE

Importance of Selection and Breeding Characteristics on Muscle Quality

11

Control and Influence
of Muscle Color

PER JONSSON

THE FIRST DIRECTOR of the Denmark Pig Progeny Testing Stations, Niels Beck, wrote in a research report in 1931 that complaints from Great Britain indicated that Danish bacon occasionally possessed a poor, pale color. At that time, a regulation was passed requiring that a muscle color score be placed on each carcass obtained from the testing station. The methods of muscle color evaluation changed slightly through the 1930's and 1940's, but from 1954 to the present the *l. dorsi* muscle has been evaluated for color characteristics. Therefore, Danish researchers have been concerned with pork muscle color problems since the early 1930's. German meat scientists (Herter and Wilsdorf, 1914) reported a pale, moist surface of pork muscle which created processing problems as far back as 1883. They also reported differences between breeds in muscle color.

Frede (1926) and Hupka (1939) used the designation "muscular degeneration" as the severest condition in muscles with pronounced, pale discoloration and watery exudation when they described acute heart problems associated with deaths in pigs. Ludvigsen (1953, 1954) described muscular discoloration in the Danish Landrace in connection with processing and canning problems and claimed that both nutritional and genetic factors were involved.

Wismer-Pedersen (1959) found a phenotypic correlation of r = —0.71 between the pH measurement in the *l. dorsi* muscle behind the last rib 45 minutes after killing and the water-holding capacity of the muscle. He also found a correlation of r = —0.86 between the same pH measurement and the corresponding concentration of lactic acid. Clausen and Nortoft Thomsen (1960) associated a high acid content of meat with pale color characteristics and reported a correlation of r = 0.6 between these traits.

Wismer-Pedersen and Briskey (1961) found it possible to produce pale, moist meat by delaying the temperature fall in the carcass after

TABLE 11.1:   The pH Measurement and Meat Color in *L. Dorsi* Muscle at Tip of Last Rib for Different Classes

Description of Muscle Cross Section Surface	Score for Meat Color	pH Measure- ment	Distribution of Meat Color Scores, percent 1960/61	Distribution of Meat Color Scores, percent 1965/66
Number of test pigs			4618	5257
Gray, same color as boiled meat. Very moist surface, rough and stringy structure	0.5	5.45	0.3	0.2
Very pale, pinkish, moist surface, rough structure	1.0	5.48	3.9	2.7
Pale pink, slightly moist surface, somewhat rough structure	1.5	5.56	15.9	14.5
Slightly paler than desirable, almost dry surface and almost normal structure	2.0	5.80	22.4	22.1
Ideal red color, dry surface, normal structure	2.5	6.19	41.8	52.0
Same as above	3.0	6.25	13.9	7.9
Slightly darker than desirable, dry surface	3.5	6.28	1.5	0.6
Same as above	4.0	6.28	0.3	0
Very dark, dry surface	4.5		0	0
Same as above	5.0		0	0

Source: R. Nortoft Thomsen and O. K. Pedersen (1961).

	color class	percent	
Pronounced too light meat color	0.5–1.5	20	17
A little too light meat color	2.0	22	22
Satisfactory meat color	2.5–4.0	58	61

killing. They concluded that the fast process of chilling the carcass postmortem caused a partial reduction on pale color characteristics of porcine muscle. Hallund (1962) confirmed these results.

RELATION BETWEEN pH AND COLOR SCORE IN PORCINE *L. DORSI* MUSCLE

Table 11.1 shows the muscle color scores and pH values obtained from test pigs and the distribution of color scores for the test years 1960–61 and 1965–66. In 1960–61 the mean muscle color score was 2.27 and the pH was 5.98. In 1965–66 the muscle color score was 2.23 and the pH less than 6.0. The frequency of "ideal red color" (2.5 points) has increased slightly. Pigs which have a muscle color score of 1 and 0.5 have a lower pH value than pigs in the 1.5 class. The reason for this is probably due to a rapid pH fall postmortem resulting in a pale muscle color before the carcasses even enter the chilling room (Clausen and Nortoft Thomsen, 1962). This is the reason the meat color score is considered as the independent variable and the pH measurement as the dependent variable.

EFFECT OF TRANSPORT ON MEAT COLOR AND pH

Ludvigsen (1954) and Wismer-Pedersen and Riemann (1960) discussed the importance of preventing pigs from fighting and biting during transport to reduce the incidence of pale, watery muscle. In 1959 the Danish Meat Research Institute developed a halter (Wichmann Jorgensen, 1959, 1961) which now is used by a number of bacon factories in

TABLE 11.2: Phenotypic Variance Within Same Day of Delivery With and Without Halter Over 14-Week Period, January–June 1960

	Sjaelland (2 km)		Fyn (14 km)		Jylland (8 km)		3 stations	
	− halter	+ halter	− halter	+ halter	− halter	+ halter	− halter	+ halter
							514	523
Castrates							castrates	
Variances within same day of delivery	0.423	0.391	0.307	0.247	0.312	0.325	0.345	0.323
Standard deviation	0.65	0.63	0.55	0.50	0.56	0.57	0.59	0.57
Decline in variance when using halter, percent		7.6		19.6		−3.9		6.6
							533	545
Gilts							gilts	
Variance within same day of delivery	0.410	0.361	0.322	0.221	0.374	0.319	0.366	0.308
Standard deviation	0.64	0.60	0.57	0.47	0.61	0.56	0.61	0.56
Decline in variance when using halter, percent		11.9		31.4		14.8		15.8

Denmark. This halter was tested in the progeny testing stations from January to July, 1960, and caused a general improvement in the muscle color score for all three testing stations (Sjaelland : $P \leq 0.20$, Fyn : $P \leq 0.001$ and Jylland : $P \geq 0.20$).

Table 11.2 shows the decrease of the intraweek variance with and without the halter. There is also demonstrated a pronounced decrease in the variance of the gilts compared to the variance of the more phlegmatic castrated males. The gilts are by nature nervous and it is very clearly shown that with increasing distance to the bacon factory the variance was diminished, whereas the castrates were indifferent to the halter treatment from the station Jylland to its bacon factory (distance, 8km.).

To get a more exact examination of the effect of transport stress on both *l. dorsi* muscle color and pH, an experiment was carried out with 54 test groups delivered from the progeny testing station Vestjylland to its bacon factory, which is only 0.5 km. from the test station. One gilt and one castrate from each of the 54 test groups were killed in their individual pens and transported dead to the bacon factory, whereas the other gilt and barrow litter mate were transported live to the factory. The results are shown in Table 11.3 (Nortoft Thomsen, 1961).

The mean muscle color improved in both the castrates and the gilts when they were killed in the pen. The standard deviation decreased in both sexes, but more in the gilts; only the variation of the pH in the muscle between gilts decreased significantly ($P < 0.048$).

EFFECT OF SEASON ON MEAT COLOR AND pH

Table 11.4 shows the estimated regressions of the mean muscle color score on temperature. Twenty-four out of 28 regression estimates showed a negative influence of the outdoor temperature, but this effect was very slight. Another study was developed to observe the causative effect of transport and season within the phenotypic variation of the test year-test station-sex subgroup of approximately 600 animals. A series of analyses of variance was carried out.

Table 11.5 shows the influence of weekday deliveries of pigs on their *l. dorsi* muscle pH and color scores postmortem. A maximum of 13.5 percent of the total phenotypic variance between pigs of the same sex delivered from the same test station in one year can be accounted for by

TABLE 11.3:   Effect of Transport on Meat Color and pH in *L. Dorsi* (one litter mate in each of the two treatments and in each sex).

	Pigs Killed at the Bacon Factory		Pigs Killed in Pen	
	54 castrates	54 gilts	54 castrates	54 gilts
Meat color score	2.19	2.06	2.27	2.25
Standard deviation	±0.518	±0.550	±0.502	±0.502
pH measurement	5.90	5.83	5.99	5.95
Standard deviation	±0.467	±0.483	±0.438	±0.370

TABLE 11.4: Influence of Testing Station Temperature on Meat Color Scores Approximately 24 Hours Postmortem (increase or decrease in sample mean for weekday of delivery per 1° C. increase. Data corrected for differences in chilled carcass weight between pigs).

Test Station	Sjaelland	Fyn	Jylland	Vestjylland
1958–59 castrates	−0.004	−0.018	−0.002	
gilts	−0.003	−0.010	−0.010	
Mean temp. of year, C.	10.8	11.0	10.2	
1959–60 castrates	−0.004	−0.020	−0.004	
gilts	−0.008	−0.017	−0.005	
Mean temp. of year, C.	10.1	10.3	8.8	
1960–61 castrates	−0.005	−0.010	+0.00002	+0.0001
gilts	−0.009	−0.007	−0.002	+0.003
Mean temp. of year, C.	10.8	10.2	9.7	10.6
1962–62 castrates	−0.004	−0.013	−0.004	−0.004
gilts	−0.007	−0.012	−0.003	+0.0002
Mean temp. of year, C.	9.9	9.4	7.2	8.3

TABLE 11.5: Relative Importance of Months and Days as Causes of Variance in Meat Color Scores and pH for Test Year 1958–59 at Different Testing Stations

	Sjaelland		Fyn		Jylland	
	Castrates	Gilts	Castrates	Gilts	Castrates	Gilts
	584	607	586	624	545	580
Meat color scores						
Months, at same station	−0.1	−0.3	6.1	4.1	4.9	−0.3
Weekdays of delivery	3.7	−0.7	2.8	−1.2	8.6	3.6
Variance among pigs killed the same day	96.4	101.0	91.1	97.1	95.6	96.7
pH in the *l. dorsi*						
Months, at same station	−0.2	2.9	9.2	5.1	−1.3	2.8
Weekdays of delivery	13.8	−0.4	4.0	5.0	8.6	7.4
Variance among pigs killed the same day	86.5	97.5	86.8	89.9	92.7	89.9

the weekly deliveries and differences between the months sampled. These causative effects associated with time cannot be traced to transport differences or differences between seasons.

The repeatability of the influence of time is shown in Tables 11.6 and 11.7. Approximately 95 percent of the total variance within a test year-test station subgroup is caused by phenotypic differences between pigs of the same sex within the same day of delivery. The conclusions drawn from Tables 11.5 to 11.7 are that specific days and specific months of delivery are not causing any systematic effect on muscle color or pH, nor on any other characteristic measured on the test pig.

Table 11.8 shows, however, that the frequencies of the plus and minus deviations within the same quarter of year give a seasonal trend. An analysis of variance will also show significant differences between quarters of year which may be designated as seasonal effect. Both color and pH are above average during the fall and winter months and below average in spring and summer.

EFFECT OF CHILLED CARCASS WEIGHT ON MUSCLE COLOR AND pH

Table 11.9 shows the repeatability of the consistently negative effects of chilled carcass weight on both muscle color and pH, though these

TABLE 11.6: **Relative Importance of Months and Days as Causes of Variance in Meat Color in Different Years and at Different Testing Stations**

	Castrates				Gilts			
	No.	Month	Week	Pig	No.	Month	Week	Pig
		(percent)	*(percent)*	*(percent)*		*(percent)*	*(percent)*	*(percent)*
1958–59:								
Sjaelland	584	—0.1	3.7	96.4	607	—0.3	—0.7	101.0
Fyn	586	6.1	2.8	91.1	624	4.1	—1.2	97.1
Jylland	545	—4.2	8.6	95.6	580	—0.3	3.6	96.7
1959–60:								
Sjaelland	628	0.7	—0.2	99.5	629	5.6	—1.0	95.4
Fyn	644	7.7	—3.7	88.6	652	6.5	9.2	84.3
Jylland	606	0.9	2.1	96.9	644	2.9	4.4	92.3
1960–61:								
Sjaelland	620	2.2	—1.4	99.2	615	1.8	—1.1	99.3
Fyn	539	—0.8	4.6	96.2	544	0.8	6.1	93.1
Jylland	609	0.7	2.5	96.9	640	0.2	0	99.8
Vestjylland	519	—1.0	4.0	97.0	524	—0.7	3.2	97.5
1962–63:								
Sjaelland	681	2.1	—0.1	98.1	684	2.3	—1.6	99.5
Fyn	620	7.7	7.3	85.8	616	9.8	1.4	89.6
Jylland	600	0.7	0.4	99.0	597	0.2	0.2	99.7
Vestjylland	591	—1.5	2.2	99.3	601	—0.7	3.9	96.8
1963–64:								
Sjaelland	653	6.9	3.0	90.1	661	6.1	0.9	93.0
Fyn	627	0.2	—0.2	100.1	628	3.4	4.1	92.4
Jylland	600	0.7	0.4	99.0	597	0.2	0.2	99.7
Vestjylland	591	—1.5	2.2	99.3	601	—0.7	3.9	96.8

TABLE 11.7: Relative Importance of Month and Days as Causes of Variance in Some Attributes of Castrates and Gilts at Different Testing Stations

	Castrates			Gilts		
	Month	Week	Pig	Month	Week	Pig
			(percent)			
Age at 20 kg. liveweight						
Sjaelland	0.1	5.8	94.1	0.9	2.9	96.3
Fyn	0.8	4.0	95.2	0.1	2.0	97.8
Jylland	2.6	3.2	94.2	1.8	6.4	91.8
Vestjylland	1.2	3.3	95.5	2.3	3.4	94.3
Body length						
Sjaelland	2.5	2.9	94.6	2.7	1.0	96.3
Fyn	1.9	2.1	96.0	2.1	3.6	94.4
Jylland	2.5	2.9	94.6	—0.4	3.7	96.7
Vestjylland	4.3	1.8	93.8	7.3	1.5	91.2
Side fat measurement						
Sjaelland	1.0	0.8	98.2	7.7	0.5	91.9
Fyn	0.5	1.1	98.3	—0.6	4.5	96.1
Jylland	0.3	0.7	99.0	0.9	1.3	97.7
Vestjylland	4.8	—1.0	96.2	2.4	2.1	95.5
Area of the l. dorsi						
Sjaelland	1.5	0.9	97.6	0.5	5.7	93.8
Fyn	0.8	1.6	97.7	1.8	3.6	94.6
Jylland	1.1	—0.1	99.0	0.1	2.6	97.3
Vestjylland	1.6	—0.9	99.3	3.0	0.5	96.5
Meat color score						
Sjaelland	6.9	3.0	90.1	6.1	0.9	93.0
Fyn	0.2	—0.2	100.1	3.4	4.1	92.4
Jylland	3.4	1.2	95.4	0.6	—1.6	101.0
Vestjylland	1.6	2.9	95.5	—0.6	3.8	96.8

TABLE 11.8: Number of Year-Station-Sex Subgroups Above and Below Average by Months for Meat Color Score and pH

			Meat color score, 1956–60								
Month	+	—	Month	+	—	Month	+	—	Month	+	—
Sept.	10	14	Dec.	22	2	Mar.	10	14	June	9	15
Oct.	18	6	Jan.	19	5	Apr.	9	15	July	3	21
Nov.	17	7	Feb.	18	6	May	8	16	Aug.	6	18

			pH measurement, 1958–59								
Month	+	—	Month	+	—	Month	+	—	Month	+	—
Sept.	5	1	Dec.	3	3	Mar.	2	4	June	2	4
Oct.	6	0	Jan.	4	2	Apr.	3	3	July	3	3
Nov.	2	4	Feb.	4	2	May	0	6	Aug.	0	6

TABLE 11.9: Relation Between Meat Color and pH in the *L. Dorsi* on the One Side and the Chilled Carcass Weight on the Other Side

	Sjaelland		Fyn		Jylland		Vestjylland	
Points for meat color	1962–63				(4990 pigs finished the test)			
Regression per 1 kg. chilled carcass weight								
♂♂	−.034 ± .01		−.049 ± .01		−.028 ± .01		−.017 ± .01	
♀♀	−.033 ± .01		−.063 ± .01		−.040 ± .01		−.017 ± .01	
	Castrates	Gilts	Castrates	Gilts	Castrates	Gilts	Castrates	Gilts
	(%)							
Variance in meat color due to differences in carcass weight. Eight subgroups of app. 600 pigs each	1.7	2.1	2.5	4.8	1.0	1.7	0.4	0.3
pH measurement 1961–62 (4,998 pigs finished the test)								
Regression of pH on chilled carcass weight:								
H+ power exponents per 1 kg.								
♂♂	−.040 ± .008		−.026 ± .008		−.017 ± .008		−.014 ± .009	
♀♀	−.015 ± .009		−.035 ± .007		−.010 ± .008		−.023 ± .009	

effects are not large. The coefficients of regression are highly significant for both.

In Figure 11.1 diagrams are shown of the effects of the chilled carcass weight, area of the *l. dorsi* muscle, and size and shape of hams on *l. dorsi* muscle color and pH. The strength of the relation between chilled carcass weight and muscle color is not changed at either a constant area of *l. dorsi* or constant size and shape of hams, as shown below:

		Castrates	Gilts
r pts. f. muscle color, chilled carcass wt.		−0.12	−0.21
r pts. f. muscle color, chilled carcass wt. *l. dorsi* area		−0.11	−0.21
r pts. f. muscle color, chilled carcass wt. pts. f. size and shape of hams		−0.08	0.18

PHENOTYPIC VARIATION AND HERITABILITY OF MUSCLE COLOR AND pH

The best estimate of the phenotypic variance is based on the summation of a sufficient number of test year-test station-sex subgroups, one year of test comprising material from four test stations and therefore eight subgroups. The variance within each subgroup is corrected for the effect from seasonal and, if necessary, chilled carcass weight differences. It is then denoted as a single estimate of the phenotypic variance. The hierarchical structure of the best estimate of the phenotypic variance is two test pigs of the same sex per test group, five test pigs of the same sex per sire half-sib family, and 12 test pigs of the same sex per breeding center (herd).

Within the elite herds were found relationships of 17.5 percent between dams mated to the same sire and 2.6 percent between sires standing at the same breeding center. The additive genetic variance between breeding centers in the material investigated was, therefore, distributed as follows:

Between breeding centers (elite herds)	= 5%
Between sires within the same breeding center	= 24%
Between dams mated to the same sire	= 21%
Between litter mates, because of no relationship between parents	= 50%

The relative causative effects which act on the phenotype of the character, are designated:

Breeding center (i.e. herd) environment	= c^2
Heritability or additive gene effect	= h^2
Maternal effect, litter environment	= l^2
Residue, i.e. percent error variance	= ir^2

The pH in the *l. dorsi* was measured by pH meters 45 minutes postmortem as a routine character in the test pigs from 1958 to 1962. Because of missing data, it was possible to obtain complete material from

The levels of significance of the regression coefficients were distributed as follows:

1954-62	P ≥ 0.05	P≤ 0.05	P≤ 0.01	P ≤ 0.001	Total
Number of $\bar{b}$ (within quarters of year)	8	8	15	21	52
Per cent	15.4	15.4	28.9	40.4	100.1

The following simple linear regressions were found:

Gilt:

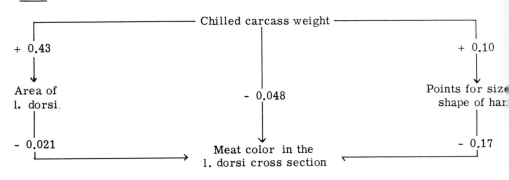

Gilt:

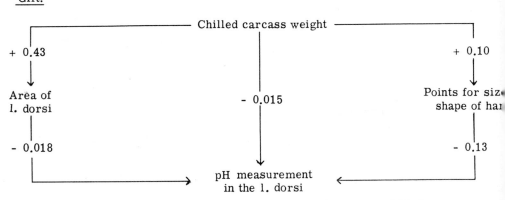

Fig. 11.1. The effect of the weight of the empty, chilled carcass on the pH and meat color in the *l. dorsi* muscle. In investigating (52 estimates of approximately 600 animals each) the regression points for meat color on the chilled carcass weight of the pig, 50 regression estimates were negative and only 2 were positive. The same regression trend was found in the pH measurement.

only one year of test, 1958–59, the results of which are given in Table 11.10 together with the points for meat color.

As under other conditions discussed previously, muscle color and pH are influenced by the different causative factors. Typical is the smaller variance in pH compared with the scores for muscle color, as shown in Figure 11.2. Especially in the upper color classes the pH has not changed very much from class to class. A pH measurement 24 hours postmortem was not available. In the four years the standard deviation for the meat color score was from 15 to 38 percent greater than the standard deviation for the pH.

An essential fact in Table 11.10 is the characteristically higher heritability in gilts than in castrates in this sample. Unfortunately the results cannot be compared with the works of Ollivier (1963), Allen *et al.* (1966), and Jensen *et al.* (1967) who worked with a pH measurement taken in the muscle 24 hours postmortem, whereas in this investigation the pH measurement used was taken 45 minutes postmortem. Also the Danish pigs are fed for the last time before slaughter in the morning, and the concentration of glycogen in the muscles is then different from that when the pigs are starved 12 or more hours before killing as was the case with the other workers.

TABLE 11.10: **Analysis of Variance of Meat Color Score and pH Measurements in the *L. Dorsi*, Test Year 1958–59.**

Variance Components, Percent	Degrees of Freedom		Meat Color Scores		pH	
	castrates	gilts	castrates	gilts	castrates	gilts
$V_{station}$	2	2	1.1	0.8	4.3	5.2
$V_{elite\ herd}$	283	281	9.5	−0.8	4.7	1.5
V_{sire}	241	239	−5.7	15.3	4.8	10.5
$V_{test\ group}$	382	384	11.7	4.5	11.8	3.6
$V_{individual}$	806	904	83.4	80.3	74.7	79.2
V_{total}	1714	1810	100.0	100.1	100.0	100.0

Meat color scores
Castrates: $y = 2.35 \pm 0.013$; Gilts $\bar{y} = 2.34 \pm 0.013$
$s_y = 0.533, s_{ind} = 0.488; s_y = 0.553, s_{ind} = 0.496$
pH measurement
Castrates: $y = 6.07 \pm 0.008$; Gilts: $y = 6.02 \pm 0.008$
$s_y = 0.350, s_{ind} = 0.305; s_y = 0.349, s_{ind} = 0.313$

Causation Components, Percent	Meat Color Scores		pH	
	castrates	gilts	castrates	gilts
Breeding center (i.e. herd) environment (c^2)	10.8	−4.0	3.9	−0.7
Heritability or additive gene effect (h^2)	−23.6	63.4	19.4	45.3
Maternal effect, litter environment (l^2)	16.7	−8.6	8.4	−5.5
Residue, i.e. % error variance (ir^2)	96.1	49.2	68.3	60.9
Phenotype	100.00	100.0	100.0	100.0

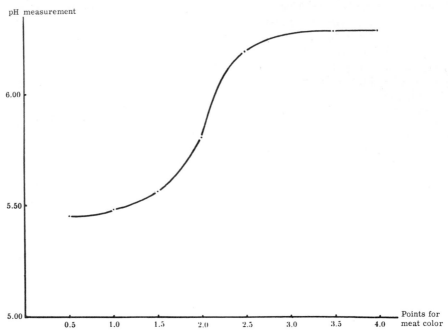

FIG. 11.2.   The pH in the *l. dorsi* at increasing values for
points for meat color at the same place in that muscle. Test
year 1960/61, 4618 test pigs. (Clausen and Nortoft Thomsen, 1962.

The pH measurement used by Ollivier was taken in the right ham
and that used by Allen *et al.* was taken in the *l. dorsi*. The estimates of
heritability given by these authors were of similar magnitude to those
given in Table 11.10 except for the estimate by Ollivier who for his
castrated males got an estimate of $h^2 = 0.94$. Thus he did not find the
difference in the expression of the additive gene effect between sires'
paternal half-sib groups of different sexes as was done in the material of
Table 11.10.

To investigate whether there is a consistent difference between
sexes in causative effects of the phenotype of meat color, the successive
test years were investigated from 1954 when the recording of this character started in Denmark. As seen in Table 11.11, there is demonstrated
quite a pronounced difference between sexes in heritability of meat color
score, but there is also demonstrated a sex-test year interaction. In the
years 1959–62, the heritability was of similar magnitude between sexes.

A difference between sexes is not found in the mean of the color
score, as can be seen in Table 11.11, but the phenotypic standard deviation of meat color is consistently larger in gilts. On an average the
phenotypic variance of the meat color is approximately 10 percent larger
in the gilts, which may be attributed to the castration effect in the male
test pigs. Considering the intensive enzyme activities in the muscle before

TABLE 11.11: **Partitioning of Phenotypic Variation Between State Recognized Breeding Centers (Elite Herds) in Meat Color Scores**

Causation Components, Percent	c^2		h^2		l^2		ir^2		Mean of Character		Standard Deviation	
	♂♂	♀♀	♂♂	♀♀	♂♂	♀♀	♂♂	♀♀	♂♂	♀♀	♂♂	♀♀
1954–55	1	10	9	−2	11	14	80	79	2.29	2.31	0.52	0.56
1955–56	2	−5	3	41	9	3	86	61	2.36	2.40	0.47	0.53
1956–57	4	1	−7	47	15	−6	88	59	2.37	2.38	0.50	0.54
1957–58	2	−3	17	44	6	−3	74	62	2.37	2.34	0.49	0.52
1958–59	11	−4	−24	63	17	−9	96	49	2.35	2.34	0.53	0.55
1959–60	−1	3	45	31	−3	3	59	64	2.30	2.23	0.54	0.57
1960–61	−1	−2	35	34	−2	2	69	66	2.27	2.29	0.51	0.55
1961–62	−3	0	43	48	2	−9	58	61	2.33	2.33	0.48	0.51
1962–63	2	0	16	46	6	−8	77	61	2.26	2.25	0.50	0.52
	2	−1	16	44	6	−3	76	60				

rigor mortis sets in, the blocking of the sex hormones at an early stage of life could influence the biochemistry of meat structure.

A parallel example is found in the phenotypic variance of the score for nasal alterations (rhinitis score) taken at slaughter. The difference between sexes in the phenotypic variance taken over a four-year period was as follows:

1956–60: $s^2_{phenotype}$ (gilts) $/ s^2_{phenotype}$ (castrates) $= 0.824/0.735 = 1.12$

For comparison is shown, for the same period of time, the ratio between sexes of the variance estimated within test groups (litters) in muscle color score.

1956–60: $s^2_{ind.}$ (gilts) $/ s^2_{ind.}$ (castrates) $= 0.235/0.217 = 1.08$

The best estimates of the partitioning of the phenotypic variance in the Danish Landrace pig are given for three characters important in selecting for the bacon type in Table 11.12.

The area of the *l. dorsi* is included in the table because the test year means of this character have shown only a slight trend of improvement since the introduction of this muscle area in 1957. As a single character the muscle area is quite important for the meat content in the whole bacon side, though Pedersen (1964) has found a phenotypic correlation of only $r = \lceil 0.47$ between the area of the *l. dorsi* and the percentage of lean meat in the carcass. The same author has found a phenotypic correlation of $r = -0.7$ between the side fat measurement and the percentage of lean meat in the carcass. Therefore the side fat measurement is included in Table 11.12 as the third character.

Discrepancies are demonstrated between heritability estimates in the years of test 1956–57, 1958–59, and 1959–60 from Table 11.11 to Table 11.12. This is because the estimates in Table 11.11 are based on the total material of test, whereas all estimates in Table 11.12 are based on sire half-sib groups with at least two test groups (litters) and breeding center groups.

TABLE 11.12: Partitioning of Phenotypic Variation Between State Recognized Breeding Centers (Elite Herds) of Danish Landrace Pig (Values Expressed in Percent)*

Year of Test	Meat Color Scores in L. Dorsi				Area of L. Dorsi Cross Section				Side Fat Measurement			
	c^2	h^2	l^2	ir^2	c^2	h^2	l^2	ir^2	c^2	h^2	l^2	ir^2
1956–57	3	23	5	68	—	—	—	—	—	—	—	—
1957–58	0	29	7	64	—	—	—	—	—	—	—	—
1958–59	−2	44	1	58	2	37	8	54	2	49	1	48
1959–60	2	23	10	66	5	7	21	68	−2	48	8	45
1960–61	−2	34	0	67	2	37	5	56	−2	40	7	49
1961–62	−1	46	−4	60	5	33	7	56	0	59	6	36
1962–63	1	31	−1	69	0	47	3	50	0	79	−7	28
1963–64	−2	36	9	57	4	51	5	41	0	54	10	36
1964–65	4	15	8	74	−2	56	6	40	1	56	4	39
	1956–65: 1,303 paternal half-sib groups				1958–65: 1,123 paternal half-sib groups				1958–65: 1,123 paternal half-sib groups			
Castrates:	0.1 ± 1.3	27 ± 6	6 ± 3	67	1 ± 2	44 ± 7	7 ± 3	49	1 ± 2	60 ± 8	5 ± 3	35
Gilts:	1 ± 1	36 ± 6	1 ± 3	63	2 ± 2	41 ± 7	6 ± 3	51	0.4 ± 1.7	52 ± 8	4 ± 3	43
Average:	0	31	3	65	2	42	7	50	1	56	4	39
Degrees of freedom	545	726	2198	3379	467	630	1900	2889	467	630	1900	2889
Standard deviation:	Castrates	Gilts			Castrates	Gilts			Castrates	Gilts		
	0.49 pts.	0.52 pts.			2.51 cm²	2.65 cm²			0.41 cm	0.34 cm		
Additive genetic	0.26 pts.	0.31 pts.			1.66 cm²	1.69 cm²			0.31 cm	0.25 cm		

*The data are corrected for the effect of the relationship between sires and that between dams; further for the influence of chilled carcass weight, seasons of year, progeny test stations, and years of test.

It is clearly demonstrated in Table 11.12 that under a system where it is necessary to restrict the test animals such that only a little more than five pigs per sire half-sib family and only 12 pigs per herd are obtained, it is necessary to include a number of test years in the estimate to get sufficient unbiased estimates of the causative parameters in the breed. This agrees with the theory given by Robertson (1960) about experimental design on the measurement of heritabilities.

Besides having a sufficient number of individuals per subgroup to get unbiased estimates of the different intraclass correlations, the years must cover some sire generations, because the sample of paternal half-sib groups sent to the test station per year is not necessarily representative for the potentialities of zygotes from the breeding centers as a whole.

Sex differences in heritabilities are not demonstrated in muscle area and side fat measurement in the overall estimates within test stations and years. In the scores for meat color it should be concluded that the sire component estimated from the castrated male data tends to be decreased, and therefore "litter environment" and error variance are correspondingly increased. In a breeding program it should, therefore, be more efficient to base the selection on data from uncastrated animals.

It has been shown previously that the effects of test stations, seasons of year, and chilled carcass weight affect meat color only slightly. Table 11.12 shows that the only two major factors which greatly influence meat color are heritability and residual error. If only gilts are included in the selection program, it is realistic to work with a heritability of 0.4 and a residual error of 0.6. If both sexes are included in the test group, the heritability is 0.3 and the residual error 0.7.

A rather strong maternal effect is found in the *l. dorsi* muscle area. This could to some extent be due to mothering abilities of prenatal nature.

The test groups of litters from the state recognized breeding centers consist of two castrated males and two females. Because of the uncertainty of the genetic variance of meat color in the castrates and also because the genetic improvement of a character is increased per year when using only two instead of four litter mates, it is of interest to investigate the genetic correlation between the sexes with respect to their performance in the three carcass characteristics (Table 11.13).

The variance components for the interaction between sire half-sib

TABLE 11.13: Genetic Correlation and Expected Gain of L. Dorsi Area and Color

	Genetic Correlation Between Castrates and Gilts	Degrees of Freedom	$h_{castr.}$	h_{gilts}	Percent Expected Genetic Gain in Castrates When Selecting Only on Gilts
Meat color score	0.97 ± 0.11	871	0.52	0.60	112
Area of *l. dorsi*	1.18 ± 0.10	693	0.66	0.64	114
Side fat measurement	0.88 ± 0.06	693	0.77	0.72	82

families and sex were very small in meat color score and side fat measurement, 0.0034 points and 0.0028 cm. respectively; the F-quotients were 1.09 and 1.15 respectively. This is the reason the corresponding genetic correlations are not unity. In the *l. dorsi* area, however, the F-quotient was consistently below unity in the different test year-test station subgroups, so no sire-sex interaction is found in this character.

In the test year 1965–66, 611 boars were tested in the four testing stations on 1,355 groups, and the breeding values of these sires were estimated for different characters as their deviation from the test year mean after having corrected the data for effects from stations, seasons, and chilled carcass weight. One hundred and ninety-four boars or 32 percent of the tested sires had two or more test groups (litters from different dams).

An investigation showed that the regression difference between the sire's breeding value for his castrate progeny and for his gilt progeny was statistically highly significant. The regression estimates are given below.

	Points for Meat Color	Area of Musc. *L. Dorsi*	Side Fat Measurement
$b \pm s_b$	-0.62 ± 0.04	-0.35 ± 0.06	-0.29 ± 0.07
t(192 d.f.)	-14.3	-6.1	-4.3

The more the mean of the character is improved, the more the difference between a sire's gilt progeny and his castrate progeny will diminish. It will, therefore, not delay a breeding program to omit the castrates from the test groups. On the contrary, this will improve the genetic gain per year. Under the Danish restriction of 5,600 pens for individual feeding per year, it is found in a model calculation (when for example 400 sires are needed for the next generation) that the genetic gain per year using four pigs in a test group is 0.60 units of the genetic standard deviation of the character in question, whereas the genetic gain is 0.68 units of that character's genetic standard deviation using two pigs in a test group. However, the genetic gain is 1.35 units of the character's genetic standard deviation when testing the performance of the breeding animal itself.

RELATION BETWEEN MEAT COLOR AND PRODUCTION CHARACTERISTICS IN DANISH LANDRACE PIGS

Figures 11.3 and 11.4 illustrate the positions of carcass characteristics measured.

In Table 11.14 estimates of correlations of eight traits with meat color scores and pH measurement are given. Data from only one year of test are included.

The reactions of these two characters with a third one are similar to the reactions against the causative effects discussed previously. The correlation for the residual sector is a measure for covariation within the litter after the elimination of the additive gene effect. The effect of the inter- and intra-allele gene action is included in this correlation.

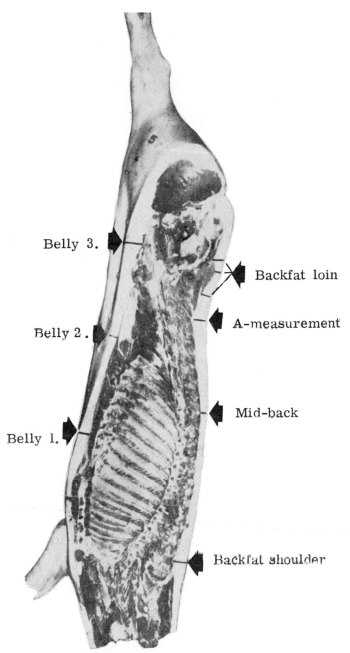

Belly 3.

Backfat loin

A-measurement

Belly 2.

Mid-back

Belly 1.

Backfat shoulder

FIG. 11.3.   Trimmed bacon side, Danish Landrace gilt.

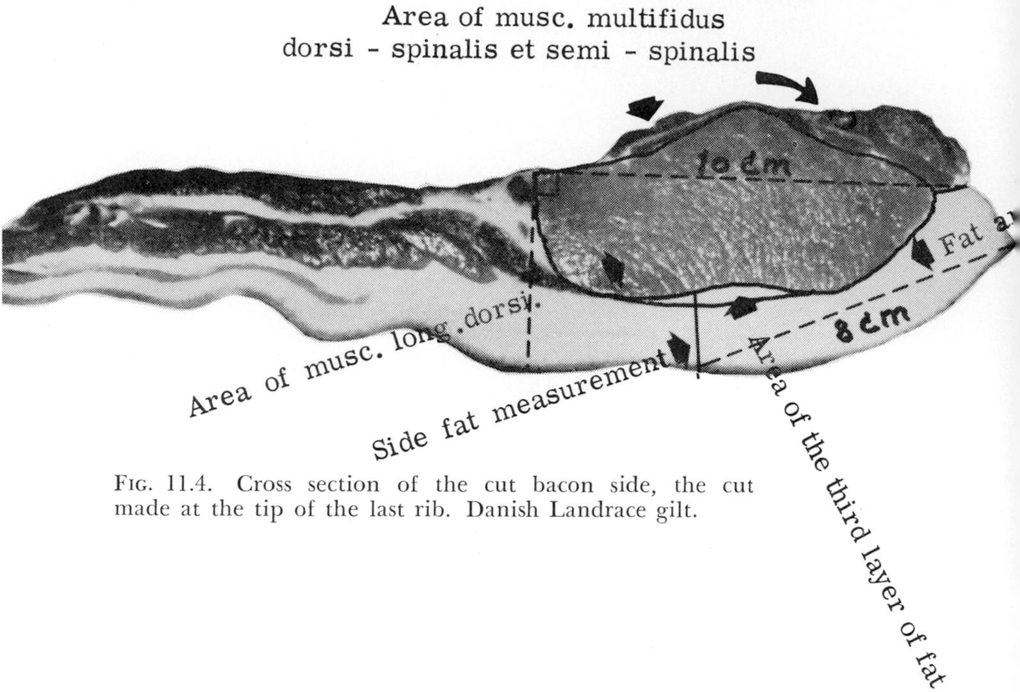

Area of musc. multifidus
dorsi - spinalis et semi - spinalis

FIG. 11.4. Cross section of the cut bacon side, the cut
made at the tip of the last rib. Danish Landrace gilt.

Meat color and pH in the muscle are negatively correlated with fast
gain and positively with feed consumption rate. At constant gain the
covariation between feed consumption and these two characters is not
changed. Length of the pig and all fat measurements are positively
correlated with color and pH in the muscle whereas meat content is
negatively correlated. None of these correlations is strong.

It is of importance to investigate whether there are phenotypically
and genetically antagonistic relationships between meat color in the
muscle and important production and carcass characteristics which estimate muscling of the pig. Table 11.15 shows that meat color is phenotypically negatively correlated with gain, size and shape of hams, and
muscle area and therefore phenotypically positively correlated with feed
consumption rate, percentage of slaughter loss, and amount of fat in
the pig. These are disadvantageous phenotypic relations, but their
trends are weak. An advantageous positive correlation is found between
meat color and length of the pig, but this relation is also weak.

The most important correlations with meat color shown here are
those with size and shape of hams and with the area of the *l. dorsi*. The
genetic correlation with size and shape of hams is rather strong and
antagonistically negative. This correlation is interesting because it de-
scribes the relation between the size of a muscle and the color of another
muscle. The strong antagonistic genetic relationship calls for direct
genetic investigation of color and structural conditions in the muscles

of the ham; the points for size and shape of hams have a heritability of
0.4 ± 0.07 in the Danish Landrace pig.

Two causative diagrams are shown for phenotypic correlations between points for meat color and different characters. These diagrams are worked out according to principles given by Hazel (1943) and Hazel *et al.* (1943).

Figure 11.5 shows causative diagrams between feed consumption rate of the pig, its side fat measurement, and its color in the *l. dorsi*. There is a primary relation between feed consumption rate and side fat measurement which, phenotypically and genetically, is statistically highly significant. The genetic and phenotypic positive relation between meat color and feed consumption rate is considered to be secondary through the covariation between feed consumption rate and fat content of the pig. The consistent positive relation between meat color and all fat measurements (Table 11.15) seems to be a biological fact, but its magnitude is

TABLE 11.14: **Phenotypic Correlations for Meat Color Score and pH Measurement at Three Pig Progeny Testing Stations, 1958–59. (Correction is undertaken for effects from chilled carcass weight, seasons of year, and test stations.)**

		Castrates	Gilts	Meat Color Score in Cross Section of *L. Dorsi*		pH Measurement *L. Dorsi* at Same Place	
$r_{phenotype}$, d.f.:		1711	1807				
$r_{residue}$, d.f.:		805	903				
				$r_{phenotype}$	$r_{residue}$	$r_{phenotype}$	$r_{residue}$
Avg. daily gain in grams from 20 to 90 kg. live weight	castrates			−0.03	+0.10	−0.08	−0.10
	gilts			−0.01	−0.12	−0.04	−0.26
Feed consumption (Scand. F.U.) per kg. live weight gain from 20 to 90 kg. live weight	castrates			+0.06	−0.02	+0.12	+0.13
	gilts			+0.05	+0.26	+0.09	+0.30
Feed consumption rate at constant gain	castrates			+0.07	−0.02	+0.11	+0.11
	gilts			+0.07	+0.23	+0.10	+0.18
Body length in cm.	castrates			+0.16	+0.19	+0.16	+0.27
	gilts			+0.19	+0.12	+0.15	+0.25
Points (0–15) for size and shape of hams	castrates			−0.19	−0.13	−0.29	−0.12
	gilts			−0.28	−0.05	−0.27	−0.03
Area of *l. dorsi* on cross section of cut bacon side, cm.³	castrates			−0.14	−0.06	−0.17	−0.16
	gilts			−0.14	−0.11	−0.14	−0.10
Area of fat on cross section of cut bacon side, cm.²	castrates			+0.09	−0.15	+0.19	+0.11
	gilts			+0.14	+0.07	+0.18	−0.04
Midback measurement, cm.	castrates			+0.02	−0.36	+0.05	−0.29
	gilts			+0.05	−0.27	+0.07	−0.40
Side fat measurement on cross section of cut bacon side, cm.²	castrates			+0.07	−0.30	+0.18	+0.02
	gilts			+0.10	−0.02	+0.16	−0.11
pH in *l. dorsi* at last rib	castrates			+0.66	+0.68		
	gilts			+0.71	+0.57		

phenotypically and genetically not strong and can be mastered through proper weighting in a selection index.

Figure 11.6 gives causation diagrams between four important characters for type of pig. The most important correlation is considered to be that between the *l. dorsi* area and color of muscle. Both the phenotypic and the genetic correlations are weak, but the positive genetic correlation between these two characters allows for strong selection in a breeding program for both size and desirable color of the *l. dorsi*.

The magnitude of correlation between muscle area and color is very similar in the three causation effects: additive gene action ($+ 0.11 \pm 0.19$),

TABLE 11.15: Meat Color in Cross Section of *L. Dorsi* Correlated With Other Characters*

Type of correlation		$r_{add.\ gen.}$	$r_{residue}$	$r_{phenotype}$	r_{total}
Degrees of freedom	♂♂	294	1302	2695	2708
	♀♀	289	1331	2700	2713
Meat color score correlated with:					
Age in days at the beginning	♂♂	−0.14 ± .51	−0.05	−0.03	−0.03
of test (20 kg.)	♀♀	+0.03 ± .39	−0.07	−0.04	−0.04
Avg. daily gain in grams from	♂♂	−0.10 ± .35	−0.07	−0.04	−0.05
20 to 90 kg. live weight	♀♀	(−4.49)	+0.12	+0.01	+0.01
Feed consumption (Scand. F.U.)	♂♂	+0.32 ± .25	+0.05	+0.08	+0.10
per kg. live weight gain from 20 to 90 kg. live weight	♀♀	+0.64 ± .17	−0.05	+0.08	+0.09
Slaughter loss as a percentage	♂♂	+0.34 ± .32	+0.01	+0.06	+0.06
of the last live weight	♀♀	+0.70 ± .09	−0.19	+0.08	+0.06
Body length	♂♂	+0.62 ± .10	−0.002	+0.20	+0.19
	♀♀	+0.56 ± .09	−0.08	+0.18	+0.16
Avg. backfat thickness	♂♂	+0.19 ± .14	+0.07	+0.11	+0.12
(avg. of 5 measurements)	♀♀	+0.24 ± .11	+0.08	+0.15	+0.15
Avg. belly thickness	♂♂	−0.33 ± .19	+0.08	−0.01	−0.01
(avg. of 3 measurements)	♀♀	−0.18 ± .20	+0.11	+0.07	+0.07
Area of fat on cross section of cut	♂♂	+0.18 ± .18	+0.13	+0.13	+0.13
bacon side	♀♀	+0.34 ± .12	+0.04	+0.19	+0.17
Midback measurement	♂♂	+0.20 ± .15	−0.02	+0.06	+0.07
	♀♀	+0.11 ± .13	+0.04	+0.08	+0.08
Side fat measurement on cross	♂♂	+0.09 ± .16	+0.08	+0.09	+0.09
section of cut bacon side	♀♀	+0.12 ± .14	+0.13	+0.15	+0.13
Fat area/total area of meat	♂♂	+0.10 ± .19	+0.14	+0.12	+0.12
	♀♀	+0.23 ± .12	+0.11	+0.19	+0.18
Points (0–15) for size and	♂♂	−0.47 ± .14	−0.12	−0.19	−0.19
shape of hams	♀♀	−0.63 ± .10	−0.06	−0.27	−0.26
Area of *l. dorsi* cross section	♂♂	+0.18 ± .20	−0.14	−0.06	−0.05
	♀♀	+0.11 ± .19	−0.19	−0.12	−0.10

* 1958–62, the four Danish Pig Progeny-Testing Stations. Data corrected for the effect from the relationship between sires and dams, chilled carcass weight, seasons of year, stations and years.

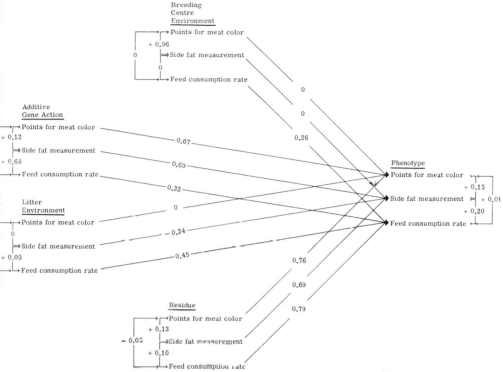

FIG. 11.5. Causative diagrams between feed consumption rate, side fat measurement, and meat color in the *l. dorsi* of gilts of Danish Landrace.

residual effect (—0.19), and phenotype effect (—0.12). The strong paths from the residual effect to the phenotype of these characters have changed the sign of the phenotypic correlation from plus to minus. The question is whether it is biologically and practically possible to change the sign of the phenotypic correlation from minus to plus.

The small negative correlation between muscle area and body length can be mastered through the high heritability in each of the two characters and selecting for both independently of one another. In the same way, the antagonistic relation between meat color and side fat has been mustered in the selection work in Denmark. However, in spite of the considerable improvement in side fat measurement, the *l. dorsi* area has not given any response though its genetic correlation with the side fat measurement is —0.7 (both sexes).

However, the advantage of a test on the animal's own performance cannot be questioned (see also Table 11.17). The matter is only to develop tools to measure at the same time muscle size and muscle quality. Some tools like the ultrasonic apparatus are being used to measure muscle size in addition to the fat layer of pigs, and it should not be impossible to develop an apparatus which can measure muscle size at different parts of the animal with sufficient accuracy. In addition attention

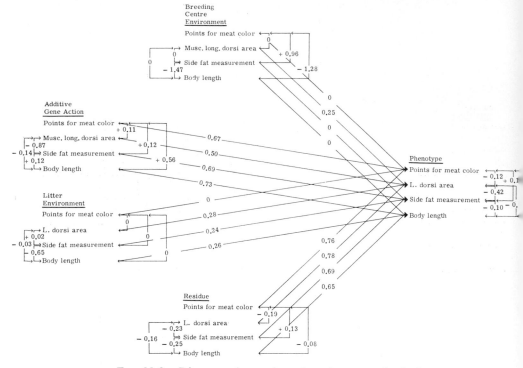

FIG. 11.6. Diagram of genetic and environmental relations between and within four important characters in gilts of Danish Landrace.

has been drawn to the possibility of quantitatively measuring specific enzyme activities in the blood of live animals in relation to muscle properties (Sybesma, 1967). If this can be practiced on a continuous scale and not only as a threshold character, test of the muscle quality properties in the live animal should be possible and a rapid improvement in breeds ensured for both qualitative and quantitative traits.

REFERENCES

Allen, E., Forrest, J. C., Chapman, A. B., First, N., Bray, R. W., and Briskey, E. J. 1967. Phenotypic and genetic associations between porcine muscle properties, *J. Animal Sci.* 25:962–66.

Beck, N. 1931. 19. Beretning om sammenlignende forsog med svin fra statsanerkendte avlscentre. 139. beretning fra forsogslaboratoriet, Kobenhavn.

———. 1933. 21. Beretning om sammenlignende forsog med svin fra statsanerkendte avlscentre. 150. beretning fra forsogslaboratoriet, Kobenhavn.

———. 1934. 22. Beretning om sammenlignende forsog med svin fra statsanerkendte avlscentre. 157. beretning fra forsogslaboratoriet, Kobenhavn.

Clausen, H., and Nortoft Thomsen, R. 1956. 44. Beretning om sammenlignende forsog med svin fra statsanerkendte avlscentre. 288. beretning fra forsogslaboratoriet, Kobenhavn.

———. 1960. 48. Beretning om sammenlignende forsog med svin fra statsanerkendte avlscentre. 317. beretning frfa forsogslaboratoriet, Kobenhavn. 127 pp.

———. 1962. 50. beretning fra forsogslaboratoriet, Kobenhavn. 159 pp.

Frede, W. 1926. Toxische Herzerkrankung bei Schweinen, Deut. tierärztl. Wochschr. 34:658–59.

Hallund, O. 1962. Kodfarvens afhaengighed af koleforlobet. Ikke offentliggjort forsogsmateriale, Slagteriernes Forskningsinstitut, Roskilde.

Hazel, L. N. 1943. The genetic basis for constructing selection indexes, *Genetics* 28:476–90.

Hazel, L. N., Baker, M. L., and Reinmiller, C. F. 1943. Genetic and environmental correlations between the growth rates of pigs at different ages, *J. Animal Sci.* 2:118–28.

Herter, M., and Wilsdorf, G. 1914. *Die Bedeutung des Schweines für die Fleischversorgung*, Berlin: Deut. Landwirtschaftgesellschaft.

Hupka, E. 1939. Seuchenhaft auftretende hühnerfleischähnliche Muskelentartungen unter den Schweinen, Deut. tierärztl. Wochschr. 47:242–44.

Jensen, P., Craig, H. B., and Robison, O. W. 1967. Genetic variation and covariation among carcass traits of swine. In press.

Ludvigsen, J. B. 1953. "Muscular degeneration" in hogs (preliminary report). 15. intern. veterin. congress, proc. repr., Stockholm.

———. 1954. Undersogelser over den såkaldte muskeldegeneration hos svin. 272. beretning fra forsogslaboratoriet, Kobenhavn.

Lush, J. L. 1954. Rates of genetic changes in populations of farm animals. Proc. 9th Intern. Congr. of Genet. Caryologia (Suppl.) 6:589–99.

Nortoft Thomsen, R. 1961. De sammenlignende forsog med svin fra statsanerkendte avlscentre, year of test Sept. 1st, 1960–August 31st, 1961. In: Årbog 1961, Landokonomisk Forsogslaboratoriums efterårsmode, pp. 202–11.

Nortoft Thomsen, R., and Pedersen, O. K. 1961. Examination of the measurements and assessments made on the back rasher with particular reference to slight of lean and muscle degeneration. European Association for Animal Production, Pig Sub-Commission. Rome.

Ollivier, L., and Mesle, L. 1963. Resultats d' un controle de descendence portant sur la qualité de la viande chez le porc. *Ann. Zootech.* 12:173–79.

Pedersen, O. K. 1964. Bestemmelse af svinenes slagtekvalitet. In: Årbog 1964 Landokonomisk Forsogslaboratoriums efterårsmode, pp. 257–67.

Robertson, A. 1960. In: O. Kempthorne, ed, *Biometrical Genetics*, London: Pergamon Press.

Sybesma, W. 1967. New methods in pig selection. Vlees en Vlecs, 7 8:223–24.

Wichmann Jorgensen, T. 1959. Use of halters during transport and penning of pigs for slaughter. Unpublished, Danish Meat Research Institute, Roskilde.

———. 1961. The experiment with halters at the Langeland bacon factory. Unpublished, Danish Meat Research Institute, Roskilde.

Wismer-Pedersen, J. 1959. Quality of pork in relation to rate of pH change postmortem, *Food Res.* 24:711–27.

Wismer-Pedersen, J. and Briskey, E. J. 1961. Relationship of post mortem acidity and temperature. *Food Technol.* 15:232–36.

Wismer-Pedersen, J. and Riemann, H. 1960. Pre-slaughter treatment of pigs as it influences meat quality and stability. Proc. 12 Res. Conf. Americ. Meat Inst. Found., University of Chicago, pp. 89–106.

12

Some Heritability Characteristics and Their Importance in a Selection Program

IRVIN T. OMTVEDT

THE SWINE INDUSTRY has made tremendous strides in producing more heavily muscled, leaner pigs in the past few years. However, the possibility that the increased incidence of pale, soft, watery pork is a result of this intense selection against fat and for greater muscling is of real concern today. For all practical purposes pork quality has been completely ignored by swine breeders in selection. But before we can justify placing emphasis on quality characters in our breeding programs, we need to know how heritable these traits are and how they are related to other traits being considered.

Quality has been described in many ways, but perhaps the definition given by Kauffman (1964) is most appropriate for the present discussion. He defined quality as the combination of traits that provides for an edible product that loses a minimum of constituent, is free of spoilage during processing, is attractive, appetizing, nutritious, and palatable. Marbling, firmness, color, and tenderness are some of the more important predictive guides in appraising pork quality, but since color was discussed in a preceding chapter, it will not be included here.

Since precise measurements for all aspects of pork quality are not well established, a review of some of the phenotypic relationships between various traits may be helpful. Arganosa at Oklahoma State University reviewed over 100 investigations including the phenotypic correlations between various pork carcass measurements. His findings are compared to the pooled, within-breed, year and sex phenotypic correlations based on 650 carcasses evaluated at Oklahoma State University in Table 12.1.

TABLE 12.1: **Phenotypic Correlations Between Carcass Traits in Swine**

Traits	Review of Published Investigations			Correlations Obtained at Oklahoma
	Range of estimates	No. of estimates	Approximate average	
Carcass backfat and:				
carcass length	—.66 to 0.32	27	—.25	—.33
loin eye area	—.66 to 0.11	24	—.26	—.05
carcass lean yield	—.72 to —.26	21	—.65	—.49
firmness score	0.13 to 0.25	2	0.19	0.06
marbling score	0.06	1		—.04
ether extract	—.06 to 0.72	4	0.32	0.02
total moisture	—.68 to 0.72	2	—.57	—.01
shear value				—.17
Loin eye area and:				
carcass length	—.29 to 0.38	25	0.08	—.12
carcass lean yield	0.25 to 0.78	19	0.54	0.47
firmness score	—.09 to —.01	2	—.05	—.25
marbling score	0.03	1		—.18
ether extract	—.60 to —.18	3	—.40	—.23
total moisture	0.41 to 0.54	2	0.48	0.12
shear value				0.16
Carcass lean yield and:				
carcass length	—.08 to 0.64	19	0.32	0.19
firmness score				—.22
marbling score				—.08
ether extract	—.84 to —.67	2	—.76	—.08
total moisture	—.73 to 0.84	4	0.10	0.03
shear value				0.19

Increased backfat thickness is associated with a decrease in carcass lean and total moisture content and with a possible increase in ether extract, firmness score, and tenderness. Loin eye area is positively correlated with lean cut yield and total moisture content and is negatively correlated with ether extract. Oklahoma results also reveal a tendency for increased loin area to be associated with increased softness and toughness and decreased marbling.

The pooled phenotypic correlations among quality measurements based on the Oklahoma data are presented in Table 12.2. Firmness was associated with an increase in marbling and ether extract and a decrease in total moisture content. Marbling score was positively correlated (0.66) with ether extract and negatively correlated (—0.48) with total moisture. A negative correlation of —0.80 was obtained between ether extract and moisture content. Most of these correlations indicate that a compatible relationship exists between most quality measurements.

Considerable research has been conducted on the inheritance of the more standard pork carcass evaluation measurements (length, backfat thickness, loin eye area, and lean cut yield), and their heritabilities are fairly well established, but investigations regardnig the inheritance of quality aspects of pork muscle are quite limited. Consequently, in an effort to shed some light on the subject, the author was forced to draw heavily on three published investigations (Smith and Ross [1965] using

TABLE 12.2: Pooled Phenotypic Correlations Among Pork Quality Measurements Based on Oklahoma Data

Traits	Correlation
Firmness score and:	
penetrometer reading	—.63
marbling score	0.48
ether extract	0.36
total moisture	—.27
shear value	0.01
Penetrometer reading and:	
marbling score	—.41
ether extract	—.40
total moisture	0.35
shear value	—.10
Marbling score and:	
ether extract	0.66
total moisture	—.48
shear value	—.12
Ether extract and:	
total moisture	—.80
shear value	—.11
Total moisture and:	
shear value	0.05

2,296 Landrace pigs sired by 250 boars tested at British progeny test stations; Allen *et al.* [1966] using 87 Yorkshire and 55 Duroc barrows from 20 sires in the Wisconsin experimental swine breeding herds; and Jensen *et al.* [1967] using 585 pigs sired by 116 boars evaluated at the swine testing station and the experimental station at North Carolina) and on unpublished data at Oklahoma based on 650 pigs sired by 89 boars in the Oklahoma swine breeding project.[1]

Previous investigations have revealed that barrows gain more rapidly than gilts, but gilt carcasses are longer, have less backfat and a higher yield of lean cuts. To complete this picture Oklahoma researchers compared the quality measurements for 275 gilts and 375 barrows, and their results are reported in Table 12.3. These results indicate that barrow carcasses were more heavily marbled, firmer, and somewhat more tender than gilt carcasses, but gilt carcasses were longer, meatier, and had less backfat.

HERITABILITY ESTIMATES

The heritability estimates and standard errors based on an analysis of the Oklahoma data including 650 carcasses from 89 sire groups from six lines of breeding are summarized in Table 12.4.

[1] Oklahoma Agricultural Experiment Station Project 1291, partially supported by a grant-in-aid from the American Meat Institute Foundation.

TABLE 12.3: Comparison of Carcass Measurements for Barrows and Gilts in Oklahoma Study

Traits	Barrows	Gilts	Difference
Length, in.	29.6	30.1	—.5
Backfat, in.	1.37	1.26	0.11
Loin area, sq. in.	4.02	4.66	—.64
Carcass lean yield, percent	53.5	56.6	—3.1
Marbling score[a]	3.8	3.3	0.5
Ether extract, percent	5.12	3.94	1.18
Firmness score[b]	4.4	3.9	0.5
Penetrometer reading, mm.	4.08	4.78	—.70
Moisture content, percent	70.7	71.2	—.5
Shear value, lb.	11.9	12.4	—.5

[a] Marbling of loin at tenth rib scored from 1 to 7 by a committee of three judges (1 = devoid; 2 = scantily; 3 = slightly; 4 = average; 5 = moderate; 6 = well; 7 = abundant).

[b] Firmness of loin at tenth rib scored from 1 to 7 by a committee of three judges (1 = very soft; 2 = soft; 3 = slightly soft; 4 = average; 5 = slightly firm; 6 = firm; 7 = very firm).

Firmness

Work reported by Johansson and Korkman (1951) and Minkema *et al.* (1963) indicated that firmness of backfat was influenced by heredity. The 1951 study showed a heritability estimate of 0.40 for backfat firmness, and the 1963 study revealed estimates of 0.07 for barrows and 0.60 for gilts. In Minkema's paper it was noted that both total and genetic variation was greater among females than among males.

In the analysis of 574 Landrace litter groups representing 250 sires, Smith and Ross (1965) obtained a heritability of 0.41 for firmness of fat scores and a genetic correlation between sexes of 0.69.

Allen *et al.* (1963) noted that heritability estimates for color firmness quality scores in the Wisconsin study based on rather limited data were essentially zero in both Durocs and Yorkshires. The North Carolina study (Jensen *et al.*, 1967) involving 585 pigs representing 268 dams and 116 sires from five breeds yielded a heritability estimate of 0.21 for firmness.

TABLE 12.4: Heritability Estimates for Some Carcass Traits Based on Oklahoma Data

Trait	Heritability	S.E.
Backfat thickness	0.53	0.16
Loin eye area	0.47	0.15
Percent lean cuts	0.62	0.18
Firmness score	0.30	0.13
Penetrometer reading	0.36	0.15
Marbling score	0.28	0.12
Ether extract	0.42	0.16
Total moisture	0.52	0.18
Shear value	0.33	0.18

Data from the Oklahoma station based on 650 pigs from 280 dams and 89 sires from six lines of breeding also revealed a moderate heritability for firmness (firmness score: 0.30 ± 0.13; penetrometer reading: 0.36 ± 0.15).

Tenderness and Moisture Content

Analyses of shear value data at North Carolina and Oklahoma gave heritability estimates of 0.25 ± 0.15 and 0.33 ± 0.18 respectively. Taste panel scores for flavor and fatness in the North Carolina study were highly heritable ($h^2 > 0.40$), but the heritability estimate for juiciness was only 0.19 ± 0.14.

All data available at present indicate that total moisture content of the *longissimus dorsi* muscle is highly heritable (North Carolina: 0.81 ± 0.18; Wisconsin: 1.0 ± 0.76 for Durocs and 0.70 ± 0.51 for Yorkshires; Oklahoma: 0.52 ± 0.18). Expressible juice is often used to measure water-holding capacity, and Jensen *et al.* (1967) calculated a heritability for expressible juice of 0.63 ± 0.17 compared to nonsignificant estimates of 0.46 ± 0.52 for Durocs and 0.77 ± 0.53 for Yorkshires based on the Wisconsin data.

Marbling and Fat Content

Based on the limited data available, ether extract values of the *longissimus dorsi* muscle are heritable. Duniec *et al.* (1961) reported an estimate of 0.50, and Allen *et al.* (1966) obtained estimates of 1.0 ± 0.76 for Durocs and 0.78 ± 0.54 for Yorkshires. North Carolina data yielded estimates of 0.86 ± 0.18 compared to 0.42 ± 0.16 for the Oklahoma study.

Marbling scores tend to be less heritable than ether extract in both the Oklahoma and North Carolina studies (0.28 ± 0.12 and 0.19 ± 0.14 respectively).

Allen *et al.* (1966) reported nonsignificant heritabilities for pH values of 0.19 ± 0.33 for Durocs and 0.52 ± 0.44 for Yorkshires, but these estimates were essentially zero in both the North Carolina and Oklahoma data.

GENETIC CORRELATIONS

Genetic correlations measure the extent to which two traits are affected by the same genes, and they are an important aspect of any breeding program. Unfortunately, very few genetic correlations have been reported and the results available are quite variable. Table 12.5 gives the genetic correlations and standard errors obtained in the Oklahoma study along with those reported by Jensen *et al.* (1967) from North Carolina.

One of the first reports pertaining to the genetic relationship between backfat thickness and marbling was published by Duniec *et al.* (1961). They obtained a heritability of 0.69 for carcass fatty tissue and a genetic correlation of 0.11 between carcass fatty tissue and chemical fat of the *longissimus dorsi*. This indicates that selection for chemical fat in the loin eye might be accomplished without producing a major change in total carcass fat content. However, Smith and Ross (1965) obtained a genetic correlation of —0.80 between carcass backfat thickness and fat distribution score. In both the North Carolina and Oklahoma studies, the genetic correlations between backfat thickness and ether extract were nonsignificant. An unexpected desirable genetic correlation of —0.56 ± 0.18 between backfat thickness and marbling score was obtained in the Oklahoma study.

Positive genetic correlations of 0.31 and 0.84 between backfat thickness and firmness score have been reported by Smith and Ross (1965) and Jensen *et al.* (1967). However, the Oklahoma data failed to reveal any significant genetic relationship between backfat thickness and firmness. The correlation between backfat thickness and shear value tended to be negative in both the North Carolina and Oklahoma data. The North

TABLE 12.5: Comparison of Genetic Correlations Among Pork Carcass Traits Based on North Carolina and Oklahoma Data

Traits	North Carolina	Oklahoma
Carcass backfat and:		
loin eye area	—.06 ± .22	—.22 ± .21
carcass lean yield	—.81 ± .12	—.60 ± .13
firmness score	0.84 ± .34	—.16 ± .25
marbling score	0.38 ± .33	—.56 ± .18
ether extract	—.09 ± .18	—.18 ± .26
total moisture	—0.1 ± .19	0.33 ± .24
shear value	—.38 ± .29	.17 ± .31
Loin eye area and:		
carcass lean yield	0.49 ± .21	0.77 ± .09
firmness score	—.22 ± .34	—.39 ± .22
marbling score	—.82 ± .43	—.01 ± .27
ether extract	—.58 ± .18	0.37 ± .23
total moisture	0.31 ± .21	—.14 ± .28
shear value	—.57 ± .34	0.41 ± .28
Carcass lean yield and:		
firmness score	—.89 ± .36	—.11 ± .24
marbling score	—.10 ± .39	0.48 ± .19
ether extract	0.19 ± .23	0.36 ± .21
total moisture	—.19 ± .23	—.23 ± .25
shear value	0.64 ± .34	0.41 ± .28
Firmness score and:		
marbling score	0.72 ± .36	0.75 ± .14
ether extract	0.03 ± .29	0.58 ± .20
total moisture	0.01 ± .30	—.60 ± .18
shear value	0.10 ± .45	0.13 ± .33
Marbling score and:		
ether extract	1.11 ± .21	0.94 ± .05
total moisture	—.96 ± .22	—.71 ± .18
shear value	—.07 ± .47	0.36 ± .33
Ether extract and:		
total moisture	—.95 ± .03	—.97 ± .01
shear value	—.07 ± .26	0.16 ± .32
Total moisture and:		
shear value	0.08 ± .27	0.18 ± .31

Carolina study did reveal a close relationship between backfat thickness and water-holding capacity as evidenced by a genetic correlation of —0.85 ± 0.15 between carcass backfat and expressible juice. Although more investigations are needed before drawing final conclusions, it appears that selection for less backfat may not seriously reduce quality of the *longissimus dorsi* muscle.

Based on Oklahoma and North Carolina results, the genetic relationships between lean cut yield and quality measures are not extremely high. Selection for increased lean yield would tend to reduce firmness, increase ether extract, decrease total moisture and tenderness, and increase water-holding capacity ($r_G = 0.73 \pm 0.21$). Loin eye area failed to consistently show any close genetic association with any of the quality traits evaluated.

The genetic correlations presented in Table 12.5 show high positive genetic relationships between firmness and marbling and between ether extract and marbling. High negative genetic correlations were obtained between total moisture and marbling and between total moisture and ether extract. Jensen *et al.* (1967) also reported a negative genetic correlation (—0.76 ± 0.30) between firmness score and expressible juice which indicates a favorable relationship between the two traits. The results available to date show no close genetic relationships between tenderness and firmness, marbling, or moisture content. Therefore, it appears the genetic relationship between firmness, marbling, and water-holding capacity of the *longissimus dorsi* poses no serious problems to the animal breeder.

CONCLUSIONS

Additional investigations are needed before drawing final conclusions on the inheritance of pork quality factors, but based on the data available at present it appears that most measures of quality are moderately to highly heritable. These heritability estimates tend to be lower than most estimates for carcass length, backfat thickness, and loin eye area, but are apparently sufficiently high to justify selection pressure in a breeding program.

The concern that selection for less backfat increases the probability of lowering quality is only partially justified. Most of the genetic relationships between backfat thickness and quality factors obtained thus far are in an unfavorable direction, but fortunately these genetic correlations tend to be quite low. The data available at the present time indicate that superior meat-type hogs with acceptable quality can be produced, but we are going to have to work at it! The relationship between backfat thickness and quality factors resembles the relationship believed to exist between backfat thickness and growth rate, but unfortunately quality can not be appraised on the live animal.

So far we have merely scratched the surface, leaving many important aspects untouched. More refined measurements of pork quality are needed, and it is hoped that additional investigations involving breeding groups with greater variation in the expression of the condition will be forthcoming. However, we have sufficient information available at the present time to justify placing some emphasis on these traits in our swine breeding program.

REFERENCES

Allen, E., Forrest, J. C., Chapman, A. B., First, N., Bray, R. W., and Briskey, E. J. 1966. Phenotypic and genetic associations between porcine muscle properties, *J. Animal Sci.* 25:962.

Duniec, H., Kielanowski, J., and Osmska, Z. 1961. Heritability of chemical fat content in the loin eye muscles of baconers, *Animal Prod.* 3:195.

Jensen, P., Craig, H. B., and Robinson, O. W. 1967. Genetic variation and co-variation among carcass traits of swine, *J. Animal Sci.* 26:204.

Johansson, I., and Korkman, N. 1951. A study of the variation in production traits of bacon pigs, *Animal Breed. Abstr.* 19:221.

Kauffman, R. G. 1964. What is pork quality? Proc. 7th Nat. Pork Industry Conf., 1964, Kansas City, Mo.

Minkema, D., Kroeske, D., and Hart, P. C. 1963. The heritability of backfat firmness in pigs from progeny testing stations, *Animal Breed. Abstr.* 31:235.

Smith, C., and Ross, G. J. S. 1965. Genetic parameters of British Landrace bacon pigs, *Animal Prod.* 7:291.

13

Variation of Quality and Quantity Factors Within and Between Breeds

ROBERT W. BRAY

CARCASS TRAITS relating to the economically important quantitative aspects of carcass value have been studied by many researchers, yet few studies have been of the magnitude to suggest variations among breeds. Thus we must turn to records provided by swine testing stations, quality pork contests, and a very limited number of research efforts relating to this subject.

Data provided by the Ohio Swine Evaluation Station provide information by breed for swine produced in Ohio, with a sizable sample for six breeds of swine. Table 13.1 does not relate significant differences among the breeds, but the means as reported have removed biases due to confounding of breed, sex, season, year, age of dam, and initial weight.

Although an analysis of the variance in these traits was not made, it would appear that the loin eye area means do vary wth breed, with Polands and Hampshires having larger loin eye areas than Durocs, Landrace, and probably Yorkshires. Although the standard deviations are not provided, it would appear that Hampshires and Polands were superior in

TABLE 13.1: Ohio Swine Evaluation Station Analysis of Data—Fall, 1959–Fall, 1965

Breed	Number in Sample	Loin Eye Area (sq. in.)	Backfat (in.)	Carcass Length (in.)	Percent Lean Cuts
Yorkshire	773	3.86	1.53	30.38	53.14
Duroc	213	3.76	1.51	29.04	52.95
Poland	270	4.53	1.38	29.07	54.90
Hampshire	686	4.25	1.36	29.67	55.14
Spotted	214	4.10	1.49	29.53	53.24
Landrace	352	3.82	1.43	30.64	53.22

percentage of lean cuts. As anticipated, this superiority in quantity of lean cuts is strongly indicated by backfat thickness and loin eye area. On the other hand, it is equally interesting to note the apparent lack of relationship between carcass length and lean cut yield. However, this poor relationship has been reported in the literature (Carpenter, 1962; Harrington and Pomeroy, 1961).

Another study which provides some indication of breed variations in traits usually associated with quantitative yields was made by Dr. R. G. Kauffman, University of Wisconsin. The data were collected from 805 carcasses originating from ten Quality Pork Contests covering a period from 1959 to 1966 in the states of Illinois, Indiana, and Wisconsin. The region represented in this study is much broader and therefore more representative of the breeds studied; however, one must recognize the shortcoming of these samples. Age of the animals was not known, and there was virtually no control of the environmental conditions under which the animals were produced. Also there is the likelihood that the sampling may have been biased due to selection of animals exhibiting the more desirable carcass traits; however, if this was so it should have taken place in all the breeds.

A significant and negative relationship between backfat thickness and lean cut yield has been established (Brown *et al.*, 1951; Whiteman *et al.*, 1953). Although the magnitude of importance of loin eye area in predicting lean cut yield is not large, it is important enough to be used in most regression equations for predicting lean cut yield in pork carcasses.

With the above in mind it is interesting to note the similarity between the data collected at the Ohio Station and those reported in Table 13.2.

The loin eye areas for Hampshires and Polands were significantly larger than those reported for the other breeds; however, note the small number of animals representing the Tamworth and Landrace breeds. The Hampshires also had a significantly thinner backfat while the vari-

TABLE 13.2: Breed Comparisons For Carcass Trait Means Data From 10 Quality Pork Contests

Breed	No. of Animals	Backfat (in.)	Loin Eye Area (sq. in.)	Length (in.)	Marbling Score
Berkshire	64	1.46	3.99	30.2	2.8
Chester	54	1.40	4.12	29.7*	2.7
Duroc	110	1.30	4.17	30.0	3.5**
Hampshire	324	1.28*	4.84**	30.4	2.2
Landrace	17	1.48	3.74	30.7	2.2
Poland	106	1.43	4.54*	29.6*	2.4
Spotted	37	1.45	4.16	29.0**	2.3
Tamworth	5	1.49	3.70	30.9	2.8
Yorkshire	82	1.47	4.09	30.8	2.5
S.D.		±0.9	±0.2	±0.7	±0.9

Study made by R. G. Kauffman, Univ. of Wis.
* Significant at 5% level.
** Significant at 1% level.

ation in this trait was not important among the other breeds. The rankings of the breeds represented in both studies for length of carcass were quite similar, with Landrace and Yorkshires being longest and Polands and Spotted swine shortest.

In an unpublished breed study at Illinois it is interesting to note certain similarities with the two previously discussed studies. The Illinois study was a growth study and made breed comparisons for various carcass traits at four different stages of growth. Although the data are very interesting for the younger animals, they cannot be compared with data from either the testing station or the Quality Pork Contests. Therefore I will relate only the data derived from carcasses in the study of about the same weight as those reported above. The following breeds were represented in each of four age groups—Berkshire, Chester White, Duroc, Hampshire, Landrace, Poland China, Spotted, Tamworth, and Yorkshire. Six to nine carcasses were studied in the two oldest age groups. Although the numbers were small in each breed group, the means followed a pattern similar to those discussed previously.

Note that again Hampshires and Polands ranked at the top in lean cut yield and that Berkshires were between these two breeds. It is also of interest to note that Durocs were low in yield of lean cuts. The same relationship between backfat thickness and lean cut yield is indicated in these data. Since the carcasses representing the third stage of growth were lighter in weight than those in the testing station, carcass contests, and the fourth growth stage of this study, the average loin eye size is not comparable to that in the other studies. Data on length showed Polands to be shortest and Landrace longest.

In thinking about breed variations in lean cut yields, one might postulate that the breeds may also vary in physiological maturity. Breeds which are larger at maturity or later in maturing might feasibly have more muscle and less fat at the weight used as the end point for carcass evaluation for Quality Pork Contests and swine testing stations.

The above three studies represent different segments of breed populations; yet it is extremely interesting to note the similarity in the comparison of breeds within each study. Although the adequacy of sampling of the breeds is still subject to question and an analysis for variance was

TABLE 13.3: Breed vs. Carcass Traits

Breed	No. of Animals	Backfat (in.)	Loin Eye Area (sq. in.)	Lean Cut Yield
Berkshire	6	1.09	3.8	52.8
Chester	5	1.32	4.1	52.1
Duroc	9	1.52	3.6	49.7
Hampshire	6	1.26	3.9	52.7
Landrace	7	1.33	3.5	51.0
Poland	8	1.15	3.7	53.8
Spotted	8	1.35	3.8	51.0
Tamworth	5	1.33	3.4	50.7
Yorkshire	7	1.31	3.4	51.6

Source: Unpublished data, R. G. Kauffman, Univ. of Ill., 1967.

not made on all the data, the indications are that breed differences in carcass quantitative traits do exist.

Very little research data exist on variations of carcass traits within breeds. On the other hand, the wide range in values for these traits as recorded for carcass shows would indicate that there are wide variations. Additionally, the establishment of significant heritability estimates for carcass traits indicate significant variations in these traits.

Pork quality has been variously defined, thus resulting in considerable confusion within the industry. To some it includes those factors associated with quantitative yields as well as those factors contributing to palatability. The meat scientist defines fresh meat quality as those factors associated with the palatability of fresh and cured products and economic losses during processing and distribution. The consumer is concerned with tenderness, juiciness, flavor, and texture of the cooked product. In carcasses from young swine, the factors most commonly associated with these traits are color, texture and firmness of muscle, and quantity of intramuscular fat (marbling). Marbling has long been considered an important trait in the palatability of beef, although recent evidence suggests that it has probably been overemphasized in our evaluation standards. Studies relating to its importance in pork indicate that intramuscular fat is favorably related to the palatability of pork.

Pork muscles, after adequate postmortem chilling, vary widely in color and gross morphology (firmness and structure). These differences in muscle color, firmness, and texture are attributable to variations in postmortem changes in muscle. The pale, soft, exudative muscle (PSE) has considerably lower water-holding capacity, which in large part accounts for the wide variation in palatability and processing quality.

A few studies have provided limited information relative to breed and strain variations in factors associated with quality of pork. One of the earliest studies relating to this subject was reported by Judge *et al.*, (1959) at the Ohio Station, using 321 hogs from the Improvement Program of the Ohio Swine Improvement Association. The hogs were treated uniformly throughout the growing-fattening period and slaughtered and chilled under identical conditions. Table 13.4 sets forth the variations observed for marbling (as measured visually) at the cross sectional surface of the *longissimus dorsi* muscle at the tenth rib.

Pigs that were grown during the fall and winter were more highly marbled. Sex differences in marbling approached significance ($P < .05$) with barrows exhibiting more intramuscular fat.

The statistical analysis of the breed data indicated highly significant differences among the breeds. The authors of this work indicate that the method of analysis prevented comparisons between breeds; however, in scanning the table one can quickly find the breeds which had high scores for this trait and those with low scores. Moderate amounts of marbling have been shown to provide an acceptable palatability in pork. Thus, if one totals the percentages by breeds of the loins possessing at least moderate quantities of marbling, it becomes apparent that Berkshires and Spotted breeds were highest in this trait, while Landrace and Poland

TABLE 13.4:   Frequencies of Degrees of Marbling

Items	Slight No.	Slight Percent	Moderate No.	Moderate Percent	Abundant No.	Abundant Percent
Season**						
Spring[a]	90	58.0	46	29.7	19	12.3
Fall[b]	56	33.7	76	45.8	34	20.5
Sex						
Barrows	64	41.0	59	37.8	33	21.2
Gilts	82	49.7	63	38.2	20	12.1
Bread[c]**						
Landrace	18	66.7	7	25.9	2	7.4
Poland China	26	65.0	8	20.0	6	15.0
Yorkshire	60	54.5	41	37.3	9	8.2
Hampshire	24	50.0	22	45.8	2	4.2
Sp. Poland China	10	24.4	19	46.2	12	29.3
Berkshire	4	13.8	13	44.8	12	41.4

Source: Ohio Study, Judge *et al.,* 1959.
[a]Dec. 1 to June 1 farrow.
[b] June 1 to Dec. 1 farrow.
[c] Only those breeds represented by 20 or more individuals are listed.
** Significant at 1% level.

China breeds were lowest. The Yorkshires and Hampshires had slightly higher percentages of their loins in the moderate to abundant marbling categories than the Landrace and Poland China breeds, yet these percentages were decidedly lower than the Berkshires and Spotted breeds.

The variation in muscle color as presented in Table 13.5 suggests breed differences.

Note the effect of season on muscle color. The observation that ambient temperature has an influence on characteristics of muscle has been reported by many researchers (Wismer-Pederson, 1959; Briskey *et al.,* 1960; Forest *et al.,* 1963).

Your attention is directed to the columns summarizing the scores for muscle classified as light and grayish pink. The light-colored pork as described here is less desirable in regard to palatability and processing traits while the grayish pink pork is considered more acceptable. The higher frequency of light-colored pork for the Poland China and Landrace breeds suggests that in the population studied, there was a difference in color between these two breeds and Berkshire and Yorkshire. The undesirable trait of a two-toned color in muscle was also of highest frequency in Poland China and Landrace breeds.

Another phase of this study reported the degree of muscle firmness by breeds. Since there was an extremely high and positive relationship between color and firmness, it was noted that the percentage of muscles scored soft was highest for the Poland China and Landrace breeds and lowest for the Yorkshire and Berkshire. However, in this phase of the study the percentage of soft muscle in Hampshires was only slightly less than in the Poland China and Landrace breeds.

Marbling is the only quality trait reported for carcasses in the sum-

TABLE 13.5:   Frequencies of Muscle Colors

	Light		Grayish Pink		Dark		Two-toned	
Items	No.	Percent	No.	Percent	No.	Percent	No.	Percent
Season**								
Spring[a]	60	38.7	75	48.4	12	7.7	8	5.2
Fall[b]	41	24.7	102	61.4	20	12.0	3	1.8
Sex								
Barrows	56	35.9	79	50.6	14	9.0	7	4.5
Gilts	45	27.3	98	59.4	18	10.9	4	2.4
Breed[c]**								
Poland China	24	60.0	13	32.5	1	2.5	2	5.0
Landrace	13	48.1	11	40.7	1	3.7	2	7.4
Hampshire	20	41.7	26	54.2	2	4.2	0	0.0
Sp. Poland China	17	41.5	22	53.7	2	4.9	0	0.0
Berkshire	6	20.7	18	62.1	4	13.8	1	3.4
Yorkshire	18	16.4	72	65.5	16	14.5	4	3.6

Source: Ohio Study, Judge *et al.*, 1959.
[a] Dec. 1 to June 1 farrow.
[b] June 1 to Dec. 1 farrow.
[c] Only those breeds represented by 20 or more individuals are listed.
** Significant at 1% level.

marization of ten Quality Pork Contests. No quality trait figures except marbling were available in the Ohio study; however, it is interesting to note that the Duroc breed had a significantly higher score. The magnitude of the marbling score for this breed in comparison with the other breed scores would suggest that Durocs generally possessed muscles that contained about 2 percent more extractable lipid. This supports an observation I have believed true as I have viewed carcasses in many Quality Pork Contests. Note also the breeds scoring lowest in marbling—Landrace, Poland China, Hampshire, and the Spotted breeds. The Ohio study and this study are not in agreement regarding the Spotted breed.

In a study reported by Allen *et al.* (1966) breed differences were reported for Yorkshire and Duroc breeds. The Wisconsin swine breeding herd, made up of a wide selection from these two breeds, provided offspring for a breed and heritability study for eight characters. These characters and breed differences are noted in Table 13.6.

Expressible juice ratio is a measurement of the water-holding capacity of muscle; higher values represent greater water-holding capacity. The ability of the protein of muscle to hold water is highly correlated to its pH or acidity. Muscles that are higher in pH values are less acid and more effectively bind water. Meat produced from muscles with relatively higher pH values are juicier when cooked and lose less weight during processing.

Although the mean values for expressible juice for Durocs was lower, it was not statistically different from that for Yorkshires. On the other hand, the pH values were significantly lower for Durocs.

The structure of muscle is affected by its acidity; greater acidity in muscle usually alters the structure in such a manner as to reflect more

TABLE 13.6:   **Means and Standard Deviations of Muscle Properties of Duroc and Yorkshire Barrows and Significance of Differences Between Breeds**

Traits	Breed	Mean	S.D.	Significance of Breed Differences
Expressible juice ratio[a]	Duroc	2.90	0.53	n.s.
	Yorkshire	3.05	0.53	
pH	Duroc	5.40	0.11	**
	Yorkshire	5.49	0.13	
Color and gross morphology score[b]	Duroc	2.27	0.61	**
	Yorkshire	2.74	0.62	
Glycogen[c]	Duroc	27.90	13.22	**
	Yorkshire	17.80	7.07	
Myoglobin[c]	Duroc	3.58	0.73	*
	Yorkshire	3.91	0.77	
Ether extract, %[d]	Duroc	23.34	5.47	**
	Yorkshire	13.10	3.62	
Moisture, %	Duroc	71.87	1.81	*
	Yorkshire	73.01	1.20	
Fiber diameter[e]	Duroc	52.1	3.6	**
	Yorkshire	59.7	5.6	

Source: Wisconsin Study, Allen *et al.*, 1966.
[a] Ratio of total area to meat film area.
[d] Based on a scale from 0.5–1.0 (extremely pale, soft, loose, and watery) to 4.5–5.0 (very dark, firm, and dry)
[c] Mg/gm of dry, fat-free tissue.
[d] Percent weight lost from dry tissue after 24-hr. continuous Soxhlet extraction with ether.
[e] Average diameter in microns of five largest fibers in five different microscopic fields.
* Significant at 5% level.
** Significant at 1% level.

light, thus making the muscle lighter in color. Color of muscle is also affected by the amount of myoglobin (red pigment) in the muscle.

Both these factors may have contributed to the lighter color of the Durocs, since this breed had greater muscle acidity and less myoglobin.

Percentage of ether extract is an objective measure of the quantity of fat in the muscle. Since the amount of ether extract and marbling score are highly related, it can be stated that in this study the Duroc breed had more marbling than the Yorkshire. This finding supports that found by Kauffman in the study of breeds in the ten Quality Pork Contests.

Moisture content of the muscle samples from Durocs was lower than for the Yorkshire. This was expected since fat in muscle reduces the moisture content of muscle, and the fat content of the Duroc breed was significantly higher.

In a series of studies at the Wisconsin Station, Chester White, Poland China, and Hampshire breeds have been compared for certain traits associated with the incidence of PSE (pale, soft, and exudative) pork. The Wisconsin researchers recognize that the breed differences they report are limited and perhaps reflect strain variations more than they do breed

TABLE 13.7: **Frequency of PSE Muscle in Various Breeds (1962 National Barrow Show)**

Breed	No. of Pigs	Percentage of PSE Pork
Hampshire	28	25
Poland China	27	25.9
Chester White	15	18
Duroc	21	14
Yorkshire	16	19
Berkshire	19	0.0
Crossbred	18	17

differences. Additionally, the sample size limits the extent to which conclusions can be drawn. Sayre *et al.* (1963) noted a higher incidence of PSE muscle in Poland China than in Chester White pigs, although the strains were restricted and PSE did occur in both breeds. In another phase of his work involving Poland China, Chester White, and Hampshire breeds, Sayre found the Chester White possessed darker muscles than either of the other two breeds at 3 hours postmortem, and Hampshires significantly darker than Polands at 24 hours postmortem.

The Wisconsin studies suggest that the strains of Chester White were superior in color and firmness to the Hampshire and Poland China strains and that the Poland China strains were usually inferior to the Hampshires.

Records taken at the 1962 National Barrow Show (Table 13.7) show the percentages of pigs of each breed that exhibited extremely low quality (pale, soft, and watery) muscle. Only breeds represented by 15 or more pigs were considered. The pigs were transported from various parts of the United States to Austin, Minnesota, for this contest. Origin, time en route, and many other considerations may have been factors influencing the incidence of PSE muscle in these pigs.

Nevertheless, there appears to be considerable evidence for suspecting that certain breeds are much more susceptible than others to the development of PSE muscle and more prone to develop PSE characteristics under controlled conditions.

It is of interest to note the similarity of findings of this survey and that observed in the Wisconsin studies for Poland China, Hampshire, and Chester White breeds.

Denmark researchers Clausen and Thomsen (1960) and Ludvigsen (1958) reported a comparison of PSE muscle in Pietran and Landrace pigs. PSE hams were found in 62 percent of the Landrace pigs and 88.9 percent of the Pietran breed. Thus the problem of PSE pork is not confined to the United States.

The quantity of evidence now available makes it difficult to draw conclusions as to breed variations in quality traits, since the number studied is small in most cases and data for certain breeds apparently are not available. However, for the breeds where data have been collected, it becomes evident that breed and strain variations are prevalent.

PSE pork appears to be prevalent in Poland China, Hampshire, and

Landrace breeds and is probably of less concern in the Chester White. Marbling is more predominant in the Duroc, but variations among the other breeds is less evident.

Undoubtedly many data have been collected at various swine testing stations as well as on progeny herds used for swine breeding research. If the question of breed variations in carcass traits is to be resolved, these data plus those from any other source must be made available for analyses. Breed associations should make pork quality data a part of the records they keep on progeny in their evaluation programs. In this way strain variations could be evaluated very rapidly.

Quality of product can be altered significantly at the processing level as well as at the producer level. On the other hand, quantitative yields are almost exclusively in the hands of the producer. The extreme variation in quantitative and qualitative characteristics of pork as it reaches the market makes it imperative to be concerned about these traits in our breeding stock as well as about how the product is processed. Thus the future of pork as reflected in sales to consumers becomes the responsibility of more than one segment of the pork industry.

REFERENCES

Allen, E., Forrest, J. C., Chapman, A. B., First, N. L., Bray, R. W., and Briskey, E. J. 1966. Phenotypic and genetic associations between porcine muscle properties, *J. Animal Sci.* 25:962.

Briskey, E. J., Bray, R. W., Hoekstra, W. G., Phillipps, P. H., and Grummer, R. H. 1960. Effect of high protein, high sucrose rations on the water binding and associated properties of pork muscle, *J. Animal Sci.* 19:404.

Brown, E. J., Hillier, J. C., and Whatley, J. A. 1951. Specific gravity as a measure of the fat content of the pork carcass, *J. Animal Sci.* 10:97.

Carpenter, Z. L. 1962. The histological and physical characteristics of pork muscle and their relationship to quality, Ph.D. thesis, University of Wisconsin, Madison.

Clausen, H., and Nortoft Thomsen, R. 1960. Report on investigations with pigs, Nat. Res. Inst. on Animal Husbandry, Copenhagen, Rept. 317.

Forrest, J. C., Gundlach, R. F. and Briskey, E. J. 1963. A preliminary survey of the variations in certain pork ham muscle characteirstics, Proc. 15th Res. Conf. Amer. Meat Inst. Foundation.

Harrington, G., and Pomeroy, R. W. 1961. The yields of cuts from Wiltshire bacon sides in relation to length and other carcass measurements, *Animal Prod.* 3:163.

Judge, M. D., Kunkle, L. E., Cahill, V. R., and Bruner, W. H. 1959. Pork Quality. 1. Influences of some factors on pork muscle characteristics, *J. Animal Sci.* 18:448.

Ludvigsen, J. 1958. Den gentiske og den ernaerangsbetingede "muskeldegeneration." Ugeskrift for Landmaenel, No. 47 and 48.

Sayre, R. N., Briskey, E. J., and Hoekstra, W. G. 1963. Comparison of muscle characteristics and post mortem glycolysis in three breeds of swine, *J. Animal Sci.* 22:1012.

Whiteman, J. V., Whatley, J. A., and Hillier, J. C. 1953. A further investigation of specific gravity as a measure of pork carcass value, *J. Animal Sci.* 12:85.

Wismcr-Pedersen, J. 1959. Quality of pork in relation to rate of pH change post-mortem, *Food Res.* 24:711.

14

Relationship of Breeding and Reproduction to Carcass Quality and Quantity Characteristics

JOHN F. LASLEY

THE DEMANDS of the consumer, if they are strong and insistent enough, sooner or later reflect themselves in the kind and type of animal produced for the market. The kind or type of animal produced under these conditions may not always be the one that is the most efficient. Ideally, the most desirable situation is one in which the kind of animal produced meets the needs of both the consumer and the producer.

Since the beginning of the discussion of the meat type hog several years ago, the question has been asked many times whether or not the meat type hog is inferior to the fatter type animal in growth rate, conversion of food to pork, and fertility. An attempt is made in this chapter to bring together experimental evidence from the literature to help answer these questions.

RELATIONSHIP OF CARCASS QUALITY AND QUANTITY TO RATE AND EFFICIENCY OF GAINS

The correlation between carcass quality and gains may be determined in three different ways: (1) phenotypic (simple) and genotypic correlations where each trait is measured in the same group of animals under similar conditions, (2) experimental station testing results, and (3) selection experiments.

Correlation Data

Phenotypic or simple correlations include those which contain both environmental and genetic effects; whereas genotypic correlations are an expression of the direction two or more traits should move when selection for one of them is effective. Genetic correlations also indicate the proportion of genes which affect one trait that also affect another.

Phenotypic correlations for postweaning daily gain and feed efficiency with carcass length, backfat thickness, and percentage of lean cuts are low, ranging from —0.20 to 0.29 (Lush, 1936; Dickerson, 1947; Dickerson and Grimes, 1947; Blunn and Baker, 1947; Fredeen, 1953; Heidenreich et al., 1961; and Biwas et al., 1966). These low phenotypic correlations suggest that there is little relationship between rate and efficiency of gains and the various carcass quality traits. However, phenotypic correlations between rates of gains and efficiency of gains are fairly high, ranging from —0.37 to —0.69 (Lush, 1936; Dickerson, 1947; and Fredeen, 1953).

Genetic correlations between rate and efficiency of gains and body length, backfat, and loin area are also low, ranging from —0.10 and 0.15 (Blunn and Baker, 1947; Fredeen, 1953; and Biwas et al., 1966). The data from these studies suggest that these traits are largely determined by different genes and selection for rate and efficiency of gains would have little effect on the carcass items mentioned. To improve both performance and carcass quality through selection, selection would have to be practiced separately for each of them.

Swine Testing Station Results

Results from carcass data and rate and efficiency of gains for barrows for 14 test periods over a period of seven years were reported by the Missouri Agricultural Experiment Station in 1966 (Table 14.1). These

TABLE 14.1:   Performance and Carcass Quality in Barrows Fed at Missouri Swine Testing Station for 14 Test Periods

Test Number	Dressing Percent	Percent Primal Cuts	Loin Area (sq. in.)	Backfat Thickness (in.)	Avg. Daily Gains (lb.)	Feed/1000 Lb. Gain
1	76.3	46.9	3.55	1.54	1.83	309
2	76.5	46.8	3.76	1.54	1.95	287
3	76.0	48.8	4.13	1.37	1.82	305
4	76.5	47.4	3.75	1.40	1.87	306
5	76.2	49.2	3.94	1.39	1.89	299
6	76.8	46.6	3.79	1.53	1.88	282
7	76.7	47.1	4.10	1.42	1.83	302
8	76.3	47.7	3.73	1.44	1.81	280
9	76.8	50.6	4.40	1.36	1.84	306
10	76.6	50.3	4.13	1.38	1.83	268
11	75.8	51.5	4.37	1.35	1.85	288
12	75.4	50.6	4.11	1.41	1.90	274
13	76.5	51.9	4.44	1.28	1.92	287
14	76.8	49.8	4.41	1.36	1.90	279
Coeff. of correlation[a]	—.05	.78**	.79**	—.68**	.00	—.61

[a] Correlations are between test number and other items.
** Significant at 1% level.

TABLE 14.2: Summary of Iowa Swine Testing Results From Barrows, Spring 1956 to Fall 1966

Test Number	Body Length	Percent Ham & Loin	Loin Area (sq. in.)	Backfat Thickness (in)	Avg. Daily Gain[a]	Feed/100 Lb. Gain[a]
1	29.1	32.3	3.22	1.64	1.89	285
2	28.9	33.2	3.50	1.61	1.95	296
3	29.2	33.5	3.40	1.60	1.80	289
4	29.1	34.5	3.80	1.51	1.79	314
5	29.4	34.3	3.62	1.51	1.80	280
6	29.1	34.9	3.81	1.50	1.76	318
7	29.5	35.3	3.63	1.50	1.80	291
8	29.1	36.2	3.94	1.48	1.87	292
9	29.3	35.6	3.77	1.48	1.77	277
10	29.3	36.2	3.94	1.55	1.94	286
11	29.3	35.6	3.87	1.48	1.80	284
12	29.2	37.3	4.08	1.41	1.87	280
13	29.7	36.8	3.96	1.35	1.89	262
14	29.6	38.8	4.22	1.39	1.99	274
15	29.9	39.4	4.13	1.36	1.96	269
16	29.7	39.8	4.25	1.35	1.97	277
17	29.7	39.0	4.07	1.38	2.00	268
18	29.4	41.0	4.24	1.32	1.96	274
19	29.2	40.5	4.35	1.29	1.92	274
20	29.1	40.5	4.57	1.40	2.17	261
21	29.4	40.4	4.29	1.34	2.16	259
22	29.5	40.5	4.52	1.33	2.20	261

[a] Pen averages.

results showed that during this period of time, growth rate had not made a significant change in spite of the fact that backfat significantly decreased and loin eye area and the percent of primal cuts increased significantly. The amount of feed required to produce 100 pounds of gain also decreased significantly. This shows that carcass quality had been improved over the years without causing slower and less efficient gains. Similar results have been obtained at the Iowa Swine Testing Stations and Consumers Cooperative Associations (Tables 14.2 and 14.3).

Selection Experiments

Several selection experiments with swine throw some light on possible genetic relationships between rate and efficiency of gain and carcass quality.

Data from the progeny testing program in Denmark involving chiefly Landrace are presented in Table 14.4. During the period from 1927 to 1962, there was a gradual improvement in the rate and efficiency of gain of pigs in spite of the fact that body length increased, bacon qualities improved, and backfat thickness decreased. Some of the improvement in rate and efficiency of gain was probably due to supplying a better environment during the growing-fattening period, but at least both performance and carcass quality were improved. This suggests that there were no important genetic antagonisms between these traits.

Hetzer and Peters (1965) reported results from ten generations of selection for high and low backfat in the Duroc breed and eight genera-

TABLE 14.3:   Summary of Farmland Swine Testing Station Results, Fall 1958 to Fall 1966

Test Number	Body Length, Barrows	Percent Ham & Loin, Barrows	Loin Area, Barrows	Backfat Thickness, Barrows	Avg. Daily Gain, Barrows	Feed/100 Lb. Gain in Pens
1	28.8	34.2	3.73	1.52	1.76[a]	300
2	29.0	35.1	3.56	1.51	1.79[a]	279
3	28.7	36.2	4.09	1.46	1.82[a]	289
4	29.3	36.7	4.01	1.47	1.76[a]	281
5	29.1	37.3	4.16	1.55	1.86	287
6	29.5	36.3	4.01	1.52	1.78	276
7	29.3	36.4	4.47	1.44	1.83	291
8	29.8	36.7	4.31	1.42	1.80	275
9	29.6	37.1	4.63	1.36	1.85	288
10	29.6	37.5	3.70	1.38	1.91	263
11	29.6	38.8	4.28	1.42	1.88	285
12	29.6	38.0	4.07	1.48	1.92	264
13	29.7	39.4	4.35	1.43	1.99	270
14	29.6	38.6	4.21	1.37	1.88	255
15	29.4	39.2	4.68	1.38	1.97	268
16	29.4	40.1	4.48	1.31	1.85	258
17	29.5	40.4	4.50	1.36	1.94	264

[a] Boar gains adjusted to barrow basis.

tions of selection for high and low backfat thickness in Yorkshires. A control line was maintained for each breed within which selection for backfat was not practiced. Selection in each breed was made almost entirely for backfat thickness at an average weight of 159 pounds. In the 10th generation of selection (159 lb. wt.) in the Duroc pigs the high-fat line measured 2.06 inches, those in the low-fat line 1.04 inches, and those in the control line 1.46 inches. When compared to the control line, there had been no change in postweaning gains in either the high or the low line. In the Yorkshire breed after eight generations of selection, the average backfat thickness in the high-fat line was 1.47 inches, in the low-fat line 0.92 inches, and in the control line 1.18 inches. Compared to the controls, there had been a slight decline in post-weaning gains in the high-fat line but not in the low-fat line.

Results from five generations of selection for backfat thickness in

TABLE 14.4:   Carcass Items and Performance of Danish Landrace Swine Over a Period of 35 Years

Year	Daily Gain (lbs.)	Feed Units per Kilogram of Body Wt.	Percent Grade A Bacon	Body Length (in.)	Backfat Thickness (in.)	Pigs per Litter Birth	Pigs per Litter 8 Weeks
1927	1.37	3.44	50	35.0	1.59	10.6	8.2
1936–37	1.38	3.28	80	36.5	1.37	10.9	8.4
1946–47	1.40	3.28	91	36.8	1.31	11.6	9.0
1956–57	1.50	2.97	91	37.2	1.23	11.5	9.5
1961–62	1.51	2.95	93	37.8	1.11	11.3	9.4

Source: Jeppesen (1962) and Clausen and Nortoft Thomsen (1963).

Poland China swine at the Missouri Agricultural Experiment Station were reported by Gray *et al.* (1965). Selections were based almost entirely on live hog backfat probes at an average weight of 179 pounds. A spring and a fall line were developed from the same original parent stock by farrowing the same sows bred to the same boars in the two seasons. The spring line pigs were then reproduced for five generations from only spring-farrowed parents. Fall line pigs were also reproduced from fall-farrowed parents. In the spring line boars after five generations of selection, the backfat was reduced from 1.07 to 0.85 inches; whereas, in the gilts it was reduced from 1.19 to 0.91 inches. In the fall line during the same period, backfat was reduced from 1.05 to 0.87 inches in the boars and from 1.12 to 0.89 inches in the gilts. The reduction in backfat did not result in a significant change in daily gains in either line.

RELATIONSHIP OF CARCASS QUALITY AND RATE OF GAIN WITH FERTILITY IN SWINE

Since the development of the backfat probe technique by Hazel and Kline (1952), some data have been obtained in relation to simple correlations between backfat thickness and fertility components at the Missouri Agricultural Experiment Station. Coefficients of correlations obtained in three studies (Lerner *et al.,* 1957; Rathnasabapathy *et al.,* 1956; and Reddy *et al.,* 1958) have shown low and positive simple correlations (0.14 to 0.28) between backfat thickness and ovulation rate in gilts slaughtered during the first half of pregnancy. This suggests that the gilts with thicker backfat tended to ovulate more ova. This may be due to the fatter gilts having a better ration and thus exhibiting a "flushing effect," thus showing that an environmental rather than a genetic effect was probably involved. Coefficients of correlation for embryonic mortality and backfat thickness in the above studies ranged from 0.15 to 0.37, indicating that thicker backfat was also related to a higher embryonic mortality rate. Thus there was a tendency for a higher ovulation rate in the gilts with the most backfat to be at least partially neutralized by a higher embryonic mortality so that there was little or no gain in litter size at slaughter in the gilts with the most backfat.

Rathnasabapathy *et al.* (1956) found a significant simple coefficient of correlation between weaning weight of gilts and ovulation rate (0.33, $P<.05$) and 154-day weight and ovulation rate (0.34, $P<.05$). Although Lerner *et al.* (1957) found a significant simple coefficient of correlation of 0.24 ($P<.01$) between body length in gilts and ovulation rate, the correlation between body length and number of embryos at slaughter was very low (0.02). Reddy *et al.* (1958) also found low and nonsignificant coefficients of correlation between body length and ovulation rate (0.04), embryonic mortality rate (—0.07), and litter size at slaughter (0.11).

Results From Selection Experiments

Genetic correlations for carcass quality and gains with fertility are scarce in the literature. The only one found was that reported by Vogt *et al.* (1963) of 0.06 between daily gains and litter size. Correlated responses of these traits in selection experiments should give some idea of the degree and direction of any genetic correlations among these traits in swine.

It seems of interest to mention the results of selection experiments for certain traits in other species of animals besides swine on fertility and reproduction. Two experiments will be mentioned because of the possibility that long-time experiments with swine might give similar results.

Lerner (1954) reported on a long-time selection experiment for longer shanks in chickens. Selection was effective as compared to a control line in which no selection was practiced. Shank length in the selected line was 9.92 cm. in 1939 when the experiment began and 10.19 cm. in 1952 when the results were reported. As the shank length was increased by selection, the index of fitness (number of offspring raised to maturity per dam) declined from 4.67 at the beginning of the experiment to 0.96 in 1952. Thus overall fertility declined as the shanks became longer. This suggests a negative genetic correlation between these two traits.

An experiment in selection for large and small body size in two unrelated strains of mice (N and C) was reported by Fowler and Edwards (1960). Selection in both lines was effective. Selection for either large or small body size in strain C did not impair fertility. In strain N, however, some of the pairs in the large and small lines, but not in the control line, were sterile. Sterility in the large line was due to low libido in the males. The females in this line did not seem to be affected. In the small line, some of the females were sterile probably because of a hypo-functioning of the anterior pituitary gland. This was indicated by a delayed estrous cycle or its complete absence. Some mice failed to ovulate after mating, and a high proportion of those that did mate had no implanted embryos at 12 days of gestation. Treatment of these females with gonadotropins and progesterone caused ovulation and increased the proportion of implanted embryos.

Hetzer and Brier (1940) made a study of litter size in large, intermediate, and small Poland China swine and found that large type sows had about 1.0 more pigs per litter than sows of an intermediate type and about 2.0 more pigs per litter than sows of the small type. They concluded that most of the type differences in litter size were of a genetic nature.

Selection for a heavy and a light 180-day weight in Hampshire swine (Krider *et al.*, 1946) was effective. However, fertility difficulties were encountered in both the fast- and slow-growing lines. About one-fourth of the females were hard to settle, and of those in this category, about 10 percent had cystic follicles. This suggests that selection for either extreme from 180-day weights might be detrimental to fertility, although a decline in fertility in both lines might have been due, to a certain extent, to an accumulation of diseases on the premises where the pigs were maintained.

Considerable interest has been expressed of late in the production of midget pigs for research purposes because of certain physiological similarities between swine and humans. The small size of midget pigs makes them much more economical to feed and handle in the laboratories as compared to the large conventional type swine. Dettmers *et al.* (1965) reported the results of an experiment in which selection was practiced for a reduction in body size in pigs over a period of 11 years. During this time, body size was reduced to 38.6 pounds at 140 days for a total reduction of about 29 percent. In spite of the reduction of body size, litter size remained unchanged. Some reduction in birth weight and 56-day weaning weight accompanied the reduction in 140-day weights.

In the USDA experiments mentioned earlier (Hetzer and Peters, 1965) selection for high and low backfat in Durocs resulted in a reduction in litter size at birth of 0.3 pigs and 0.2 pigs per generation in the high-fat and the low-fat lines respectively, as compared to the controls. In the Yorkshire line a decline of 0.1 pig per generation was observed in the high-fat line as compared to the control line. No decline in litter size at birth has occurred in the low-fat line.

Five generations of selection for thinner backfat in a spring and a fall line of swine at the Missouri Agricultural Experiment Station failed to result in any decline in ovulation rate or litter size in either line as backfat thickness was reduced.

Data in Table 14.4 show that litter size at birth and weaning in Landrace swine between 1927 and 1962 in Denmark increased to a certain extent even though rate of gain and efficiency of gain improved, backfat decreased, and overall carcass quality improved during the period.

CONCLUSIONS

The conclusions from this study are that many of the same genes that cause rapid gains also cause efficient gains, but rate and efficiency of gain are not influenced by many of the same genes that determine carcass quality and quantity. It is possible, however, that effective long-time selection experiments for thinner backfat or meatiness in swine might eventually result in less desirable rate and efficiency of gain in swine.

Evidence from selection experiments with chickens, mice, and swine suggests that selection for extremes in body form and size and carcass quality may result in lowered fertility in some experiments with a middle-of-the-road approach giving the most desirable results. We would like to postulate here that a certain balance between gonadotropins and other anterior pituitary hormones is necessary for optimum fertility, and an upset in this balance by selection for extremes could be detrimental to fertility and survival of the young in swine.

It appears that the consumer demand for more lean and less fat in pork products is compatible (within certain limits) with more efficient production in swine as long as breeding stock are selected for top performance. Some evidence suggests, however, that it is possible to go too far in selection for more lean and less fat with reduced fertility being the end result. It is also possible that too much lean in proportion to the amount of fat may have other undesirable effects such as increasing the incidence of soft, pale, watery pork and decreasing the resistance to disease. We are not sure about these possible relationships, but it seems desirable in livestock production to avoid extremes as much as possible.

REFERENCES

Biwas, D. K., Hurt, P. V., Chapman, A. B., First, N. L., and Self, H. L. 1966. Feed efficiency and carcass desirability in swine, *J. Animal Sci.* 25:342–47.

Blunn, C. T., and Baker, M. L. 1947. The relation between average daily gain and some carcass measurements, *J. Animal Sci.* 6:424–31.

Casey, Bob. 1967. Summary of farmland swine testing results. Personal communication.

Clausen, H., and Nortoft Thomsen, R. 1963. Report on pig testing 1961–62. Copenhagen.

Dettmers, A. E., Rempel, W. E., and Comstock, R. E. 1965. Selection for small size in swine, *J. Animal Sci.* 24:216–20.

Dickerson, G. E. 1947. Composition of hog carcasses as influenced by heritable differences in rate and economy of gain, Iowa Agr. Exp. Sta. Res. Bull. 354.

Dickerson, G. E., and Grimes, J. C. 1947. Effectiveness of selection for efficiency of gain in Duroc swine, *J. Animal Sci.* 6:265–87.

Fowler, R. E., and Edwards, R. G. 1960. The fertility of mice selected for large or small body size, *Genet. Res. Comb.* 1:393–407.

Fredeen, J. T. 1953. Genetic aspects of Canadian bacon production, Can. Dep. Agr. Publ. 889.

Gray, R. C., Tribble, L. F., Day, B. N., and Lasley, J. F. 1965. Five generations of selection for thinner backfat, *J. Animal Sci.* 24:848 (Abstr.).

Hazel, L. N. 1967. Summary of Iowa Swine Testing Station results from 1956 spring–1966 fall. Mimeograph, personal communication.

Hazel, L. N., and Kline, E. A. 1952. Mechanical measurement of fatness and carcass value in live hogs, *J. Animal Sci.* 11:313–18.

Heidenreich, C. J., Tribble, L. F., Zobrisky, S. E., and Lasley, J. F. 1961. Carcass evaluation in live hogs, Mo. Agr. Exp. Sta. Res. Bull. 766.

Hetzer, H. O., and Brier, G. W. 1940. Extent to which type differences among swine affect litter size, Proc. Am. Soc. Animal 135–38.

Hetzer, H. O., and Peters, W. H. 1965. Selection for high and low fatness in Duroc and Yorkshire swine, *J. Animal Sci.* 24:849 (Abstr.).

Jeppesen, R. P. 1962. Beretning am svine avlens ledelse (Report on pig breeding in Denmark). Copenhagen.

Krider, J. L., Fairbanks, B. W., Carroll, W. E., and Roberts, E. 1946. Effectiveness of selection for rapid and for slow growth rate in Hampshire swine, *J. Animal Sci.* 5:3–15.

Leavitt, R. K., Angell, C., and Stephenson, D. 1966. Fifteenth semi-annual rep. of Mo. Swine Evaluation Sta.

Lerner, E. H., Mayer, D. T., and Lasley, J. F. 1957. Early embryonic mortality in strain crossed gilts, Mo. Agr. Exp. Sta. Res. Bull. 629.

Lerner, I. M. 1954. *Genetic Homeostasis*, New York: John Wiley & Sons, Inc.

Lush, J. L. 1936. Genetic aspects of the Danish system of progeny-testing swine, Iowa Agr. Exp. Sta. Res. Bull. 204.

Rathnasabapathy, V., Lasley, J. F., and Mayer, D. T. 1956. Genetic and environmental factors affecting litter size in swine, Mo. Agr. Exp. Sta. Res. Bull. 615.

Reddy, V. B., Lasley, J. F., and Mayer, D. T. 1958. Genetic aspects of reproduction in swine, Mo. Agr. Exp. Sta. Res. Bull. 666.

Vogt, D. W., Comstock, R. E., and Rempel, W. E. 1963. Genetic correlations between some economically important traits in swine, *J. Animal Sci.* 22:214–17.

15

Limits for Rapidity of Genetic Improvement for Fat, Muscle, and Quantitative Traits

LAUREN L. CHRISTIAN

THE YEARLY IMPROVEMENT in carcass and production traits of swine is largely dependent upon choosing replacements that are superior to their predecessors. It is obvious that at some levels of the swine industry this aspect of production has received considerable attention. In Iowa five central testing stations are currently in operation, furnishing 1–2 percent of the boars needed yearly in commercial production. The improvement observed at the Ames station through 11 years of testing is shown in Table 15.1. The increase from 32.3 to 40.5 in percent of ham and loin of carcass weight on the barrows slaughtered is remarkable, particularly when this change has occurred with an apparent increase in other performance traits. Some of these fat and muscling differences are clearly illustrated (Fig. 15.1). Although these changes cannot be totally attributed to genetic improvement due to unequal breed contribution to the the different years, it most certainly indicates the desire of breeders to obtain comparative evidence on performance traits, a trend which is almost certain to continue as swine producers become larger, fewer, and now specialized.

The yearly rate at which a breeder can improve his herd in a desired direction is due to three factors: (1) heritability of the selected traits, (2) intensity of the selection practiced, and (3) the generation interval.

Traits of swine vary in their heritability. Reproductive traits have generally been characterized by low heritabilities and thus do not respond well to selection in a direct manner. Genetic improvement in these traits is largely dependent upon crossbreeding procedures. Conversely the pro-

UNDESIRABLE   **DESIRABLE**

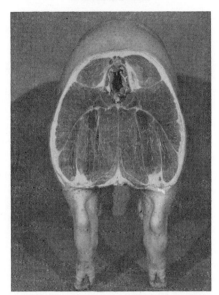

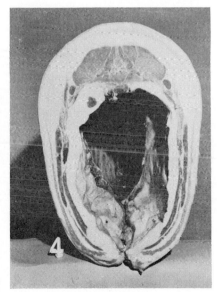 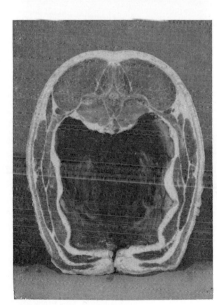

FIG. 15.1.   Pork carcass cross sections of ham and loin regions showing muscle-fat deposition.

TABLE 15.1:   Eleven Years of Testing at Ames, Iowa, Station, 1956–1966

	Pen Average		Boar Average		Barrow Cutout			
	Gain	Eff.[a]	Probe	Index	Length	Back-fat	Ham & loin (%)	Loin eye
56S	1.89	285	1.46	101	29.1	1.64	32.3	3.22
56F	1.95	296	1.31	109	28.9	1.61	33.2	3.50
57S	1.80	289	1.24	113	29.2	1.60	33.5	3.40
57F	1.79	314	1.11	112	29.1	1.51	34.5	3.80
58S	1.80	280	1.22	118	29.4	1.51	34.3	3.62
58F	1.76	318	1.19	106	29.1	1.50	34.9	3.81
59S	1.80	291	1.25	119	29.5	1.50	35.3	3.63
59F	1.87	292	1.17	125	29.1	1.48	36.2	3.94
60S	1.77	277	1.19	128	29.3	1.48	35.6	3.77
60F	1.94	286	1.20	130	29.3	1.55	36.2	3.94
61S	1.80	284	1.17	125	29.3	1.48	35.6	3.87
61F	1.87	280	1.06	140	29.2	1.41	37.3	4.08
62S	1.89	262	1.08	149	29.7	1.35	36.8	3.96
62F	1.99	274	1.04	154	29.6	1.39	38.8	4.22
63S	1.96	269	1.08	156	29.9	1.36	39.4	4.13
63F	1.97	277	.92	157	29.7	1.35	39.8	4.25
64S	2.00	268	.96	160	29.7	1.38	39.0	4.07
64F	1.96	274	.98	160	29.4	1.32	41.0	4.24
65S	1.92	274	.95	163	29.2	1.29	40.5	4.35
65F	2.17	261	1.08	172	29.1	1.40	40.5	4.57
66S	2.16	259	1.01	175	29.4	1.34	40.4	4.29
66F	2.20	261	.96	179	29.5	1.33	40.5	4.52

[a] Pounds of feed consumed per 100 pounds liveweight gain.

duction traits of gain and efficiency have been found to be moderate in heritability and carcass traits in the moderate to high range. The latter traits have been found to respond well to mass selection procedures.

Response to selection for change in backfat thickness is perhaps best exemplified by the results of Hetzer and Peters (1966). Selection for increased and reduced backfat was practiced for 12 generations in Durocs and for 10 generations in Yorkshires. These results are summarized in Tables 15.2 and 15.3. The almost symmetrical response in the two directions has been in close agreement with the selection intensities and the heritabilities involved and assures one's faith in the power of selection to change a trait.

The effect of changing backfat thickness upon other carcass and production traits is most encouraging. On a 200-lb. weight adjusted basis, low-fat Durocs yielded approximately 15 lb. more lean cuts and 20 lb. fewer fat cuts than the high-fat line. The respective differences between high- and low-fat lines of Yorkshires were 8 lb. and 13 lb. Low-fat lines of both breeds excelled or were similar to the fat and control lines for litter size farrowed, litter size raised, birth weight, and growth rate. Thus there is no evidence to suggest genetic antagonisms between reduced backfat and other production traits. In fact, favorable associations may exist with some traits.

TABLE 15.2: **Mean Performance of 12th Generation Durocs and 10th Generation Yorkshires, 1966**

Trait	Duroc			Yorkshire		
	High	Low	Control	High	Low	Control
No. of litters	18	17	15	19	15	18
Litter size:						
Birth	7.2	9.1	8.3	8.2	7.5	8.3
56 days	6.1	6.6	6.0	6.4	5.9	7.1
Litter weight:						
Birth	12.3	19.9	16.2	15.9	17.0	19.2
56 days	193	260	231	239	222	257
Pig weight:						
Birth	1.71	2.18	1.94	1.94	2.28	2.31
56 days	32.0	39.5	38.5	37.5	37.5	36.4
Daily gain:						
56 days–175 lb.	1.36	1.51	1.48	1.32	1.21	1.34
175 lb. backfat probe	2.34	1.11	1.53	1.75	0.97	1.24

A similar selection study is being conducted by Gray *et al.* (1965) with Poland Chinas. After five generations of selection, backfat thickness in the spring farrowed line has been reduced from 27.2 to 23.6 mm. in boars, and from 30.0 to 25.1 mm. in gilts. In the fall line, five generations have reduced backfat from 26.6 to 21.8 mm. in boars, and in gilts from 28.5 to 22.1 mm. These changes in backfat thickness have occurred without significant reduction in the rate or efficiency of gain or fertility. There was observed a significant increase in the percent of lean in the carcass of the selected pigs as compared to the parent generation.

Hazel (1965) investigated the sources of improvement in ham and loin percentage by relating the selection differential practiced in boars for mechanical probe, sib carcass data, and progeny carcass data to the heritabilities and genetic correlations involved. These data, shown in Table 15.4, indicate that (1) the genetic gain realized is consistent with the reach achieved and the parameters involved and (2) about 40 percent of the realized change has resulted from selecting on the basis of mechanical probe, about 20 percent on the basis of carcass data on 2.5 sibs, and about 40 percent on the basis of carcass data on 8.5 progeny per sire.

TABLE 15.3: **Mean of Carcass Traits for 12th Generation Durocs and 10th Generation Yorkshires, 1966**

Trait	Duroc			Yorkshire		
	High	Low	Control	High	Low	Control
No. of pigs	11	11	11	11	11	11
Slaughter wt.	211	211	214	210.5	212.5	209.5
Lean cuts, % of liveweight	34.0	41.4	39.0	38.2	42.6	39.2
Fat cuts, % of liveweight	21.7	11.9	14.6	16.8	10.3	13.3
Carcass length	26.3	29.6	29.0	29.2	30.2	30.0
Backfat thickness	2.80	1.50	1.95	2.11	1.26	1.50
Loin eye area	2.76	4.16	4.06	3.47	4.84	3.84

TABLE 15.4:   Genetic Gain Expected in Percentage of Ham and Loin

Pigs Born in	Due to Selection for		
	Probe	Full sibs	Progeny test
1962 F	.484	0	0
1963 S	.346	.007	0
1963 F	.331	.302	.820
1964 S	.506	.127	.542
1964 F	0	.346	.222
Total	1.667	.782	1.584

Regression of genotype for ham and loin percent on probe is —3.64, 2.5 full sibs slaughtered, 8.5 progeny slaughtered.

What is hindering the industry from moving from the present situation where only 35 percent of the commercial hogs have less than 1.60 inches of average fat thickness to a level comparable to those of pigs under central test? Why is the average loin eye of the industry less than four square inches and the average ham-loin percent less than 40 when loins in excess of eight square inches are on record and carcasses in excess of 50 percent ham and loin are known to exist? The answers to these questions, neither simple nor completely known, are in part due to the following:

1. Selection pressure is being exerted on economically unimportant traits, thus decreasing the reach attainable in important traits. Equal selection on n traits decreases the intensity of selection on a single trait by $\dfrac{1}{\sqrt{v}}$.

2. Undue consideration is being given to lowly heritable traits. Selection for increased litter size, for example, will be rather fruitless.

3. Closing a herd (or even a breed) can be a detriment to genetic progress since it fails to incorporate outside stock with superior merit. Fredeen (1966) demonstrates that where boars are replaced annually from the top half of a breed and coupled with the best 25 percent of the females produced within the herd (based upon individual performance), improvement would be superior to the best closed herd system possible. The Iowa State teaching herd has used the technique of bringing in outside seed stock coupled with intraherd selection. The yearly changes in production traits are shown in Table 15.5. This system has in this case brought about steady improvement in most traits.

4. More of our seed stock herds must utilize performance testing. Less than 2 percent of the potential seed stock produced each year can be tested under central conditions. This number is hardly a representative sample upon which to establish the relative merit of a herd, nor does it supply an adequate number of tested boars to meet the commercial demands. The success of central testing and herd improvement is dependent upon intraherd selection.

5. There is need for an objective means of evaluating the muscling in

TABLE 15.5: Average Performance of Swine Teaching Herd, 1960–1966

Year	No. of Litters	Avg. 154-day Weight	No. Slaughtered	Slaughter Weight	Days to 200 Lb.	Length	Backfat (200 lb.)	Loin Eye Area	Percent Ham and Loin
1960	83	133	120	208	197	29.3	1.48	3.90	36.0
1961	89	135	285	211	195	29.6	1.39	4.05	36.7
1962	95	170	200	209	171	29.9	1.36	4.19	38.2
1963	112	183	214	210	165	29.7	1.36	4.52	39.4
1964	107	177	186	211	167	29.5	1.31	4.80	40.2
1965	101	173	217	211	170	30.0	1.28	4.77	40.7
1966	121	195	266	207	159	29.6	1.21	5.00	41.5

the live hog to be used in conjunction with the backfat probe. For traits of high heritability such as backfat thickness and muscling traits, selection upon individual performance will give greater per year improvement when litter mate carcass data are not used, since the latter decreases the selection pressure applied to the replacements. Although the backfat probe is a reliable estimator of backfat in the live hog, it is possible that as backfat is decreased to lower levels, differences in muscling may play a larger role in carcass cutout variation. Continued effort must be devoted to improving ultrasonic or other methods of estimating muscling in the live hog so as to reduce the need for sib or progeny testing which prolong the generation interval and/or limit the selection intensity.

6. We must establish the degree to which selection for purebred performance is preventing, if at all, the optimum utilization of combining ability between lines or breeds. Louca and Robinson (1967) present evidence to suggest that selection for 154-day weight in purebreds would not be effective in improving the performance of crossbreds and suggest the use of selection for combining ability for the most rapid progress in this trait. The results of Stanislaw et al. (1967) are in close agreement with the North Carolina results for postweaning gain but suggest that for 56-day weight and backfat probe direct selection within purebreds would be the most effective selection method.

Will selection for improvement in quantitative traits give rise to increased undesirability of qualitative traits of pork muscle? This problem could represent a limitation to the rapidity of genetic improvement for quantitative traits. At present there is no direct experimental evidence to indicate a negative genetic association between these traits; however, a high incidence of PSE has been reported in herds under intense selection for meatiness, and death loss is observed when pigs from these herds are subjected to excessive stress at or near market weight. There is a definite need for further investigation in this area.

The potential for rapid improvement of quantitative traits in swine rests with the producers themselves. The efforts of the producer who practices continuous selection for economically important traits of high heritability, with the major emphasis upon individual performance, will be rewarded by consistent improvement.

REFERENCES

Fredeen, H. T. 1966. Breeding for pig improvement: Prospects for genetic progress, Pig Industry Development Authority, London, England.

Gray, R. C., Tribble, L. F., Day, B. N., and Lasley, J. F. 1965. Five generations of selection for thinner backfat, *J. Animal Sci.* 24:848 (Abstr.).

Hazel, N. L. 1965. Selection for meatiness in swine, Twenty-ninth Ann. Rep. Regional Swine Breeding Laboratory, Ames, Iowa.

Hetzer, H. O., and Peters, W. H. 1966. Selection for high and low fatness in Duroc and Yorkshire swine, Thirteenth Ann. Rep. Regional Swine Breeding Laboratory, Ames, Iowa.

Louca, A., and Robinson, O. W. 1967. Components of variance and covariance in purebred and crossbred swine, *J. Animal Sci.* 26:267.

Stanislaw, C. M., Omtvedt, I. T., Willham, R. L., and Whatley, J. A., Jr. 1967. A study of some genetic parameters in purebred and crossbred populations of swine, *J. Animal Sci.* 26:16.

PART SIX

Physiological Stress Related to Production Practices and Muscle Quality

16

Modern Production Practices and Their Influence on Stress Conditions

J. WISMER-PEDERSEN

THE INCREASED EFFICIENCY of meat production in the last twenty years has originated from steady improvements in feed conversion and better nutrition of the animals. Advancement in hygiene and design of environment during the growth and fattening period have brought additional benefits. The result has been more meat at reasonable prices to the public. Although the public has appreciated these benefits, it has often been inferred that modern efficiency in meat production tends to lower the meat quality. The meat of the "old days" when production methods were simple often stands in the memory of elderly consumers as being better than the meat of our industrial age.

With regard to pork this complaint is not new. German butchers spoke very critically about muscle quality in relation to modern production practices in the years prior to World War I (Herter and Wilsdorf, 1914). They accused the meat of being pale and watery because the pigs had become "refined," kept without natural exercise and fed diets not compatible with good meat quality.

STRESS CONDITIONS

Today we have similar discussions about pale watery meat in swine carcasses, notably in the loin and ham muscles. This quality is in general due to violent postmortem glycolysis and related to stress conditions in the pig immediately prior to slaughter (Ludvigsen, 1954; Wismer-Pedersen, 1959b; Briskey, 1964; Bendall and Lawrie, 1964). Stress in relation to meat quality may be defined as the sum of all the strains caused by any kind of vital reaction throughout the body at any one time. These reactions are the results of stressors in the environment. It is only by the intensity of their manifestations that we can recognize

FIG. 16.1. Interior of large modern pig house (Landbrugets Informationskontor, Copenhagen).

the presence and gauge the intensity of stress. We do not offhand know whether pigs under primitive conditions suffered more stress than pigs under modern production practices (Fig. 16.1).

STRESS ON MUSCLE QUALITY AT LOW ULTIMATE pH

We are interested in stress manifestations on the ultimate muscle quality through its impact on the rate and extent of the carbohydrate metabolism in the muscle. When the musculature has reduced or depleted glycogen depots so that little or no lactic acid can be produced postmortem, we will have muscle quality characteristics of high ultimate pH, dark color, and high water-holding capacity (Callow, 1938, 1939; Madsen, 1942; Gibbons and Rose, 1950; Rose and Peterson, 1951; Wismer-Pedersen, 1959a). This meat quality was formerly considered disadvantageous because of the reduced keeping quality, especially of cured products. In modern meat processing it is usually regarded as a favorable quality although the pigs might have suffered considerable stress in the antemortem period. The adverse effects of stress on meat quality are most obvious when the musculature has sufficient glycogen depots so the ultimate pH falls below 6.

We shall first consider to what extent the modern pig is likely to develop pale watery meat on the more or less hazardous assumption that primitive breeds are resistant to it (Janicki and Walczak, 1954). This is of interest in relation to the possible consequences of the selection for improved feed conversion and meatiness which has been considered to have aggravated the incidence of pale watery meat (Ludvigsen, 1954; Kielanowski, 1957) and which might entail reduction in the adaptation energy of the animals. Furthermore the effects of possible stressors in the management of the pigs will be considered with the exemption of temperature effects (Judge, 1967). In the words of Henry and Billon (1959) these are "agressions mineures" as opposed to "agression majeure," by which they mean the slaughter process. These "agressions mineures" may either increase or decrease the adaptation energy of the animals at time of slaughter and the manifestation of pale watery meat which we for convenience shall call PSE (Briskey, 1964).

GROWTH HORMONE EFFECTS

Several decades of selection have brought about considerable changes in the performance of several of our breeds. An example is the Danish Landrace pig. Table 16.1 shows the average change in daily gain and feed efficiency over the past 15 years for the pigs in the Danish pig progeny testing stations, and Table 16.2 shows the corresponding change in some of the important carcass data (Clausen *et al.*, 1967). The genes governing these economic characters may do so by controlling the rates at which glands concerned with growth secrete the hormones specific for various aspects of metabolism. The genes may, however, also affect other anatomical features important for muscle development potentials.

TABLE 16.1: Average Results of Growth Observations on Danish Pig Progeny Testing Stations, 1950–1965, Compared With Results From Growth Hormone Injection Experiment

	Year	Daily Gain (lb.)	Lb. Feed/Lb. Gain
T. & A. controls		2.19	3.84
	1950/51	1.46	3.14
	1952/53	1.46	3.06
	1954/55	1.49	3.03
	1956/57	1.50	2.97
	1958/59	1.51	2.96
	1960/61	1.53	2.91
	1962/63	1.48	2.97
	1964/65	1.51	2.93
T. & A. GH treated pigs		2.26	3.10

Source: Clausen *et al.* (1967); Turman and Andrews (1955).

TABLE 16.2: Some Carcass Data From Danish Pig Progeny Testing Stations, 1950–1965, Compared With Data in Growth Hormone Injection Experiment

Year	Dressing Percent	Body Length (cm.)	Avg. Backfat Thickness (cm.)	Meat Color Score
T. & A. controls	72.7	74.4	4.50	
1950/51	73.7	93.2[a]	3.40	
1952/53	73.5	93.4	3.43	
1954/55	73.3	93.8	3.26	2.30
1956/57	73.2	94.4	3.12	2.38
1958/59	73.2	95.1	2.97	2.35
1960/61	73.1	95.7	2.85	2.27
1962/63	72.8	96.2	2.66	2.28
1964/65	72.4	96.1	2.54	2.22
T. & A. GH treated pigs	69.5	77.7	3.56	

Sourcce: Clausen *et al.* (1967); Turman and Andrews (1955).
[a] From *os pubis* to *atlas.*

We will consider first the pituitary growth hormone. Baird *et al.* (1952) showed that the anterior pituitaries of a genetical line of pigs selected for rapid growth had a higher content of growth hormone compared to a corresponding line of pigs selected for slow growth. Turman and Andrews (1955) studied the effect of injecting purified growth hormone preparations in pigs. The pigs responded by requiring significantly less feed per unit gain and grew at a slightly faster rate than corresponding pigs injected with saline. The carcasses were considerably meatier than the controls. In Table 16.1 and 16.2 are the average figures of Turman and Andrews' results shown in comparison with the development in the Landrace pigs. There is a remarkable similarity in the figures which makes it tempting to conclude that a considerable part of the change in the Landrace pig is due to a genetically controlled increase in growth hormone production. From Table 16.2 we also learn that the average meat color score has decreased slightly during the years. The score is given after subjective evaluation on a scale from .05 to 5. The relationship between color score and pH_1 (pH 45 minutes after slaughter) is shown in Figure 16.2 (Clausen and Nortoft Thomsen, 1962). Scores under 2.5 are associated with pH_1 under 6.2 which denote meat with reduced water-holding capacity (Wismer-Pedersen, 1956b). The color was evaluated in the loin eye at the last rib. We may ask what impact this possible increased growth hormone production may have on the susceptibility to develop PSE.

Ludvigsen (1955) and Henry *et al.* (1958) suggested that an increased production of growth hormone should decrease release of ACTH and the thyrotropic hormone from the anterior pituitary and thus depress the activity of the adrenal cortex and the thyroid gland. The corticoids from the adrenal cortex play a central role in the adaptative mechanism of the animal, and several observations have indicated that pigs with severe PSE have degenerative changes in the adrenal cortex (Henry and

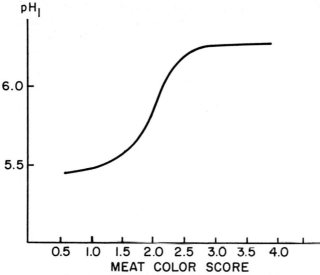

FIG. 16.2. Relationship between pH_1 and meat color score (Clausen and Norloft Thomsen, 1962).

Billon, 1959; Cassens *et al.*, 1965). Topel *et al.* (1967) showed that lower levels of glucocorticoids in the blood were associated with the PSE condition. The adrenal regulation of the mineral balance has also been suspected. An increased concentration of potassium in the blood from PSE pigs was found by Ludvigsen (1954), Henry (1957), and Henry *et al.* (1958) and ascribed to mobilization of potassium from the muscle tissue. However, Briskey *et al.* (1959), Wismer-Pedersen (1960), and Topel *et al.* (1967) found no consistent difference in potassium and sodium content of muscle and blood relative to ultimate muscle structure. The growth hormone by itself may, however, have an impact on the hormonal regulation of glucose content in the blood. Injection of purified growth hormone gave higher blood sugar levels (Turman and Andrews, 1955) as well as glucose uptake by muscle and synthesis of glycogen (Recant, 1952; Russell, 1953; Huggins and Ottaway, 1961). Budding *et al.* (1956) also noted a better glucose tolerance in rapid growing swine than in corresponding slow growing. An increased production of growth hormone may thus have an activating effect on the carbohydrate metabolism and indirectly or directly a depressing effect on secretion of glucocorticoids. The hormone may thus interfere with the adaptive mechanism of the pig. Activation of enzymes in muscle involved in glycolysis by the growth hormone has also been observed (Krebs and Fischer, 1955; Russell and Wilhelmi, 1960).

EFFECT OF THYROID GLAND

The thyrotropic hormone should also be considered. Ludvigsen (1954) suggested that the PSE condition was due to a decrease in the function of the thyroid gland. The increased incidence of PSE in the summer coincided with low activity of the gland, and feeding iodinated casein improved the muscle structure of pigs with tendency for PSE. Correspondingly feeding of methylthiouracil increased frequency of PSE. However, direct determination of protein-bound iodine (PBI) in the blood serum failed to show lower values in pigs with tendency to develop PSE (Sorensen, 1958). On the other hand Judge *et al.* (1965) found higher PBI in blood from pigs with severe PSE, and Topel and Merkel (1966) were unable to produce significantly increased level of PSE by feeding goitrogens. It is therefore doubtful that the function of the thyroid has a central position in development of PSE. Ozinska and Kielanowski (1960) analyzed meat color score and other observations on the pigs from the Danish pig progeny testing stations. They made the interesting observation that there was a significant correlation between low meat color scores and high feed efficiency for pigs slaughtered in the summer but not for those slaughtered in winter or for the overall average results for the whole year. The increased PBI in winter may have counteracted the effects of the growth hormone to some extent (Gawienowski *et al.*, 1955). The higher incidence in the summer may also be due to a higher degree of excitement of the pigs (Wismer-Pedersen, 1959b) as well as to a lower secretion of ACTH by the pituitary gland in the summer (Ludvigsen, 1955). The effect of increased growth hormone production may thus more easily be observed when the pigs are subjected to an elevated degree of stress immediately before slaughter. The increased stress may originate from an increased stressor intensity combined with reduced adaptive energy.

INTERACTION BETWEEN MEAT COLOR AND OTHER CARCASS CHARACTERISTICS

To evaluate the proposed effect of growth hormone on the performance of pigs we may study the correlations between meat color score and other observations made from the Danish pig progeny testing stations (Jonsson, 1965). Table 16.3 shows some of the important results. The

TABLE 16.3: Correlation Coefficients Between Meat Color Score and Some Data From Danish Pig Progeny Testing Stations, 1958–1962

	$r_{phenotypic}$		$r_{add. gen. effect}$	
	Gilts	Castrates	Gilts	Castrates
Daily gain	+0.007	—0.035		
Lb. feed/lb. gain	+0.075*	+0.083**	+0.642 $\mp$ 0.174	+0.323 $\mp$ 0.249
Dressing pct.	+0.079*	+0.062*		
Backfat thickness	+0.151**	+0.106**	+0.243 $\mp$ 0.114	+0.192 $\mp$ 0.140
Carcass length	+0.176**	+0.199**	+0.560 $\mp$ 0.092	+0.620 $\mp$ 0.103
Area of *l. dorsi*	—0.121**	—0.056	+0.107 $\mp$ 0.194	+0.183 $\mp$ 0.200
Score for meatiness in split carcass	—0.205**	—0.127**	—0.291 $\mp$ 0.115	—0.282 $\mp$ 0.156
Score for size of hams	—0.205**	—0.191**	—0.634 $\mp$ 0.097	—0.468 $\mp$ 0.142

Source: Jonsson (1965).
* $P \leq 0.05$
** $P \leq 0.01$

phenotypic correlation coefficients support the growth hormone theory except for carcass length. Comparative high positive correlations are found between carcass length and meat color score. This means that the rather short meaty pigs with well-developed hams show the highest frequency of PSE. We have an illustration to this point in the comparatively high frequency of PSE in the Pietrain breed (Clausen and Nortoft Thomsen, 1962). Topel *et al.* (1967) also found a highly significant negative correlation coefficient between muscle area and morphology score in their study. The thickness of the muscles seems therefore especially important for the manifestation of PSE. However, it is remarkable that the genetic correlation with the muscle area is positive. The effect of the growth hormone must be regarded as one aspect associated with improvement of muscling in pigs. In selection for muscling, genes other than those governing production of growth hormones must also be considered. Among these are the gene combinations affecting the number of muscle fibers in various muscles. The number of fibers in a particular muscle is usually regarded as fixed at birth. Thus growth of the muscle is predominantly due to growth in length and thickness of the fibers (Staun, 1963). Staun (1967) has measured the fibers in the *longissimus dorsi* of pigs from the Danish pig progeny testing stations. He found that the fiber diameter did not affect the muscle area as much as the number of fibers. As the genetic correlation between number of fibers and muscle area is positive, the selection for meatiness might thus automatically have involved selection for an increased number of fibers in the muscle. Table 16.4 shows the correlation coefficients between meat color score and fiber measurements on samples from 1,368 pigs. The phenotypic correlation coefficients are very low, slightly negative between meat color and fiber diameter, slightly positive between meat color and number of fibers in the muscle area. The genetic correlation coefficients show the same tendencies. From these results it appears that selection for meatiness through increased growth of the muscle fibers may bring about an increased tendency to develop PSE. If on the other hand the increased meatiness can be obtained through increase in number of fibers, meat color should not be adversely affected. Allen *et al.* (1966) found a negative phenotypic correlation co-

TABLE 16.4: **Correlation Coefficients Between Meat Color Score and Muscle Fiber Measurements in *L. Dorsi* From Danish Pig Progeny Testing Stations**

	Meat Color Score	Area of Muscle	Number of Fibers	Fiber Diameter
Meat color score		—0.11	+0.03	—0.04
Area of muscle	—0.82		+0.49	+0.16
Number of fibers	+0.07	+0.21		—0.50
Fiber diameter	—0.28	—0.80	—0.42	

Above diagonal: phenotypic correlation coefficients.
Below diagonal: genetic correlation coefficients.

Source: Staun (1967).

efficient between fiber diameter and expressible juice in the meat. The composition of the muscle fibers must also be considered. Allen *et al.* (1966) found a positive although nonsignificant heritability estimate of myoglobin concentration in the *longissimus dorsi* which was significantly negatively correlated with amount of expressible juice in the meat.

Krzywicki and Ratcliff (1967) showed that a highly significant negative correlation exists between pH_1 and the phospholipid content in the myofibrillar and reticular fraction of the muscle fiber (Fig. 16.3). The phospholipids are primarily constituents of the muscle cell membranes. Factors in the composition and function of the membranes may thus be factors of importance for metabolism of the fiber. Porter and Franzini-Armstrong (1965) have suggested that the sarcoplasmic reticulum is responsible for the rapid synthesis of ATP via the pathway of anaerobic glycolysis. Little is known about the hereditary characteristics of phospholipids in muscle, but these factors in the metabolism of muscle fiber should be considered in future breeding programs. They are in fact automatically taken care of when the breeders take the meat quality characteristics into consideration when selection is made for improved meatiness. The total deposition of intramuscular fats appears to be unimportant for the tendency to develop PSE (Sink *et al.*, 1967).

NUTRITIONAL FACTORS

Much concern has been shown in Germany as to the possible causes of "acute heart death" of pigs which suddenly died in transport or during

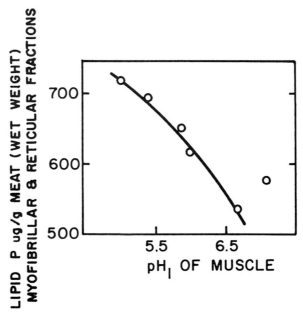

FIG. 16.3. The sum of lipid P in the myofibrillar and reticular fractions of the *longissimus dorsi* related to pH_1 (Krzywicki and Ratcliff, 1967).

feeding and on dissection showed pale watery musculature. It was proved by Hupka (1952) and Richter and Oslage (1955) that this kind of PSE could be produced experimentally by potato feeding without sufficient protein supplement. The pigs on the deficient diet, however, showed poor growth and appetite and cannot be compared to pigs under normal commercial conditions. When the protein supplement is sufficient to sustain normal growth, further protein supplement has no effect on meat quality.

With regard to the carbohydrate composition of feed, it has been a common trend in Danish experiments that a high content of sucrose increases the frequency of PSE (Clausen *et al.*, 1957). The reason may be that long-term sugar feeding (from 20 to 90 kg. liveweight) increased the glucose tolerance and readily mobilizable glycogen deposits in the muscle which may increase the frequency of PSE (Meyer *et al.*, 1962). In general, there is a tendency for higher glycogen depots in muscle where postmortem glycolysis is accelerated (Briskey and Wismer-Pedersen, 1961) although there are breed differences in this respect (Sayre *et al.*, 1963).

In general the content of vegetable fats in the feed appears not to have any influence on the muscle quality. However, a number of observations have appeared in the literature on the occurrence of carcasses with pale watery muscles after feeding the pigs unsaturated fats with low content of vitamin E (Adamstone *et al.*, 1949; Obel *et al.*, 1953; Thafvelin, 1960; Lannek *et al.*, 1961; Lindberg and Orstradius, 1961; Orstradius *et al.*, 1963; Tanhuanpää, 1965). This so-called nutritional muscle degeneration (NMD) is associated with dystrophic changes in the musculature and with consequent appearance of glutamic acid transaminase (GAT) in the blood. The NMD is mostly observed on feeding grain grown in northern Scandinavia and harvested under rainy conditions. This grain contains a rather high amount of unsaturated fatty acids and a low level of vitamin E. Of most importance, however, was that the selenium content of the grain also was low (Lindberg and Tanhuanpää, 1966). Feeding fish silage with a high content of unsaturated fatty acids which should put considerable pressure on the vitamin E reserve in the muscle failed to produce NMD under Danish conditions where no selenium deficiency exists (Clausen *et al.*, 1961). In a Swedish experiment feeding of barley deteriorated on storage produced pale watery muscle without any change in the GAT values of the blood (Thomke *et al.*, 1966). In a similar experiment with feeding of mouldy barley grown in Denmark, no effect on meat quality was observed (Clausen *et al.*, 1965). The damage to muscle tissue from lack of tocopherol and selenium might be due to their importance for aerobic metabolism. When no deficiencies exist the addition of vitamin E and selenium has no effect on the occurrence of PSE (Thomke *et al.*, 1965). In general we must conclude that the occurrence of PSE under normal production conditions does not appear connected with any known nutritional deficiency. It is interesting to note that stress imposed on animals through stressors in feed or environment often has no effect on muscle quality. The feeding of mouldy barley produced considerable stress which manifested itself through degenerative changes in the kidneys. Only very low and mostly insignificant correlation coefficients have been found between the degree of nasal alteration due to atrophic rhinitis and meat color score for the pigs from the Danish progeny testing stations (Jonsson, 1965). Only when the stress involves increase in body temperature as result of pneumonia infection may the meat quality be adversely affected (Sybesma, 1966).

EFFECT OF CONFINEMENT

It has often been suggested that the incidence of PSE was associated with the confinement of pigs and the lack of adequate exercise (Herter and Wilsdorf, 1914; Cohrs, 1942). Giving the pigs access to open-air pens where they could get exercise resulted in slight improvement in meat color (Herter and Wilsdorf, 1914; Ludvigsen, 1955). It appears, however, that effective exercise is required in order to obtain significant improvements. Lannek et al. (1967) subjected pigs from 30 to 90 kg. liveweight to exercise twice a week in 10-minute periods on a moving belt with a speed of 2 m/sec while a corresponding control group remained undisturbed. Prior to slaughter half of the pigs in each group were exposed to exercise on the moving belt. The untrained pigs showed signs of fatigue after 2–3 minutes, and all the pigs were then slaughtered immediately. The results showed that the short antemortem treatment gave lower water-holding capacity and paler color of the meat for both groups, but a highly significant improvement in these quality characteristics was achieved through the regular training period. The trained pigs were considerably better than the untrained pigs regardless of the antemortem treatment (Table 16.5). An interesting method to bring about physical exercise of the pigs was suggested by Skjervold et al. (1963). They gradually lifted the feeding troughs with increasing body size of the pigs during the feeding period. Only the effect of exercise on the meatiness of the carcass was studied. In a similar Danish experiment (Clausen et al., 1963) the meat quality was also considered. These results are shown in Table 16.6. The exercise gave no improvement in meatiness but tended to improve the meat color score. However, the effect was not so dramatic as in the forced exercise experiment by Lannek et al.

Variation in the size of sties does not appear to affect the ultimate muscle quality. Comparison between the performance of pigs divided in 12 sties with 8 pigs per sty was made with a corresponding group of 96

TABLE 16.5: Effect of Forced Exercise on Medial Ham Muscle Quality

Group	No. of Pigs	Expressible Juice (v/w%)	Optical Density (high value = dark color)
Trained	11	1.30 ∓ 0.35[a]	0.933 ∓ 0.062
Untrained	9	8.35 ∓ 1.10[b]	0.622 ∓ 0.080[bc]
Trained-antemortem stress	10	5.75 ∓ 1.45[b]	0.769 ∓ 0.077[b]
Untrained-antemortem stress	8	13.25 ∓ 1.85[c]	0.435 ∓ 0.062[c]

Source: Lannek et al. (1967).
Note: Values with like superscripts are not significantly different.

TABLE 16.6: Effect of Lifting Feeding Troughs on Pig Performance and Meat Color Score

Group	1	2	3	4	5
Trough position	normal	lifted			
Number of pigs	10	10	10	10	10
Number of feedings per day	3	3	4	5	6
Daily gain in g	568	558	543	540	555
Lb feed/lb gain	3.15	3.23	3.31	3.36	3.25
Percent lean meat in carcass	58.5	57.8	57.6	57.2	57.8
Meat color score[a]	2.15	2.80	2.20	2.40	2.55

Source: Clausen *et al.* (1963).
[a] Statistically significant difference between groups 1 and 2.

pigs in one sty with the same total area. The experiment did not reveal any difference in meat color due to treatment (Clausen *et al.*, 1958).

We may conclude that training the pigs during the feeding period might improve the ultimate muscle characteristics but the exercise must be effective.

REFERENCES

Adamstone, F. B. *et al.* 1949. Response of swine to vitamin E-deficient rations, *Ann. N.Y. Acad. Sci.* 52:260.

Allen, E. *et al.* 1966. Phenotypic and genetic associations between porcine muscle properties, *J. Animal Sci.* 25:962.

Baird, D. M., Nalbundov, A. V., and Norton, H. W. 1952. Some physiological causes of genetically different rates of growth in swine, *J. Animal Sci.* 11:292.

Bendall, J. R., and Lawrie, R. A. 1964. Watery pork: a discussion of symptoms and causes, *Fleischwirtschaft* 16:411.

Briskey, E. J. 1964. Etiological status and associated studies of pale, soft, exudative porcine musculature, *Advan. Food Res.* 13:89.

Briskey, E. J. *et al.* 1959. The chemical and physical characteristics of various pork ham muscle classes, *J. Animal Sci.* 18:146.

Briskey, E. J., and Wismer-Pedersen, J. 1961. Biochemistry of pork muscle structure, *J. Food Sci.* 26:306.

Budding, I. M., Davenport, M. E., and Schooley, M. A. 1956. The glucose tolerance test in swine and its implications, *J. Animal Sci.* 15:234.

Callow, E. H. 1938. The after effects of fasting, *Ann. Rept. Food Invest. Board* (UK), p. 54.

———. 1939. The pH of muscle tissue, *Ibid.* p. 27.

Cassens, R. C. *et al.* 1965. Porcine adrenocortical lipids in relation to striated muscle characteristics, *Proc. Soc. Exp. Biol. Med.* 120:854.

Clausen, H. *et al.* 1957. Bilag til forsogslaboratoriets efetrårsmode. Copenhagen.

———. 1958. *Ibid.*

———. 1961. *Ibid.* p. 148.

———. 1963. *Ibid.* p. 261.

———. 1965. *Ibid.* p. 106.

———. 1967. 55. beretning om sammenlignende forsog med svin. 360. beretning fra forsogslaboratoriet. Copenhagen.

Clausen, H. and Nortoft Thomsen, R. 1962. 50. beretning om sammenlignende forsog med svin fra statsanerkendte avlscentre. 331. beretning fra forsogs-laboratoriet. Copenhagen.

Cohrs, P. 1942. Patologische Anatomie und Pathogenese der wichtigsten Schweinekrankheiten, *Deut. Tierärztl. Wochsch.* 50:1.

Gawienowski, A. M., Mayer, D. T., and Lasley, J. F. 1955. The serum protein-bound iodine of swine as a measure of growth potentialities, *J. Animal Sci.* 14:3.

Gibbons, N. E., and Rose, D. 1950. Effect of ante-mortem treatment of pigs on the quality of Wiltshire bacon, *Can. J. Res.* F 28:438.

Henry, M. 1957. Mobilisation du potassium cellulaire chez le porc et qualites charcutieres de la viande. 3. European Meeting of Meat Research Workers. Roskilde.

Henry, M., and Billon, J. 1959. Nouvelle observations sur l'influence des agres-sion non specifiques sur la qualite de la viande der porc. 5. European Meet-ing of Meat Research Workers. Paris.

Henry, M., Romani, J. D., and Joubert, L. 1958. La myopathie exudative de-pigmentaire du porc. Maladie de l'adaptation. Essai pathogenique et con-sequences pratique. *Rev. Pathol. Gen. Physiol. Clin.* 696:355.

Herter, M., and Wilsdorf, G. 1914. Die Bedeutung des Schweines für die Fleischversorgung. Heft 270. DLG. Berlin.

Huggins, A. K., and Ottaway, J. H. 1961. Purification and properties of hypo-glycemic peptide from ox growth hormone, *J. Endocrinol.* 23:193.

Hupka, E. 1952. Fütterungsversuche zur Auslösung des enzootischen Herztodes bei Schweinen, *Deut. Tierärztl. Wochsch.* 19:145.

Jonsson, P. 1965. Analyse af egenskaber hos svin af dansk landrace. Thesis, Royal Vet. and Agricultural College. Copenhagen.

Judge, M. 1967. Future for Pork Conference.

Judge, M. D. *et al.* 1965. Thyroid I-131 uptake and serum-bound iodine in relation to pale, soft, exudative porcine muscle, *J. Animal Sci.* 24:864.

Kielanowski, J. 1957. in "Probleme der Steigung der tierischen Producktion," Tagungsberichte Nr. 8, p. 120. Deutsche Akademie der Landwissenschaften. Berlin.

Krebs, E. G., and Fischer, E. H. 1955. Phosphorylase activity of skeletal muscle extracts, *J. Biol. Chem.* 216:113.

Krzywicki, K., and Ratcliff, P. W. 1967. The phospholipids of pork muscle, and their relation to the post-mortem rate of glycolysis, *J. Sci. Food Agr.* 18:252.

Lannek, N. *et al.* 1961. Production of vitamin E deficiency and muscular dystro-phy in pigs, *Res. Vet. Sci.* 2:65.

Lannek, N., Lindberg, P., and Rülcker, C. 1967. Transportmuskeldegeneration hos svin. Svensk Veterinär Tidning. In press.

Lindberg, P., and Orstradius, K. 1961. Production of muscular dystrophy in pigs by feeding cottonseed oil, *Acta Vet. Scand.* 2:60.

Lindberg, P., and Tanhuanpää, E. 1965. Retention of selenium in tissues of swine after a single intramuscular administration of sodium selenite, *Acta Vet. Scand.* 6, suppl. 3.

————. 1966. Nutritionell betingad muskeldegeneration hos svin. Proc. 10. Nordic Vet. Congress II, 832.

Ludvigsen, J. 1954. Undersøgelser over den såkaldte "muskeldegeneration hos svin. 272. beretning fra forsøgslaboratoriet. Copenhagen.

————. 1955. Undersøgelser over den såkaldte "muskeldegeneration" hos svin. 279. og 284. beretning fra forsøgslaboratoriet. Copenhagen.

Madsen, J. 1942. Undersøgelser over svinekødets holdbarhed efter forskellig fodring. 11. beretning fra den kgl. Vet.-og Landbohøjskoles Slagterilaboratorium. Copenhagen.

McMeekan, C. P. 1940–41. Growth and development in the pig, with special reference to carcass quality characters, *J. Agr. Sci.* 30:276, 31:1.

Meyer, J. A. *et al.* 1962. Glucose tolerance in swine as related to post-mortem muscle characteristics, *J. Animal Sci.* 21:543.

Obel, A. *et al.* 1953. Om s. k. toxisk leverdystrofi hos svin, Proc. 6. Nordic. Vet. Congress, 94.

Orstradius, K., Norström, G., and Lannek, N. 1963. Combined therapy with vitamin E and selenite in experimental nutritional muscle dystrophy, *Cornell Vet.* 53:60.

Ozinska, Z., and Kielanowski, J. 1960. Relationship between meat colour and feed efficiency in pigs, *Animal Prod.* 2:209.

Porter, K. R., and Franzini-Armstrong, C. 1965. The sarcoplasmic reticulum, *Sci. Am.* 212:3, 72.

Recant, L. 1952. Fed. Proc. 11:272.

Richter, K., and Oslage, H. J. 1955. Zur Frage der Fleischqualität und ihrer Beeinflussung durch die Fütterung, Züchtungskunde 27:3, 99.

Rose, D., and Peterson, R. 1951. Depletion of carbohydrate reserve by starvation and exercise, *Can. J. Technol.* 29:421.

Russell, J. A. 1953. CIBA Foundation Colloq. *Endocrinol.* 6:193.

Russell, J. A., and Wilhelmi, A. E. 1960. Endocrines and muscle. *Structure and Function of Muscle.* G. H. Bourne, ed. Academic Press. Vol. 2.

Sayre, R. N., Briskey, E. J., and Hoekstra, W. G. 1963. Effect of excitement, fasting and sucrose feeding on porcine muscle phospholylase and post-mortem glycolysis, *J. Food Sci.* 28: 472.

Sink, J. D. *et al.* 1967. Lipid composition of normal and pale, soft, exudative muscle, *J. Food Sci.* 32:258.

Skjervold, H., Standal, N., and Bruflot, R. 1963. Effect of one form of exercise on the body development in pigs, *J. Animal Sci.* 22:458.

Sørensen, P. H. 1958. Meddelelser fra Sterilitetsforskningsinstitutet. Copenhagen.

Staun, H. 1963. Various factors affecting number and size of muscle fibers in the pig. *Acta Agr. Scand.* 13:3, 293.

———. 1967. Den genetisk betingede variation i muskelfibrenes diameter og antal i m. long. dorsi hos svin af Dansk landrace. 13. N. J. F. kongres. Copenhagen.

Sybesma, W. 1966. Lungenentzündungen bei Schweinen und deren Folgen für die Fleischqualität. 12. European Meeting of Meat Research Workers Sandefjord.

Tanhuanpää, E. 1965. *Acta Vet. Scand.* 6, suppl. 3.

Thafvelin, B. 1960. Role of cereal fat in the production of nutritional disease in pigs, *Nature* 188:1169.

Thomke, S., Dahl, O., and Persson, K.–Å. 1965. Tocopherol and selenium in pig rations, including an assessment of meat quality parameters. *Acta Agr. Scand.* 15:262.

Thomke, S., Pira, C., and Persson, K.-Å. 1966. The effect of feeding storage deteriorated and normal barley, soaked and unsoaked, on the growth and carcass quality of pigs. 12. European Meeting of Meat Research Workers. Sandefjord.

Topel, D. G., and Merkel, R. A. 1966. Effect of exogenous goitrogens upon some physical and biochemical properties of porcine muscle and adrenal gland, *J. Animal Sci.* 25:1154.

Topel, D. G., Merkel, R. A., and Wismer-Pedersen, J. 1967. Relationship of plasma 17-hydroxycorticosteroid levels to some physical and biochemical properties of porcine muscle, *J. Animal Sci.* 26:311.

Turman, E. J., and Andrews, F. N. 1955. Some effects of purified anterior pituitary growth hormone on swine, *J. Animal Sci.* 14:7.

Wismer-Pedersen, J. 1959a. Some observations on the quality of cured bacon in relation to ante-mortem treatment, *Acta Agr. Scand.* 9:69.

———. 1959b. Quality of pork in relation to rate of pH change post-mortem, *Food Res.* 24:711.

———. 1960. Effect of cure on pork with watery structure. *Food Res.* 25:789.

17

Influence of Stress Syndrome on Chemical and Physical Characteristics of Muscle Postmortem

E. J. BRISKEY and D. LISTER

BERNARD (1878) recognized a hundred years ago that the maintenance of homeostasis was a fundamental characteristic of the living animal, and as a result of this, life could continue under a whole range of environments and resist, to a large extent, a wide gamut of adverse treatments. The individual treatments or factors which are capable of causing disturbances to this harmony are called "stressors," while the disequilibrium or loss of harmony caused by the "stressors" is "stress." "Stress" of course involves muscle because, as a tissue, muscle is not only an integral part of the animal body, dependent on a blood supply, but it also has nervous and hormonal connections with other tissues and organs.

For many reasons a pig is subject, particularly in the period before and associated with slaughter, to numerous factors or stressors which bring about a disequilibrium or loss of coordination. These factors may include sound, temperature, humidity, atmospheric pressure, nutrition, shock, fear, light, fatigue, anoxia, and emotional excitement. However, regardless of the specific nature of the "stressor," Selye (1936) observed that they induced, for the most part, a rather similar "stress response." Specifically when subjected to a "stressor" an animal discharges hormones

Published with the approval of the Director of the Wisconsin Agricultural Experiment Station.

The University of Wisconsin work which has been cited in this review, has been supported in part by Public Health Service Research Grant UI 00266–09 from the National Center for Urban and Industrial Health and by a special research grant from the American Meat Institute Foundation.

from its adrenal gland in an act of resistance. These hormones, cate-cholamines from the inside (medulla) and 17-hydroxycorticosterone and 11-deoxycorticosterone from the outside (cortex) of the adrenal gland, elic-it various responses in the animal which have been collectively referred to by Selye as the "general adaptation syndrome." In brief, this syndrome may represent an adrenal-hypothalamus-pituitary response. It is not our purpose to delve into the intricate nature of stress and stress response, much of which is at best controversial, but instead it is our objective to discuss briefly animal-to-animal variation or tolerance and then move directly into a discussion of the effect of stressors on pig muscle.

Let us consider a general situation where many animals are exposed to a stressor of a specific intensity. We all know, from what is so loosely passed off as biological variation, that much variation in response will be found among these animals—a few may die while most survive and re-cover, or most may die while a few recover. Why do we have this differ-ence—this variation in tolerance? We know that tolerance declines with age or disease, but we do not necessarily understand the fundamental mechanisms involved. We also know that tolerance is not reflected in sur-vival alone—it may in fact be reflected by a slight alteration in the tissue. Muscle is particularly vulnerable because an adrenergic response or lib-eration of catecholamine can have a pronounced effect on the circula-tion of blood in the tissue. What really matters is whether the main-tenance of the blood flow is adequate to provide the required oxygen and nutrients. The adrenergic response can bring about vasoconstriction —the blood supply may be reduced—in fact at different points in the muscle, anoxia or a stagnant anoxic condition may develop. In the proc-ess of responding, a muscle usually contracts, breaking down some of its chemical energy, but normally a resting situation is quickly restored because the blood brings adequate oxygen and glucose. If, however, the stressor continues, or the response is exaggerated by constriction, or the muscle's ability to resynthesize its chemical energy by the more efficient aerobic system is exceeded, lactic acid production ensues. This probably represents a more general "stagnant anoxia" or "oxygen debt." These statements are a totally inadequate expression of "stress response" as far as the whole body is concerned but rather are given only with the in-tent of showing their relation to muscle.

MUSCLE VARIATION

Muscle may be described as red or white, a white muscle having mostly white fibers with only a few red fibers. These white fibers are myoglobin-poor and have a poor capacity for aerobic metabolism; how-ever they are abundantly provided with stores of high energy compounds which may be called upon as and when a need arises and are geared for anaerobic metabolism. Red muscles are adapted for aerobic metabolism and are capable of long sustained action but have little reserve capacity (George and Berger, 1965). Consequently we may expect stress to have a different effect on white than on red muscle.

ANIMAL VARIATION

It has been observed that pigs of certain strains die when unavoidably excited in a warm environment whereas pigs of other strains seem to possess the ability to maintain homeostasis during such exposure (Forrest *et al.*, 1967). Those animals which cannot withstand excitement in a warm environment have been called "stress-susceptible" whereas those which can withstand exposure to a warm environment have been categorized as "stress-resistant" (Judge *et al.*, 1967a). When a "stress-susceptible" pig is exposed to a stressor, its muscle will ultimately become pale, soft, and exudative (PSE). Briefly during and after exsanguination, lactic acid accumulates quickly or pH decreases while the temperature remains at or near body temperature. The combination of this low pH and high temperature brings about a denaturation of the proteins and muscle becomes pale (white), soft, and exudative (Briskey, 1964; Briskey *et al.*, 1966a, b; Lister *et al.*, 1967a, b; and Sair *et al.*, 1967). However, when a "stress-resistant" animal is exposed to a stressor such as a warm environment it will withstand the treatment and have essentially normal changes in its muscle postmortem.

A number of studies have been completed in our laboratory on "stress-susceptible" and "stress-resistant" pigs (Forrest *et al.*, 1967; Judge *et al.*, 1967a, b; Sair *et al.*, 1967; Lister *et al.*, 1967a, b).

ENDOCRINE STUDIES

These "stress-susceptible" animals are by no means limited to, but in our situation have come from, the Poland China breed, while our "stress-resistant" pigs have come from strains of the Chester White breed. Cassens *et al.* (1965) used a histochemical method to study the adrenal cortices of animals in relation to their "stress susceptibility." These workers found some evidence of adrenal abnormality in "stress-susceptible" pigs. The adrenal cortices tended to contain small quantities of uniformly dispersed lipid granules, but large masses of lipid were found in the zona reticularis. More recently Judge *et al.* (1967c) found that the number of lipid masses in the zona reticularis increased markedly when "stress-susceptible" pigs were exposed to fluctuating temperatures.

Ludvigsen (1954) reported that exercise causes a greater accumulation of lactate in the muscles of some pigs than in others. He also postulated that the pigs which accumulated the high levels of lactate produced insufficient amounts of adrenal corticoids because the administration of cortisol restored their ability to convey the lactate from the muscles to the blood stream. Judge *et al.* (1967a) conducted a study to specifically compare the quantities of various adrenal steroids and catecholamines in the urine, the levels of protein bound iodine (PBI) in the serum, and I^{131} uptake in the thyroids of pigs which could be classified as "stress-susceptible" or "stress-resistant." PBI values increased more rapidly in "stress-susceptible" than in "stress-resistant" animals when they were all held at warm temperatures. Mean values of 17-ketosteroids and 17-OH-corticosteroids tended to be lower, PBI higher, and thyroid I^{131} uptake lower in "stress-susceptible" than in "stress-resistant" pigs. Collectively these data gave some support to the view that these pigs suffer a degree of adrenal insufficiency accompanied perhaps by some failure of circulating thyroid hormone to stimulate oxidative metabolism in their striated musculature.

PHYSIOLOGICAL RESPONSE

In related work Forrest *et al.* (1967) studied (1) the changes in heart and respiratory rates and venous blood pO_2, pCO_2, and pH of "stress-susceptible" compared to "stress-resistant" animals during exposure to a warm environment and (2) the changes in the above parameters as well as cardiac output, blood pressure in the pulmonary artery and aorta, and body temperature in similar animals observed under anesthesia.

The heart rates before treatment (immediately prior to initiating the experiment and while pigs were in standing positions) were, in general, considerably higher than the resting rates (taken during sleep); however, the pretreatment rates of the "stress-susceptible" animals were slightly higher than those of the "stress-resistant" animals at the same time period. The "stress-susceptible" animals which were subjected to the warm environment (42°C.) exhibited a sharp increase in heart rate, reaching an average of about 270 within 10 minutes of the beginning of treatment. The elevated heart rates were followed immediately by declines. The "stress-susceptible" animals which were maintained in the warm environment showed increased respiration during the first 10 minutes of exposure, followed by a sharp decline which most certainly would have led to respiratory arrest if the pigs had been allowed to remain in the chamber. The "stress-resistant" animals reacted to the warm environment in an entirely different manner and showed continuous moderate increases in respiration rates so that by the end of the treatment period the rates were significantly higher than those found in control animals.

The "stress-susceptible" animals showed significant increases in blood pCO_2 during treatment and concomitant drastic decreases in pO_2 values during the same period. The pH of the blood in these treated "stress-susceptible" animals also decreased significantly to below 6.8. Conversely, during treatment the "stress-resistant" animals maintained blood pH levels, while values for pO_2 seemed to be increased and those for pCO_2 decreased. The muscles of the "stress-susceptible" animals became PSE postmortem while the "stress-resistant" animals maintained normal musculature. Hyperthermy appeared to contribute to tissue hypoxia in the "stress-susceptible" animals and represents a phenomenon of obvious import to the circulatory and respiratory functions. Other stressors probably also elicit adverse responses from "stress-susceptible" animals. The recent observation of Judge *et al.* (1967a) that "stress-susceptible" animals exhibit some adrenocortical insufficiency may contribute significantly to the result of the present study. It follows that if animals were unable to respond with increased adrenal catecholamine output, hypercapnic acidosis developed. Our observations in "stress-susceptible" animals might suggest that the stress in these animals was potentiated by their inability to respond with an increased adrenal hormone output.

In a study of the susceptibility of these animals to physical restraint, Judge *et al.* (1967b) restrained all the legs of Poland China and Chester White pigs for three and five hours, using litter mates as unrestrained controls. In all Poland China muscles the five-hour restraint caused pH increases beyond the increases caused by three hours of restraint, but in some Chester White muscles, restraint for five hours resulted in less pronounced pH increases than restraint for three hours. The ratings of color and gross morphology of the muscles at 24 hours postmortem when compared with duration of restraint show differences which were consistent with the pH differences. Poland China muscles became darker, firmer, and drier as the duration of restraint increased, whereas muscles from Chester White animals subjected to prolonged restraint (five hours) resembled the muscles of unrestrained Chester White animals. These results demonstrate once again that pigs of differing genetic backgrounds respond to antemortem stressors in different ways. The breed differences were so pronounced that a single treatment (five-hour restraint) resulted in generally opposite effects on the muscles of Poland China compared with those of Chester White animals. The patterns of response indicated that the effects of stress in Poland China animals became more severe with duration of restraint, and there was no evidence that these animals could resist the stressor. However, the Chester White animals apparently possessed defense mechanisms which enabled them to withstand the stressors and restore the original conditions in the muscles.

EFFECTS OF STRUGGLE AND STIMULATION VERSUS ANOXIA

Since it is now established that the PSE condition develops in association with a high production of lactic acid while the muscle temperature remains high, it follows that it must inevitably be caused by muscular stimulation and/or anoxia. Lister *et al.* (1967 a, b) recently conducted extensive studies to examine the way in which pigs which are susceptible to stress (strains of Poland China) and those which are less susceptible (strains of Chester White) are affected by the two most commonly cited causes of the PSE condition, namely muscular stimulation and anoxia. The experiments were designed in such a way as to allow the effects of one of these to be examined uncomplicated by the effects of the other. In the first experiment the effects of anoxia were examined in completely resting anesthetized pigs. Anoxia was produced by allowing the animals to breathe nitrogen for a time before they were slaughtered. For comparison purposes a group of pigs was allowed to breathe pure oxygen. The animals were anesthetized by injection with a mixture of dial with urethane and nembutal via an ear vein. In this condition we arranged for the pigs to breathe the various gases by way of an endotracheal tube. Biopsy samples were removed as quickly as possible from anesthetized subjects and dropped straight into liquid nitrogen. Additional samples were taken immediately after exsanguination and at one and three hours subsequently. Details of treatment and analytical procedures can be found in the reports of Lister *et al.* (1967 a, b).

The administration of oxygen or nitrogen produced very little difference in the amounts of lactic acid in the samples from Chester White pigs (Lister *et al.*, 1967a). However when Poland China pigs were permitted to breathe nitrogen before death, their level of lactic acid in the *longissimus dorsi* muscle increased markedly, particularly in the samples taken at biopsy and immediately postmortem. In other words, the *longissimus dorsi* of a Poland China pig is susceptible to anoxia despite the fact that this muscle is said to be characteristically white, relying mainly on the anaerobic production of energy. Additionally, the initial amount of lactic acid was very important in deciding the rate of accumulation of lactic acid during the two or three hours after death or the intensity of the PSE condition in the muscle.

To follow the effect of complete relaxation or importance of struggle or stimulation on the incidence of the PSE condition, we anesthetized, incubated, and injected Poland China and Chester White pigs with d-tubocurarine chloride (Lister *et al.*, 1967b). Curarization of the Chester White resulted in high levels of chemical energy (ATP and CP) and low levels of lactic acid, whereas there was very little effect in the Poland China—in fact these Poland China muscles still became extremely PSE. The amount of CP is very closely related to the amount of lactic acid in muscle (Lister *et al.*, 1967b).

How the two breeds, which are more or less susceptible to the development of the PSE condition, differ in their response to struggle anoxia can be seen through an analysis of the amount of lactic acid which is attributable to struggle and stimulation. Approximately 65 percent of the total amount of lactic acid in the muscle of a Chester White animal conventionally slaughtered may result from struggle. Conversely 65 percent of the lactic acid in the Poland China muscle which becomes PSE can be assumed to be associated with anoxia produced by exsanguination alone.

It is therefore apparent that while the muscle of the Poland China breed suffers a greater production of lactic acid as a result of the anoxia caused by exsanguination, that of the Chester White suffers more from stimulation in the period associated with slaughter. These data would seem to indicate that the *longissimus dorsi* of the Poland China is more susceptible to anoxia than that of the Chester White breed, and consequently the act of exsanguination alone is sufficient to cause a relatively large change in the pH of the muscle. Any effect of stimulation before death can only be even more harmful, but it is interesting to note that stimulation itself is less productive of lactic acid in the Poland China that it is in the Chester White, and this would seem to indicate that so long as the blood supply to the muscle is intact, the facility for the production of high-energy phosphate compounds by aerobic means is maintained. In order to try to give some quantitative assessment of the aerobic state in these muscles we looked at the levels of myoglobin and succinic dehydrogenase by chemical analysis (Lister *et al.*, 1967b). The amounts of myoglobin were not different, but the amounts of one of the key oxidative enzymes—succinic dehydrogenase—were very different. Usually high levels of oxidative enzymes are found in association with elevated abilities to store oxygen. This is not always the case, however, for where there is a particularly good blood supply to the fibers, there is no real need for appreciable storage of oxygen. This situation may occur in the Poland China and also contribute in this breed to a high susceptibility to anoxia. In order to tie up these findings with the histological picture we sectioned the muscles and stained for red (aerobic) and white (anaerobic) fibers and also serially sectioned and stained for succinic dehydrogenase and cytochrome oxidase. The number of fibers with these latter stains were compatible with the red fiber component for the Chester White and Poland China. It was also clear that the fibers of the Poland China were bigger. While it may be argued that the differences in the levels of the various enzymes are not sufficient in themselves to account completely for particular degrees of aerobic activity, they are in line with what might be expected from a general consideration of the results and are included as indicators of the nature of the metabolism until more complete evidence is available.

We were able to measure the areas of individual fibers from standard enlargements and to assess the total area of red and white fibers in standard sections.

Lister *et al.* (1967a, b) concluded that the condition of the muscles of some pigs which results in their presenting a pale, soft, and exudative character is brought about by the excessive stimulation of individual pigs before slaughter or, more consistently, as a breed susceptibility to the condition by a combination of the anoxic effects of exsanguination and a smaller one of stimulation. The pH of the muscle resulting from either of these causes is germane to the subsequent characteristics of the process of rigor mortis.

Since lactic acid production in the Poland China seemed to be associated with anoxia, Sair *et al.* (1967) attempted to differentiate between the effect of antemortem or pre-exsanguination and exsanguination anoxia.

It was postulated that an adrenergic response in these susceptible pigs to an external stressor could produce considerable vasoconstriction in the microcirculatory system of the muscle. This adrenergic response, representing the release of norepinephrine and epinephrine, would cause the constriction of vascular smooth muscle in the skeletal muscle bed. This constriction would subsequently cause a decrease in the rate of blood flow per unit of time through the musculature which would result in a decreased oxygen supply or a stagnant anoxic condition. The *longissimus dorsi* of Poland China pigs possesses a greater capacity for aerobic metabolism (Lister *et al.*, 1967a, b) and a lower capability for anaerobic metabolism than the Chester White and would be affected more by stagnant anoxia than the Chester White.

The rationale supporting the experimental approach of Sair *et al.* (1967) was that by either blocking the alpha receptor in vascular smooth muscle to the constrictor action of norepinephrine and epinephrine or by actively stimulating the beta dilatory receptors to antagonize the constrictor effect, it may be possible to prevent the stagnant anoxic condition.

In general these results of the work of Sair *et al.* (1967) indicated that treatment with alpha-blocking agents and/or anesthesia and beta-stimulating agents leads to a slightly higher initial level and a slower depletion of high-energy phosphate compounds and a reduced accumulation of lactic acid after death. The fact that the lactic acid values were significantly (P < .01) lower at the time of death in the *longissimus dorsi* of pigs treated with alpha-blocking and beta-stimulating agents showed that these agents were effective in reducing the vasoconstriction and thereby avoiding some of the stagnant anoxic condition. As previously pointed out, anoxia could result before death due to low levels of oxygen reaching the tissues through a stagnant anoxic mechanism or at the time of death due to blood removal. Through extensive studies on samples biopsied before death and excised at the time of death (immediately after exsanguination) from animals subjected to oxygen, nitrogen, anesthesia, and curare, Lister *et al.* (1967a, b) showed that approximately 60 percent of the production of lactic acid in muscle is associated with anoxia resulting from the process of exsanguination. That the initial lactate levels were still substantial in animals treated with these alpha-blocking and beta-stimulating agents is therefore reasonable, because it is difficult to visualize a mechanism by which exsanguination anoxia would be aided by a mere dilation or prevention of constriction. Nevertheless the reduction in the concentration of lactic acid at the time of death is both significant and appropriate in terms of what might be anticipated. It seems that it could certainly prevent borderline cases from becoming PSE.

As previously pointed out, Lister *et al.* (1967a) have estimated that approximately 65 percent of the lactic acid in the muscle at the completion of exsanguination is associated with anoxia resulting from blood removal. Nevertheless even a slightly lower lactic acid concentration in muscle, caused by an inhibition of what otherwise might be an adrenergically caused vasoconstriction, indirectly affects the subsequent changes which will take place in the muscle after death. This is most easily visualized in the work of Lister *et al.* (1967a, b) which shows a high association between slight increases in lactate and decreases in CP. Consequently a slight increase in initial lactic acid, especially in the 30–40 μm range, is crucial in determining the intensity of the development of the PSE condition. Therefore, while these vaso-active agents definitely reduce the intensity of the development of the PSE condition, they cannot give complete assurance against its development because of the limited extent to which anoxia before death, compared with that associated with bleeding, contributes to the total accumulation of lactic acid at slaughter.

In an animal which is not extremely vulnerable to anoxia (i.e., Chester White—small red fibers, low cytochrome oxidase, and low succinic dehydrogenase [Lister *et al.*, 1967b]) anesthesia alone would give almost complete assurance that this PSE condition would never develop. However, in an animal which is vulnerable to anoxia (i.e., Poland China, more highly geared for aerobic metabolism—large red fibers, high levels of cytochrome oxidase and succinic dehydrogenase [Lister *et al.*, 1967b]), the elimination of struggle, even with anesthesia and curarization to eliminate subsequent stimulation, will not totally protect against the development of the PSE condition.

In summary, there are many environmental and handling factors which have pronounced influences on quality of meat from pigs and in extreme cases may even terminate in death before the pig approaches the slaughter floor. We have pointed out the hormonal response of the pig to some of these stressors and have substantiated that these responses may vary widely in both kind and magnitude. Additionally it is important for us to keep in mind that, even when the hormonal responses may be similar, wide variations in basic properties of muscles may cause this hormonal response to have varied influences on meat quality. Therefore there is no reason to expect a particular stressor to be detrimental to 100 percent of the pigs going to slaughter. It is important to keep in mind that the mere act of removing blood, by itself, can bring about poor meat quality in pigs with a potential for these characteristics.

We believe that we are approaching the threshold of an understanding of the basic phenomena involved with the development of pale, soft, exudative muscle. We trust that within the near future we will be able to bring this condition under reasonable control for the benefit of the entire pork industry.

REFERENCES

Bernard, Claude. 1878. *Leçons sur les phénomènes de la vie communs aux animaux et aux végétaux.* P. 50, J. B. Bailliere, Paris.

Briskey, E. J. 1964. Etiological status and associated studies of pale, soft, exudative porcine musculature. Vol. 13, 89:189. E. M. Mrak, and G. F. Stewart. (eds.). *Advances in Food Research,* Academic Press, Inc., New York.

Briskey, E. J., Cassens, R. G., and Trautman, J. C. 1966a. *Physiology and Biochemistry of Muscle as a Food,* Univ. of Wisconsin Press.

Briskey, E. J., Kastenschmidt, L. L., Forrest, J. C., Beecher, G. R., Judge, M. D., Cassens, R. G., and Hoekstra, W. G. 1966b. Biochemical aspects of post-mortem changes in porcine muscle. *Agr. and Food Chem.* 14, 3, 201.

Cassens, R. G., Judge, M. D., and Briskey, E. J. 1965. Porcine adrenocortical lipids in relation to post-mortem striated muscle characteristics. *Proc. Soc. Exp. Biol. Med.* 120, 854:856.

Forrest, J. C., Will, J. A., Schmidt, G. R., Judge, M.D., and Briskey, E. J. 1967. Homeostasis in Animals *(Sus domesticus)* during exposure to a warm environment. *J. Appl. Physiol.* (In Press).

George, J. C., and Berger, A. J. 1965. *Avian Myology.* Academic Press, New York.

Judge, M. D., Briskey, E. J., Cassens, R. G., Forrest, J. C., and Meyer, R. K. 1967a. Adrenal and thyroid function in "stress susceptible" pigs *(Sus domesticus).* Am. *J. Physiol.* (In press).

Judge, M. D., Cassens, R. G., and Briskey, E. J. 1967b. Muscle properties of physically restrained stressor-susceptible and stressor-resistant porcine animals, *J. Food Sci.* 32, 5, 565.

Judge, M. D., Howe, J., and Martin, R. J. 1967c. Unpublished information.

Kastenschmidt, L. L., Hoekstra, W. G., and Briskey, E. J. 1968. Post-mortem levels of glycolytic intermediates and co-factors in "fast" and "slow-glycolyzing," *J. Food Sci.* (In press).

Lister, D., Sair, R. A., Cassens, R. G., Moody, W. G., Hoekstra, W. G., and Briskey, E. J. 1967b. Metabolism of striated muscle of pigs injected with d-tubocurarine chloride (Submitted).

Lister, D., Sair, R. A., Will, J., Schmidt, G. R., Cassens, R. G., Hoekstra, W. G., and Briskey, E. J. 1967a. Adenosine triphosphate and lactic acid in striated muscle of pigs breathing oxygen or nitrogen (Submitted).

Ludvigsen, J. 1954. Undersogelser over den sakaldte "muskeldegeneration" hos svin Beretning fra Forsøgslaboratoriet Udgivet af Statens Husdygrugsudvalg. 1:272.

Sair, R. A., Lister, D., Hoekstra, W. G., and Briskey, E. J. 1967. Vaso-active agents and the metabolism of porcine striated muscle (Submitted).

Selye, Hans. 1936. A syndrome produced by diverse nocuous agents, *Nature* 138:32.

18

Influence of Controlled Environmental Temperature and Humidity

M. D. JUDGE

THE RESEARCH to be described in this chapter was conducted in the psychrometric chambers at the Purdue Center for Refrigeration Research and Climate Control. A number of controlled-environment chambers are available in which air temperature (—30 to +130° F.), humidity (10 to 100 percent relative), floor temperature (—30 to +130° F.), and light intensity may be independently controlled by automatic programming equipment. In each of two chambers up to 24 pigs may be accommodated under prescribed conditions facilitated by the capability of admitting up to 10,000 cubic feet per minute of conditioned air.

Our research in these facilities has been designed (1) to identify the elements of the climatic environment that are responsible for the known seasonal differences in pork quality and (2) to characterize the development of porcine muscle from animals reared in close confinement under contrasting climate conditions. The experiments have provided information on the effects of two climatic variables during animal growth and development. These are (1) the constancy of the temperature and (2) the level of the humidity. In subsequent reference to these conditions, the term "constant" will denote stable temperature conditions whereas "alternating" will denote three-day periods at two alternating temperatures. The humidity levels have been termed "low," "moderate," and "high" for relative humidity of 15–30 percent, 40 percent, and 85 percent respectively. The initial studies utilized pigs of the Hampshire, Landrace, and Poland China breeds, but more recent experiments have used Poland China pigs exclusively. Data on a total of 197 animals will be used in this presentation. All pigs were barrows and most of them were placed in the environmental chambers shortly after weaning and were slaughtered when they weighed approximately 200 lbs. Most were stunned

with a captive-bolt pistol while in the chambers with no prior handling
and with minimal excitement.

EFFECT OF TEMPERATURE ACCLIMATION
ON HEAT STRESS RESPONSES

An experiment was conducted to determine if we could induce a
degree of heat stress susceptibility and to determine if such an environmentally induced stress response would be associated with postmortem
muscle properties. Groups of Landrace pigs were acclimated to constant
temperatures of either 29 or 18°C. and a third group was subjected to alternating temperatures of 29 and 18°C. These animals were subsequently
heat-stressed by raising the temperature for all groups to 37–40°C. Their
rectal temperatures and respiratory rates were used as indices of their
stress responses. A few days after the heat stress they were slaughtered
and their muscle properties observed.

The results of the study showed that the pigs could be preconditioned
to exhibit heat stress responses since those pigs previously held at the
cool temperature (18°C.) had higher body temperature and respiratory
rates during heat stress than the other groups (Table 18.1). However, as
a group these animals did not have a higher incidence of the pale, soft,
exudative (PSE) muscle condition than the other groups. Within the
acclimated groups however, those pigs with pronounced stress responses
had PSE muscles. We have concluded that the heat stress responses that
are associated with the PSE muscle condition are inherent with the animal and are probably not induced by the environment. If this were not
true, it seems logical that the stress and excitement of handling cool-ac-
climated pigs would result in a high incidence of PSE in the winter
months, the reverse of the seasonal differences reported. Heat stress susceptibility per se does not indicate a propensity for pigs to develop PSE

TABLE 18.1: Effect of Environmental Temperature on Physiological Responses to Heat Stress

Item	29°C	Alternating 29–18°C	18°C	F
Body temperature, °C.[b]				
Nonstressed	39.3	39.3	39.3	0.1
Heat-stressed	39.3	40.0	40.7	13.0**
Inspirations/min.				
Nonstressed	69.4	56.0	40.1	3.9
Heat-stressed[c]	145.4	146.3	175.2	4.7*
Increased[d]	76.0	90.3	135.1	11.6**

Souce: Addis *et al., J. Animal Sci.* 26:466, 1967.
[a] Means not underlined by the same line are significantly ($P < .05$) different.
[b] Rectal temperature.
[c] Avg. of maximum values attained during two periods of heat stress (4 hr. at 37–40°C.).
[d] Avg. of heat-stressed minus nonstressed values.
** $P < .01$; * $P < .05$.

TABLE 18.2: Effect of Environmental Temperature on the Correlations Between Physiological Measurements and Postmortem Muscle Properties

	High 29°C			Alternating 29–18°C			Low 18°C		
Item	Carcass temp[a]	Color-structure[b]	Juice loss[c]	Carcass temp[a]	Color-structure[b]	Juice loss[c]	Carcass temp[a]	Color-structure[b]	Juice loss[c]
Body temperature[d,e]									
Nonstressed	0.35	0.73*	-.16	0.33	0.01	0.33	-.18	-.08	0.15
Heat-stressed[f]	0.46	0.16	0.44	0.37	-.28	0.32	0.27	0.42	0.54
Respiratory rate[e]									
Nonstressed	0.14	0.63*	-.55	0.55	0.15	0.10	0.80**	-.54	0.41
Heat-stressed[f]	0.82**	0.28	0.17	0.27	0.39	-.05	0.77**	-.73*	0.61
Increase[g]	0.53	-.31	0.59	-.35	0.07	-.11	0.64*	-.72**	0.62
Multiple correlation	0.85	0.38	0.74	0.64	0.68	0.44	0.97	0.76	0.83
S.E. of estimate	0.45	0.29	2.60	0.43	0.36	7.03	0.20	0.29	3.33

Source: Addis et al., J. Animal Sci. 26:466, 1967.
[a] Internal ham temperature, 45 min. postmortem.
[b] Avg. of scores for color and structure of l. dorsi and g. medius muscles using the system of Forrest et al. (1963).
[c] Juice loss by l. dorsi muscle as percent total moisture after heating and centrifugation.
[d] Rectal temperature.
[e] Simple correlation coefficients.
[f] Avg. of maximum values attained during two periods of heat-stress (4 hr. at 37–40°C).
[g] Avg. of heat-stressed minus nonstressed values.
** P < .01; * P < .05.

muscles, but within a group those pigs that exhibit the highest respiratory rates and body temperatures are inherently more stress-susceptible and more likely to have PSE muscles.

These relationships should be useful in predicting postmortem muscle properties by observing heat stress responses. Our research indicates that prediction equations for PSE score, muscle temperature, and muscle-free water can be developed by using the respiratory rate and body temperature data observed during heat stress of acclimated pigs (Table 18.2). This prediction was not possible among pigs subjected to alternating temperatures prior to heat stress. The absence of temperature acclimation in these pigs apparently upsets the stability of the heat stress responses and makes it impossible to identify which pigs are inherently stress-susceptible.

EFFECT OF TEMPERATURE ACCLIMATION AND HUMIDITY ON POSTMORTEM MUSCLE PROPERTIES

A breed comparison was made to determine the muscle quality of strains of Hampshire and Poland China pigs which had been reared under several temperature and humidity conditions (Table 18.3). This study revealed wide differences in the apparent response (observed as structure score with low scores representing PSE muscle) of the two breeds to the environments (Fig. 18.1). The quality of Hampshire muscle was relatively uniform among the treatment groups but Poland China muscle was quite variable. In the latter breed the combination of alternating temperature (29, 18°C.) and low humidity (30 percent) produced severely PSE muscle. All low humidity groups had more of the PSE muscles than any high humidity (85 percent) group, and the combination of high temperature (29°C.) and high humidity produced muscle that was normal in virtually all animals. It is interesting that the environment that produced the highest incidence of PSE muscle (alternating temperature and low humidity) and the one that produced the most normal muscle (high temperature and high humidity) were both adverse for growth rate, and the pigs were smaller at slaughter than those of other more optimum growth

TABLE 18.3: **Effects of Environmental Temperature and Humidity During Growth on Muscle Properties of Two Breeds**

Group	Ambient Temperature (°C)	Relative Humidity (%)	Number of Animals	
			Poland China	Hampshire
H[a]L[b]	29	30	6	6
LL	18	30	6	6
AL	29, 18[c]	30	6	6
HH	29	85	6	6
LH	18	85	6	6
AH	29, 18[c]	85	6	6

Source: Thomas *et al.*, *J. Food Sci.* 31:309, 1966.
[a] Designates high, low, or alternating temperature.
[b] Designates high or low percent relative humidity.
[c] Three-day periods at each temperature.

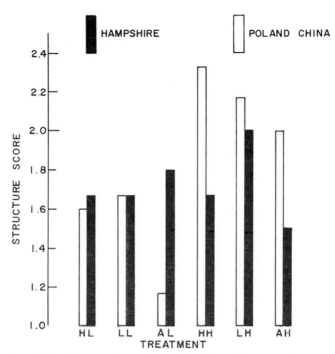

BREED −TREATMENT INTERACTIONS
DORSI STRUCTURE SCORE

FIG. 18.1. Interaction of breed and environmental treat
ment for structure score of *longissimus dorsi* muscle (low
scores indicate pale, soft, exudative muscles). See Table 18.3
for description of treatments. (From Thomas *et al., J. Food
Sci.* 31:309, 1966)

environments (low temperature [18°C.] and low humidity; low temperature and high humidity).

The above results were studied further and confirmed by use of objective methods for measurement of muscle quality. Groups of Landrace
pigs were subjected to high (85 percent), low (30 percent), and alternating (85, 30 percent) humidity, all in combination with a high temperature
(29°C.) environment. The results showed that the Landrace animals
were similar to Poland China animals in their ability to retain normal
muscle when reared in high humidity. There was a tendency for pigs
reared in low or alternating humidity to develop the PSE condition in the
longissimus dorsi muscle (Table 18.4).

The rate of postmortem change was observed in the muscles of Poland China pigs in experiments which included constant (21° or 27°C.)
and alternating (29, 13 or 32, 21°C.) temperatures in combination with
moderate (40 percent) or low (20 percent) humidity. Measurements of
pH (probe electrode) and light reflectance (Spectronic-20 spectrophotom-
eter) of the muscles revealed that the pigs reared in alternating tempera-

TABLE 18.4:   **Effect of Environmental Humidity in a Warm (29°C.) Environment on Muscle Color and Gross Morphology and Processing Characteristics**

	Environmental Humidity			
Muscle Property	High (85%)	Alternating (85–30%)	Low (30%)	F[a]
Color—gross morphology[b]				
l. dorsi	2.46	1.72	1.54	2.8
g. medius	2.28	1.90	2.46	0.9
Juice loss[c]	33.6	35.2	33.9	0.8
Emulsifying capacity[d]	41.5	42.8	42.4	0.3

Source: Addis *et al.*, *J. Animal Sci.* 26:705, 1967.

[a] F.05 = 3.32;   F.01 = 5.39.

[b] 1 = pale, soft, exudative; 3 = normal; 5 = dark, firm, dry (Forrest *et al.*, 1963).

[c] Juice loss as percent total moisture after heating and centrifugation *l. dorsi* muscle).

[d] Milliliters oil emulsified per gm. fat-free *biceps femoris* muscle.

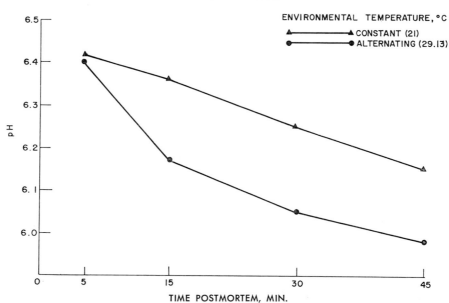

FIG. 18.2.   Rates of postmortem pH decline of *longissimus dorsi* muscle from pigs reared in constant and alternating temperatures. (From Addis, P. B., Ph.D. thesis, Purdue Univ., 1967)

tures had more rapid glycolysis (Figs. 18.2 and 18.3) and paler muscles (Fig. 18.4) than those reared in constant temperatures, but this was true only in the presence of moderate humidity. When the humidity was low, both temperature groups had the rapid glycolysis (Fig. 18.3) and light reflectance values (Fig. 18.4) that are typical of PSE muscle.

The differences described above in muscle glycolytic rate and subsequent morphology were apparently the result of differences in metabolic capabilities of the muscles in the postmortem period rather than differences in muscle temperature or other physical influences. This statement is supported by the finding that the muscles that became PSE, as a group, did not have higher temperatures in the immediate postmortem period than the muscles that were ultimately normal (Figs. 18.5 and 18.6). Consequently the PSE muscle did not result directly from the preslaughter environment.

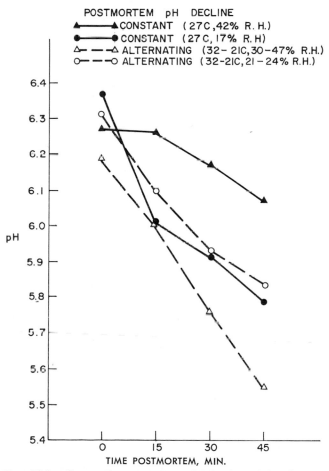

FIG. 18.3. Rates of postmortem pH decline of *longissimus dorsi* muscle from pigs reared in constant and alternating temperatures at two humidity levels. (From Howe *et al.*, submitted)

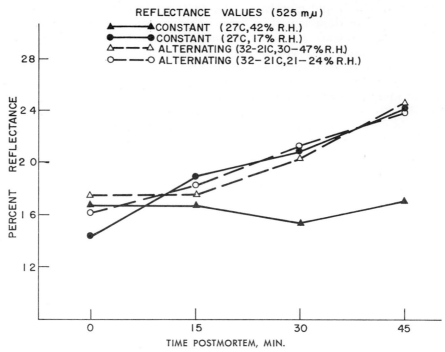

Fig. 18.4.   Postmortem changes in light reflectance by *longissimus dorsi* muscle from pigs reared in constant and alternating temperatures at two humidity levels. (From Howe
et al., submitted)

Chemical and histochemical data were collected to determine the
existence of environmental influences on the development or differen-
tiation of muscle. Muscle fiber types were studied using a stain (Sudan
Black B) which is taken up by fibers having a high capacity for oxidative
metabolism. The ratios of the poorly stained (anaerobic) fibers to the
stained fibers were calculated within muscle bundles. The data suggested
that the alternating temperatures during growth favored high ratios of
light to dark muscle fibers (presumably resulting in anaerobic type
muscles) but the differences in constant and alternating temperature
groups were masked when the humidity was low (Table 18.5).

The histochemical data cited above are supported by myoglobin
analyses. The muscles from the alternating temperature group with high
light-to-dark fiber ratios also had significantly less myoglobin than those
of the constant temperature group (Table 18.5).

We have concluded that temperature acclimation in pigs favors the
development of muscle that has the capacity for storage of large quantities
of oxygen and possibly a greater capability to sustain aerobic metabolism
in the postmortem period. Such muscle would not undergo the rapid
shift to anaerobic conditions postmortem that is typical of PSE muscle.

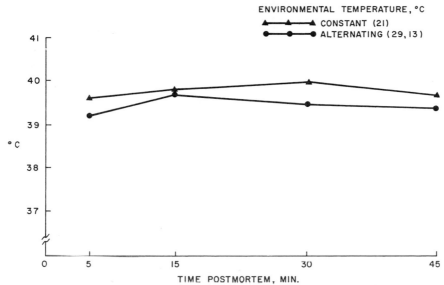

FIG. 18.5. Postmortem changes in temperature of *longissimus dorsi* muscle from pigs reared in constant and alternating temperatures. (From Addis, P. B., Ph.D. thesis, Purdue Univ., 1967)

EFFECT OF TEMPERATURE ACCLIMATION AND HUMIDITY ON MORPHOLOGY OF ADRENAL GLAND

Several studies have been completed in a number of laboratories which indicate that the PSE muscle condition is associated with inadequate function of the adrenal cortex (Ludvigsen, 1957; Henry *et al.*, 1958; Judge *et al.*, 1966; Topel and Merkel, 1967). It has also been suggested that this adrenal condition may be evidenced by the presence of large lipid masses in the cells of the zona reticularis (Cassens *et al.*, 1965). Our studies therefore included histological observation and scoring of the abundance of these degenerative cells (Cassens *et al.*, 1965). The average scores were calculated for the Poland China pigs whose muscle properties were previously described. A direct relationship seemed to exist between adrenal lipid score and rapidity of muscle pH decline in the postmortem period (Table 18.6). A higher incidence of the degenerative adrenal cells existed in the pigs reared in alternating temperatures as compared to those in constant temperature, but these differences were partially masked when the humidity was low. The adrenal alterations were especially severe in pigs reared under low humidity conditions.

Assuming that these pigs were inherently stress-susceptible at the beginning of the experiments, their hormone output from the adrenal cortex was probably marginal at that time. The imposition of conditions of stress during their growth period may have hastened the degenerative

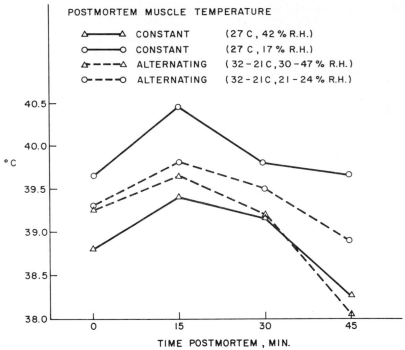

FIG. 18.6. Postmortem changes in temperature of *longissimus dorsi* muscle from pigs reared in constant and alternating temperatures at two humidity levels. (From Howe *et al.,* submitted)

TABLE 18.5: **Effect of Environmental Temperature and Humidity on Muscle Fiber Types and Myoglobin Content**

Ambient Temperature (°C)	Relative Humidity (%)	Light:Dark Fibers[b]		Myoglobin[c]	
		L. dorsi (ratio)	*G. medius* (ratio)	*L. dorsi* (mg/gm)	*G. medius* (mg/gm)
27	42	4.2 ⎤ **	2.7	3.94 ⎤ **	3.78 ⎤ **
32,21[a]	38	5.4 ⎦	3.3	2.52 ⎦	2.39 ⎦
27	17	4.5	2.9	2.64	3.33
32,21[a]	23	4.5	2.7	2.25	2.97

[a] Alternating three-day periods at each temperature.
[b] From Howe *et al., J. Food Sci.* (submitted).
[c] From Thomas and Judge (in preparation).
** $P < .01$.

TABLE 18.6: Effect of Temperature Acclimation and Humidity on Adrenal Lipid Scores and Their Relation to Muscle pH Decline

Ambient Temperature (°C)	Relative Humidity (%)	pH Decline	Adrenal Lipid (score)	
21	40	normal	0.26	**
29,13[a]	40	rapid	0.56	
27	42	normal	0.13	
32,21[a]	38	rapid	0.44	**
27	17	rapid	1.17	
32,21[a]	23	rapid	1.44	

Source: Howe *et al.* (in preparation).
[a] Alternating three-day periods at each temperature.
** P < .01.

changes that might occur more slowly in the adrenal glands under optimal conditions. The high-stress environments therefore may cause rapid physiological aging of the animals and result in their inability to resist a secondary stress.

EFFECT OF TEMPERATURE ACCLIMATION AND HUMIDITY ON RELATIONSHIP BETWEEN QUANTITATIVE AND QUALITATIVE MUSCLE PROPERTIES

Swine management research conducted at Purdue University has provided information on the performance and carcass attributes of large numbers of pigs reared in several confinement systems. In many of these trials we have observed that the housing systems which seem to impose environmental stress tend to result in slower growing but leaner animals (Kadlec *et al.*, 1966). In addition it has been reported that among Danish pigs (which are reared in close confinement), the short, muscular animals with thin backfat tend to have poor muscle quality (Clausen and Nortoft Thomsen, 1956; Ludvigsen, 1960). Therefore we were interested in the degree to which muscularity was associated with muscle quality in our animals reared in controlled conditions.

Quantitative carcass data were collected on the Landrace pigs described previously which had been subjected to different humidity levels in combination with a warm (29°C.) temperature. The liveweight gain by these animals was relatively low, indicating that all the environments were adverse to growth (Table 18.7). When humidity levels were compared, the trends in the data indicated that on the basis of weight gain and backfat thickness the well-being of the animals in high humidity was equal to or greater than that of the low or fluctuating humidity groups.

TABLE 18.7: Effect of Environmental Humidity in a Warm (29° C.) Environment on Weight Gain and Quantitative Carcass Traits

Item	Environmental Humidity High (85%)	Alternating (85–30%)	Low (30%)	F[a]
Liveweight gain, kg/day	0.40	0.35	0.38	1.1
Backfat thickness, cm.	3.25	3.02	2.92	1.8
Carcass length, cm.	77.2	78.0	78.0	0.3
Area of *l. dorsi*, cm.²	23.0	24.1	24.6	0.6
Ham and loin yield, %[b]	37.5	38.2	37.3	2.0
Ham and loin edible portion yield, %[b,c]	28.4	29.4	27.6	2.7

Source: Addis *et al., J. Animal Sci.* 26:705, 1967.
[a] F.05 = 3.32; F.01 = 5.39.
[b] Percent carcass wt.
[c] Muscle plus maximum of 0.6 cm. of fat.

TABLE 18.8: Relationships Between Quantitative Carcass Traits and Muscle Color and Morphology of Animals Reared in a Warm (29° C.) Environment[a]

Carcass Trait	Group[b]	Color—Gross Morphology[c] L. dorsi	G. medius
Backfat thickness	H	0.32	—.74**
	L	0.27	0.19
	A	0.18	0.18
Carcass length	H	0.33	0.36
	L	0.01	0.71*
	A	0.06	0.27
Area of *l. dorsi*	H	—.08	—.36
	L	—.16	—.19
	A	—.23	0.12
Ham and loin yield[d]	H	—.05	0.55
	L	—.27	—.39
	A	—.22	—.25
Ham and loin edible portion yield[d,e]	H	0.13	0.60*
	L	0.09	0.11
	A	0.37	—.54

Source: Addis *et al., J. Animal Sci.* 26:705, 1967.
[a] Correlation coefficients, df = 9.
[b] Environmental humidity treatments; H = 85%; L = 30%; A = 85 and 30% alternating relative humidity.
[c] 1 = pale, soft, exudative; 3 = normal; 5 = dark, firm, dry (Forrest *et al.*, 1963).
[d] Percent carcass wt.
[e] Muscle plus maximum of 0.6 cm. of fat.
* P < .05.
** P < .01.

Several of the quantitative carcass measurements or percentages were associated with subjective and objective measures of muscle quality (Tables 18.8 and 18.9). Surprising, however, were the positive relationships between muscularity and muscle quality in the pigs reared in high humidity.

Since the above findings with Landrace pigs could have resulted from a specific breed-environment interaction, we were interested in the quantitative-qualitative relationship in other breeds. The carcasses of the Poland China and Hampshire pigs in the high humidity groups of the experiment described previously (Table 18.3) were evaluated. In this instance there were pronounced differences in growth among the groups (Table 18.10). The group with the least restriction of growth was that grown in constant low (18°C.) temperature.

The correlations between quantitative carcass traits and measures of quality were significant in certain of the groups (Table 18.11). Several significant relationships existed in the groups reared in high (29°C.) or alternating temperatures, but there were no significant correlations among pigs reared in low temperature. There may also have been treatment effects on the direction of the correlations in the high and alternating temperature groups but they were inconsistent.

These results may have important implications in the design of

TABLE 18.9: **Relationships Between Quantitative Carcass Traits and Processing Characteristics of Muscle of Animals Reared in a Warm (29° C.) Environment**[a]

Carcass Trait	Group[b]	Juice Loss[c]	Emulsifying Capacity[d]
Backfat thickness	H	0.19	—.49
	L	—.05	—.33
	A	—.15	—.02
Carcass length	H	—.42	0.31
	L	—.21	0.26
	A	—.35	0.13
Area of *l. dorsi*	H	—.27	0.22
	L	0.65*	0.04
	A	0.16	—.39
Ham and loin yield[e]	H	.39	0.61*
	L	0.18	—.46
	A	0.50	—.61*
Ham and loin edible portion yield[e,f]	H	—.46	—.53
	L	—.94	0.16
	A	0.19	.17

Source: Addis *et al.*, *J. Animal Sci.* 26:705, 1967.

[a] Correlation coefficients, df = 9.

[b] Environmental humidity treatments; H = 85%; L = 30%; A = 85 and 30% alternating relative humidity.

[c] Juice loss as percent total moisture after heating and centrifugation (*l. dorsi* muscle).

[d] Milliliters oil emulsified per gm. fat-free *biceps femoris* muscle.

[e] Percent carcass wt.

[f] Muscle plus maximum of 0.6 cm. of fat.

* P < .05.

TABLE 18.10: Effect of Temperature Acclimation at High (85%) Humidity on Carcass Weight and Composition

Item	Environmental Temperature High (29° C.)	Alternating[a] (29, 18° C.)	Low (18° C.)	F
Carcass wt., kg.	61.3	64.5	70.0	10.4**
Carcass length, cm.	74.2	74.7	75.2	1.0
Backfat thickness, cm.	3.38	3.25	3.35	0.7
Area of *l. dorsi*, cm.[2]	26.3	26.8	28.8	2.1
Ham and loin yield, %[b]	37.7	38.3	37.6	0.6
Ham and loin edible portion yield, %[b,c]	29.6	29.6	29.4	0.1

Source: Addis, Ph.D. Thesis, Purdue Univ.
[a] Three-day periods at each temperature.
[b] Percent carcass wt.
[c] Muscle plus maximum of 0.6 cm. of fat.
** $P < .01$ (All treatments were significantly different from each other).

TABLE 18.11: Effect of Temperature Acclimation at High (85%) Humidity on Relationship of Carcass Weight, Measurements, and Composition to Processing Qualities of Muscle[a]

Measurement	Treatment[b]	Juice Loss[c] H[e]	PC[f]	Fat Emulsified[d] H	PC
Carcass weight	H	0.00	0.35	0.10	0.57
	L	—.31	—.38	—.67	—.04
	A	0.31	—.82*	—.98**	—.79
Carcass length	H	—.71	—.63	—.40	—.37
	L	—.25	—.21	—.05	0.07
	A	0.52	—.53	—.89*	—.51
Backfat thickness	H	0.91*	0.76	0.43	0.59
	L	—.63	—.40	—.42	—.20
	A	—.82*	—.91*	0.28	—.05
Area of *l. dorsi*	H	—.21	0.13	—.29	0.07
	L	0.44	—.24	0.69	—.59
	A	0.71	—.59	—.90*	—.62
Ham and loin yield[g]	H	—.78	—.07	—.82*	—.45
	L	0.38	0.60	—.11	—.43
	A	0.16	0.14	—.25	0.18
Ham and loin edible portion[g,h]	H	—.80	—.10	—.75	—.51
	L	0.43	0.49	—.12	—.36
	A	0.45	—.68	—.23	—.64

Source: Addis, Ph.D. Thesis, Purdue Univ.
[a] Correlation coefficients, df = 4.
[b] Treatment groups: H = 29° C., L = 18° C., and A = 29, 18° C., alternating.
[c] Juice loss as percent total moisture after heating and centrifugation of *l. dorsi* muscle.
[d] Ml. fat emulsified/gm. fat-free *biceps femoris*.
[e] Hampshire.
[f] Poland China.
[g] Percent carcass weight.
[h] Muscle plus maximum of 0.6 cm. of fat.
** $P < .01$.
* $P < .05$.

swine production systems since they suggest that environmental factors influence muscle quality of muscular animals. In general, we believe that environmental conditions or production systems which restrict growth are partially responsible for the poor muscle quality observed in muscular pigs. It may be possible, in addition, to design systems in which the environment actually favors high muscle quality in muscular animals. The latter point in particular requires further study.

POSSIBLE MECHANISMS BY WHICH ENVIRONMENTAL CONDITIONS INFLUENCE DEVELOPMENT OF PORCINE MUSCLE

The data collected in our experiments with pigs in environmental chambers do not provide clear-cut explanations for the exact physiological adjustments which result in the described influences on the musculature. We may be justified in suggesting some plausible explanations, however, based on the easily observable responses and the indirect evidence available. Two possibilities are described which may be involved singly or jointly.

1. Certain environmental conditions hasten the degeneration of the adrenal cortex, the function of which is already marginal due to an inherited susceptibility to stress. Since many of the actions of the adrenal hormones are exerted directly or indirectly on the circulatory system (Schayer, 1964), it is likely that the buildup of heat in the bodies of stressed pigs may be traced to partial failure of the circulatory system. Environmental conditions such as fluctuating temperatures may therefore ultimately affect fluid balance and the efficiency of the microcirculation in the muscles.

2. Respiration rate, adjusted on the basis of the need to dissipate heat, influences the availability of oxygen to the inefficient circulatory system of a stress-susceptible animal. Support for this contention is available from the respiratory patterns observed throughout the growth periods of the Poland China pigs previously discussed. When pigs were exposed to a constant temperature and moderate humidity, their average respiration rate tended to increase with time as their growth and increased body size increased their need for heat dissipation (Fig. 18.7). This was the group of animals with normal rates of muscle pH decline and the lowest incidence of adrenal lipid invasions. The same relationship for respiration rate and body size was observed in the alternating temperature group reared in moderate humidity (Fig. 18.8). In this case the fluctuations in respiration rate caused by temperature fluctuations became more pronounced with time. However in the constant (Fig. 18.9) and alternating (Fig. 18.10) temperature groups reared in low humidity, the respiration rates were stable with time or actually decreased. It is possible, consequently, for conditions of environment to influence the frequency of respiration and presumably the volume of air intake over an extended period of time. This is consistent with the finding of Gold *et al.* (1964) that the environmental temperature influences the sensitivity of mice to the toxic effects of oxygen.

RESPIRATION RATE

REARING ENVIRONMENT : 27 C, 42 % REL. HUMIDITY

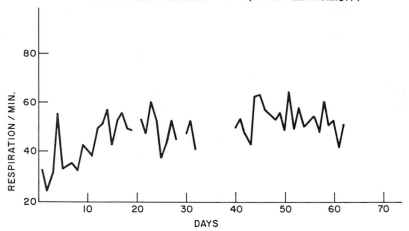

FIG. 18.7. Average respiration rate for pigs reared in constant temperature and moderate relative humidity. (From Thomas and Judge, in preparation)

RESPIRATION RATE

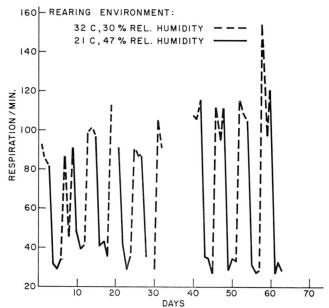

REARING ENVIRONMENT:

32 C, 30 % REL. HUMIDITY – – –
21 C, 47 % REL. HUMIDITY ——

FIG. 18.8. Average respiration rate for pigs reared in alternating temperatures and moderate relative humidity. (From Thomas and Judge, in preparation)

202

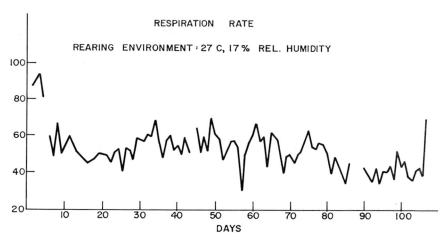

FIG. 18.9. Average respiration rate for pigs reared in constant temperature and low relative humidity. (From Thomas and Judge, in preparation)

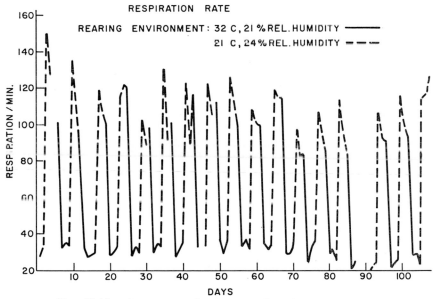

FIG. 18.10. Average respiration rate for pigs reared in alternating temperatures and low relative humidity. (From Thomas and Judge, in preparation)

Stimulation of respiration, if occurring as shown in Figures 18.7 and 18.8, might prevent the tendency for muscles to differentiate into the anaerobic type by providing a rich oxygen supply to the tissues. Alternatively, such an effect on respiration might enlarge the oxygen storage capacity by increased synthesis of myoglobin in muscles designed primarily for aerobic metabolism and would thus delay the time of development of anaerobic conditions postmortem.

REFERENCES

Addis, P. B. 1967. Acclimation during growth in relation to biochemical reactions and post-mortem properties of porcine muscle, Ph.D. Thesis, Purdue Univ., W. Lafayette, Ind.

Addis, P. B., Johnson, H. R., Heidenreich, C. J., Jones, H. W., and Judge, M. D. 1967. Effect of humidity level in a warm growing environment on porcine carcass composition and quality, *J. Animal Sci.* 26:705.

Addis, P. B., Johnson, H. R., Thomas, N. W., and Judge, M. D. 1967. Effect of temperature acclimation on porcine physiological responses to heat stress and associated properties of muscle, *J. Animal Sci.* 26:466.

Cassens, R. G., Judge, M. D., Sink, J. D., and Briskey, E. J. 1965. Porcine adrenocortical lipids in relation to striated muscle characteristics, *Proc. Soc. Exp. Biol. Med.* 120:854.

Clausen, H., and Nortoft Thomsen, R. 1956. Report on investigations with pigs. Nat. Res. Inst. on Animal Husbandry, Copenhagen, Rept. 288.

Gold, A. J., Silver, E. C., and Hance, H. E. 1964. Influence of environmental temperature on toxicity of oxygen, *Aerospace Med.* 35:563.

Henry, M., Romani, J. D., and Joubert, L. 1958. La myopathie exudative depigmentaire du porc maladie de l'adaption essai pathogenique et consequences pratiques, *Rev. Pathol. Gen. Physiol. Clin.* 696:355.

Howe, Jean M., Addis, P. B., Howard, R. D., and Judge, M. D. 1967. Induction of rapid post-mortem glycolysis in muscle and adrenocortical lipid in pigs reared in controlled environments, *J. Animal Sci.* 26:895.

Howe, Jean M., Thomas, N. W., Addis, P. B., and Judge, M. D. 1967. Effects of temperature acclimation in two humidity environments on porcine muscle properties, *J. Food Sci.* (submitted).

Judge, M. D., Briskey, E. J., and Meyer, R. K. 1966. Endocrine related postmortem changes in porcine muscle, *Nature* 212:287.

Kadlec, J. E., Morris, W. H. M., Bache, D., Crawford, R., Jones, H., Pickett, R., Judge, M. D., Dale, A. C., Peart, R. M., Friday, W. H., Haelterman, E. O., and Boehm, P. N. 1966. Comparison of swine growing-finishing building systems, Purdue Univ. Agr. Exp. Sta. Res. Bull. 816.

Ludvigsen, J. 1957. On the hormonal regulation of vasomotor reactions during exercise with special reference to the action of adrenal cortical steroids, *Acta Endocrinol.* 26:406.

————. 1960. Maladaption syndromes in pigs, Proc. 2nd Intern. Ann. Nutr. Conf., Madrid, Spain.

Schayer, R. W. 1964. A unified theory of glucocorticoid action, *Perspectives Biol. Med.* 8:71.

Thomas, N. W., Addis, P. B., Johnson, H. R., Howard, R. D., and Judge, M. D. 1966. Effects of environmental temperature and humidity during growth on muscle properties of two porcine breeds, *J. Food Sci.* 31:309.

Thomas, N. W., and Judge, M. D. Effect of growing environment on the myo-globin content of porcine skeletal muscle. In preparation.

Topel, D. G., and Merkel, R. A. 1967. Effect of exogenous prednisolone and methylprednisolone upon plasma 17-hydroxycortico-steroid levels and some porcine muscle characteristics, *J. Animal Sci.* 26:1017.

19

Association of the Stress Syndrome to Sudden Death Losses and Postmortem Characteristics

E. J. BICKNELL

IN RECENT YEARS an increase of unexplained deaths in market-sized swine has been observed in Iowa. An investigation was initiated by workers at Iowa State University to study the possible correlation of stress to death and certain blood and skeletal muscle changes.

These deaths which occur in pigs from 20 kg. to market weight (85–105 kg.) usually occur without warning. However, in most cases there is a history indicating that the animals have recently sustained a stressing experience. We have called this disease Porcine Stress Syndrome (PSS). Sudden deaths have been observed in susceptible swine when they were removed from confinement housing and transported to new quarters. As a result of PSS, dead hogs may frequently be found in trucks following transportation from farm to market. Many deaths from this condition eventuate following a sudden rise in atmospheric temperature or a rapid change from a cold to a warm environment. Probably one of the most common circumstances for stimulating PSS is fighting. Whenever strange animals are mixed there is a struggle to establish the social order of the pen. Susceptible hogs have died after two minutes from this type of stress. A survey made by Christian *et al.* (1967) revealed that approximately 33 percent of the purebred swine breeders in Iowa have lost pigs under stressing conditions.

German workers have described a disease in swine that they have termed *Herztod* which has many characteristics similar to PSS. *Herztod* is described as a syncope with sudden death and myocardial involvement. Sudden death in the Danish Landrace hog was reported by Ludvigsen

(1954) in which losses were associated with degeneration of skeletal muscle. This muscular degeneration was defined as an alteration of skeletal muscle to a grayish color resembling that of chicken muscle. This musculature was very juicy, had a sour odor, and the muscle bundles separated easily. A definite diagnosis of the disease in the live pig was impossible; however, in the suspects a higher body temperature, slight cyanosis, and muscular tremors were reported. Pigs with these signs could not withstand even minor stress.

These same signs have been observed in pigs studied by Topel *et al.* (1968). In many cases, pigs that have died suddenly manifested signs of excitability and tail tremors. Necropsy examination performed in most cases an hour or less after death revealed congestion of the parenchymatous organs. The heart had stopped in systole, as there was almost no lumen in the left ventricle. In some cases there were pale streaks in the musculature of the left ventricle. The *longissimus dorsi* (Fig. 19.1), *gluteus medius,* and *semimembranosus* muscles were very pale and edematous (watery); other muscle groups retained the normal color, thus resulting in a two-toned appearance. The *longissimus dorsi* muscle in PSS hogs can be easily separated from the surrounding tissues as compared to normal hogs.

Histopathologic examination of tissues from PSS hogs has failed to demonstrate any consistent, significant lesions. To date, only light microscopy has been used in the study at Iowa State. It is hoped that electron microscopy will be employed especially in the examination of skeletal muscle of PSS hogs.

Monetary losses in millions of dollars to the meat packing industry due to pale watery porcine muscle have been reported by Briskey (1964). It is believed that the animals reported in this chapter possess these same characteristics. The hogs observed in this work were very muscular in type and possessed very small backfat thickness. It has been reported by

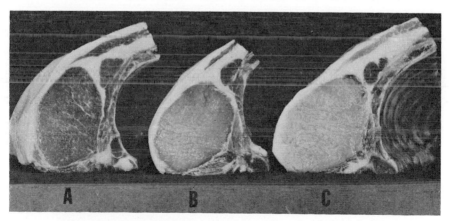

FIG. 19.1. Variability in porcine *l. dorsi* muscle color and firmness characteristics. A. Desirable, B. Intermediate, C. Undesirable PSS.

Topel *et al.* (1967) that the relationship between the area of the *longissimus dorsi* muscle and pale watery characteristics is significantly correlated. Animals which apparently have died of this condition in the field are from outstanding swine producers who have concentrated their efforts in producing pigs with rapid growth rates, feed efficiency, and superior muscling. It should be pointed out that many outstanding pigs which possess these same attributes do not have the PSS characteristics. A selection program for these economic traits can still be carried out, but caution should be taken when breeders start to encounter sudden deaths.

REFERENCES:

Christian, L. L., Bicknell, E. J., Preston, K. S., and Topel, D. G. 1967. Incidence of sudden deaths in swine. Unpublished data.

Ludvigsen, J. 1954. Undersgelser over den sakaldte "muskeldegeneration" hos svin I. 272. beretning fra forsøgelaboratoriet. København.

Topel, D. G., Bicknell, E. J., Preston, K. S., Christian, L. L., and Matsushima, C. Y. 1968. Sudden death in swine and its relationship to blood and muscle changes (Preliminary report), *Modern Veterinary Practice* (Submitted).

Topel, D. G., Merkel, R. A., and Wismer-Pedersen, J. 1967. Relationship of plasma 17-hydroxycorticosteroid levels to some physical and biochemical properties of porcine muscle, *J. Animal Sci.* 26:311–15.

PART SEVEN

Labor Problems

20

Labor Situations Facing the Producer

PAUL R. ROBBINS

IF THE FARM LABOR FORCE should decrease as much in absolute amount in the next 15 years as it has in the past 15, there would be no farm labor force by the early 1980's.

U.S. farm employment in May, 1967, totaled 5.3 million, down 4 percent from a year earlier and down more than 1.5 million workers or almost 25 percent from the 1961–65 average.

Decline in total farm labor force is reflected in a decline in both family labor and hired labor. The decline in the U.S. hired farm labor force in recent years has averaged about the same as decline in the total farm labor force.

Percentage decrease in the labor force of the Corn Belt in recent years has been about in line with national trends. In the first half of 1967 the total farm labor force of Indiana, Illinois, and Iowa was 495,000, down 5 percent from a year earlier. The hired labor force in these three states during the past year declined about 4 percent. In the next few years we are likely to see a slightly more rapid decline in operator and family labor than in hired labor.

Why the rapid decline in the farm labor force in the Corn Belt? Many factors could be listed, but the most important one without question is the abundance of good off-farm employment opportunities. Off-farm employers have been bidding strongly for farm workers in recent years. Off-farm wage rates have been so high that many farm operators have been unwilling or unable to meet the competition in bidding for labor.

Table 20.1 indicates an average weekly farm labor wage only about 40 percent as high as contract construction and about 50 percent as high as the average for all manufacturing workers.

During the past 25 years the spread in earnings between farm workers and industrial workers has widened considerably (Table 20.2).

Average figures do not tell the whole story. Average earnings to

TABLE 20.1:   Average Earnings of Production Workers in United States, 1967

Industry	Salary	
	Nearest dollars per week	Dollars per hour
Contract construction	143	3.99
Manufacturing (av. for all)	111	2.78
Motor freight transportation	133	3.20
Wholesale trade	114	2.82
Retail trade	69	1.97
Hired farm workers (without room and board)	59	1.34

farm laborers include stoop labor and other farm jobs that require little training or skill. Thus many good hog producers offering wages considerably higher than the averages shown in Tables 20.1 and 20.2 are still having difficulty in getting and keeping good employees.

Many farmers realizing the keen competition for labor have been not only pushing up wage rates but also improving working conditions, updating fringe benefits, etc. in an effort to attract and hold competent employees. All indications point to a continued very tight farm labor situation in the foreseeable future. There will be a need for even greater efforts on the part of farm operators if they are to attract and hold the caliber of labor needed.

SWINE PRODUCERS AND LABOR COSTS

Perhaps the first question a swine producer should answer regarding labor is whether or not he can justify hiring it. Certainly many swine growers cannot justify an additional full-time employee because their efficiencies are too low or their volume is too small to make additional labor profitable. Table 20.3 indicates a need to gross an additional $20,000 to $35,000 or to farrow and raise an additional 500 to 800 market hogs, depending largely on efficiency level, in order to have a residual of $6,000 to labor and management. Labor and management return in Table 20.3 is a residual to operator's and family labor and management as well as hired labor. If efficiencies increase or decrease as more hogs are raised, the relation of labor and management income to gross income would change.

TABLE 20.2:   Farm Wages as a Percent of Industrial Wages and Average Hourly Wage Rates in the U.S.

Year	Farm Wages as Percent of Industrial Wages	Farm Workers (dollars)	Industrial Workers (dollars)	Difference (dollars)
1950	39	.56	1.44	.88
1960	36	.82	2.26	1.44
1965	36	.95	2.61	1.66
1966	38	1.03	2.69	1.66

Source: *The Farm Cost Situation 1967 Outlook Issue,* USDA.

TABLE 20.3: **Additional Gross Income Needed To Pay a $6,000 per Year Employee on a Large Indiana Hog Farm, 1963–66**

Large Hog Farms (1100–1500 hogs raised annually)	Gross Income (dollars)	Labor and Management Return (dollars)	Percent of Gross That Is Return to Labor and Management	Gross Needed To Return $6,000 to Labor and Management (dollars)
Avg. all farms	87,500	21,700	25	24,000
More profitable half	104,000	31,000	30	20,000
Less profitable half	71,000	11,700	17	35,000

Source: Indiana Farm Business Summaries

FILLING LABOR NEEDS

Following are various alternatives being pursued by good swine producers in an effort to meet needed labor requirements.

1. *Substitution of capital for labor* has been going on for many years but still offers real opportunities on many farms. As labor costs continue to rise, opportunities for substituting additional capital for labor will be presented. Technology is currently available in swine housing and materials handling which permits one man to at least double pork production without increasing the labor input. Many top hog farmers have already converted to the high capital-low labor setups. These labor-saving facilities necessitate large capital investments, they have few alternative uses, obsolescence will likely be quite high, and a high level of management is required. However, we are likely to see a fairly rapid shift in hog production to large, specialized, highly mechanized, and automated setups. Good up-to-date technical information on capital-labor

TABLE 20.4: **Direct Labor and Capital Requirements per Market Hog Produced Under Low Capital-High Labor and High Capital-Low Labor Hog Production Systems[a]**

	Investment per Pig Capacity (dollars)		Hours of Direct Labor per Pig	
	High capital	Low capital	High labor	Low labor
Farrowing:[b]				
Crates, slotted floors, fed inside	49	. . .	. . .	.28
Outside individual houses	. . .	20	17	
Nursery:				
Total slats	29	. . .	. . .	.11
Portable houses	. . .	23	.43	. . .
Finishing:				
Enclosed slotted floors	46	. . .	. . .	.55
Pasture—portable houses	. . .	16	.90	. . .
Totals	124	64	1.80	.94

[a] Based on research being conducted at Purdue University and reported in Purdue Research Bulletin No. 816 and Research Progress Report No. 267.

[b] Assumes 8 pigs weaned per litter.

substitutions in swine production is badly needed to guide farmers in making these investments, because capital is certainly not without cost.

2. *The purchase of labor as a package along with other inputs* will help meet the tight labor problem. Custom application of fertilizers, custom harvesting, off-farm processing of feeds, and bulk delivery of feeds to the feeders are examples of labor purchases along with the purchase of a product or the services of machinery and equipment. Such labor purchases will permit greater output with a fixed farm labor supply and may help greatly in meeting peak labor requirements.

3. *The hiring of part-time labor* may offer real possibilities, especially near industrial areas. There are many nonfarm workers with farm backgrounds; some have had considerable experience with machinery and equipment. What incentive would be required to induce more of these people to work part-time on the farm? A relatively few days of very high cost hired labor to meet peak requirements is often less costly than a full-time employee who isn't really needed full time.

Another possibility for hiring part-time help would be the sharing of a hired employee by two or more farmers.

ATTRACTING AND KEEPING FULL-TIME EMPLOYEES

The rapid decline in the hired farm labor force would indicate that nonfarm competition is winning the race for prospective employees.

What are some of the things that swine producers might do to improve their chances of getting and keeping productive, dependable, full-time employees?

First and foremost, they must be willing to pay a competitive wage. Farm wage rates must be competitive with nonfarm opportunities. If the wage package offered by the farmer is not competitive with other job opportunities, the more capable, aggressive workers will move to nonfarm opportunities, leaving the marginal workers for the farm labor force. The swine production industry in the years ahead will be big business with big investments and opportunities for big profits and big losses. Hiring poorly qualified labor to put into these complex businesses is a pretty sure way of incurring big losses. The caliber of labor required to look after a large modern automatic hog facility is quite different from the scoop-shovel labor used in hog production under less modern systems. Thus the modern swine producer in the future must be willing and able to attract and keep high-caliber employees.

The cash wage package may be more attractive to a prospective employee if it is on an hourly rather than a weekly or monthly basis. Most nonfarm employers hire labor on a basic hourly wage for a specified number of hours per week. There is usually a bonus of $1\frac{1}{2}$ to 2 times the basic rate for any overtime. Employees usually do not resent working overtime if they are receiving extra compensation. Employees do resent long hours, uncertain quitting time, no regular days off—especially when the extra effort is not rewarded with overtime pay.

Wages and hours should be thoroughly discussed and agreed upon. Most nonfarm jobs operate on a basic eight-hour day and 40-hour week.

Since the farm employee usually does not have to commute to and from his job, there is some justification for considering a longer basic work week (perhaps 45 hours) on the farm.

Fringe benefits are an important part of the pay for most farm employees. The value of fringe benefits was estimated at $826 per farm employee on about 150 Indiana farms in 1964. Had the employees bought all of these items at full retail prices, the values would have been even higher. Many farm employees tend to compare farm wages with factory wages and overlook the value of extras furnished on the farm. By some means the value of perquisites furnished the employee should be called to his attention occasionally. Some employers itemize the value of the perquisites and attach it to the paycheck from time to time. Other farm operators furnish no houses or other extras, preferring to give the hired man his total pay in cash. This enables the hired man readily to compare his income with nonfarm opportunities. It allows him also to choose his home, perhaps even own it, and permits him to buy food items most desired by his family. However, it is often desirable to have the hired man live on the farm. Since there is often housing available on the farm, the hired man may get a real bargain by being furnished a house and farm produce. Also there may be tax savings to the hired man if part of his pay is in the form of housing and other extras provided on the farm.

In updating fringe benefits, farmers should consider dropping the extras sometimes not really desired by employees, such as the privilege of keeping a milk cow or chickens. Some new fringe benefits may need to be added. For example, the cost of hospital-medical insurance for an employee and his family would be less than $30 per month.[1] This is an item worthy of consideration in the wage agreement. Whether it is paid entirely by the employer or shared jointly is an item for bargaining.

Many nonfarm employers provide disability income insurance. This would provide for a minimum monthly income in case of disability. The estimated cost of such a policy would be in the range of $5 to $10 per month.[2]

Many nonfarm employers are required by bargaining associations of employees to contribute to retirement income and life insurance programs.

As was true for items furnished by the farm, the value of other fringe benefits should frequently be called to the employee's attention.

Good labor relations mean many things to many people. Most farmers who employ a substantial amount of hired help will likely agree that *people* are one of their big problems—and often the biggest problem. Many farmers have made much more rapid progress in learning how to increase corn yields, wean more pigs per litter, etc. than they have made in learning how to deal with hired help.

---

[1] L. H. Brown, "Making Farm Labor Competitive," Special Paper #1, Rural Manpower Center, Michigan State University.
[2] *Ibid.*

Good labor relations among other things mean:

1. Mutual respect, trust, and loyalty.

2. A cooperative, friendly attitude and ability to get along with others.

3. Knowing the jobs to be done and how to supervise the hired man in doing them.

4. Planning ahead so as to reduce hasty decisions and confusion.

5. Giving orders in a clear concise manner so the employee knows what is expected of him.

6. Praise and expression of gratitude for a job well done.

7. Reviewing written agreements from time to time.

8. Upgrading the employee's image. He is not a hired hand or hired man; he is at least an employee, or perhaps, a swine herdsman, assistant manager, swine technician, or partner.

INCENTIVE PLANS

Four major types of incentive plans are in operation on Corn Belt farms.

1. Plan based on tenure. Employee receives an additional $5 to $20 per week if he stays on the job a stipulated time. The main advantage of this plan is its simplicity. The employee knows exactly what must be done to receive the extra payment. However, this plan may not stimulate the employee to take added responsibility or put forth added effort stimulated by some other plans.

2. Physical production plan such as:

    a. 10–25 cents per feeder pig bought and fed out.

    b. 25 cents–$1.00 per pig weaned.

    c. $1.00–3.00 per pig weaned above eight in a litter.

    d. $2.00–5.00 per market hog sold above seven per litter.

Major advantages of physical production plans are: easy to understand, easy to compute payments, payments are easily linked to time of performance (when pigs are weaned, market hogs sold, etc.).

Major disadvantages are: costs are largely disregarded and unfortunate circumstances often eliminate payments.

3. Plan based on a percent of gross income, either from one enterprise or total farm, such as:

    a. 0.5–1 percent of hog sales, less cost of feeder pigs.

    b. 10 percent of feeder pig sales above $90 per litter.

    c. 1–4 percent of gross income from hogs, including inventory changes.

Plans based on a percent of gross income exhibit about the same advantages and disadvantages as do plans based on physical production.

4. Plan based on percent of net income such as:

    a. 2–10 percent of taxable income as computed for income tax purposes.

The major advantage of net income plans is that costs are taken into consideration. Thus a percent of net income is the most inclusive of any of the plans.

Major disadvantages are: the plan may be difficult to understand, payments may be difficult to compute, the farm operator may not want his employee to know this much about his earnings, the plan can lead to conflict of interest.

The success of an incentive plan is difficult to predict. Personalities must be congenial and there must be mutual respect. Many incentive plans have failed because they violated important management principles. Under proper conditions, incentive plans have worked and are currently working in a satisfactory manner.

Successful incentive plans do not "just happen"—they result from careful planning and study. It is extremely important that the plan be well understood by both parties. The hired man must be able to understand what is expected of him in order to receive payment. Putting the plan in writing is important. However, even the most carefully devised plan does not guarantee that the hired man will work harder or take more responsibility, but many hired men will put forth greater effort if proper incentives are offered.

Incentive payment plans should be in addition to and not in place of such important things as good wages, good labor relations, adequate housing, good buildings and equipment to work with, and vacation and time off.

Fairly small payments made at frequent intervals or as soon as a particular job is accomplished are probably more effective in stimulating incentive than larger payments made at the end of the year.

The hired man should be given considerable responsibility in those enterprises from which he is to receive incentive payment. Only by assuming responsibility does he really have an opportunity to influence the size of the payment. On the other hand, the operator should put sufficient safeguards into the agreement to protect himself against uneconomical practices that might arise.

Incentive plans based on physical production or a percentage of gross income are fairly widely used, adapted to a wide range of conditions, easily understood, and usually require only limited record keeping. But these types of plans are most susceptible to the stimulation of uneconomical practices.

Payment plans based on a percentage of net income should be very carefully scrutinized before being put to use. Net income is difficult to define, complete records are required, the hired man must know about one's financial affairs, and the making of management decisions may be hampered. However, with proper safeguards and adequate record keeping, a percent of net can be a very good plan—especially with a top-notch, aggressive employee.

The plan based on tenure may not stimulate the employee to take the added responsibility or put forth the extra effort desired, but it has advantages and avoids many of the disadvantages that other plans present. Until a farmer is fairly certain of the employee's capabilities, ambitions, character, etc., a simple plan is probably advisable. After the employee has been on the job for a sufficient period to demonstrate his value to the business, a more complicated and involved plan may be considered.

Multiple management farms are likely to increase in the years ahead. Farm businesses are rapidly becoming so large, capital investments so high, and managerial requirements so great that many of the top farms now have multiple management and often multiple ownership. Farming at best is a risky business, but when the decision making for a highly specialized, modern setup of a quarter-million-dollar investment depends entirely on the health and well-being of one individual, it is indeed a risky business. As farms continue to get larger and more complex, multiple management farms are almost sure to increase. Many of the multiple management farms are actually composed of a father and one or more sons or sons-in-law, or perhaps two or more brothers. However, a partnership arrangement with a good neighbor boy or some other well-qualified individual may offer real possibilities in providing needed labor and management. Before going into such an agreement one would want to carefully choose his partner, understand the hazards of partnerships, and use good legal counsel to avoid pitfalls.

A major concept in most partnership agreements is the sharing of net farm income between the partners on the basis of labor, management, and capital contributed by each partner. Table 20.5 illustrates a method for dividing net farm income on large Indiana hog farms cooperating in Purdue's record analysis program during the 1963–66 period. In this

TABLE 20.5: **Division of Net Income Between Partner A and Partner B Where Partner B Furnishes Only His Labor and Management, Indiana Hog Farms, 1963–66**

	Large Hog Farms	
	More profitable half	Less profitable half
Tillable acres	369	346
Hogs raised	1,468	1,053
Total investment	$247,000	$224,900
Months of labor	26	25
Annual Contributions of Partner A		
Real estate investment @ 5%	$ 8,495	$ 8,265
Operating capital invested @ 6%	$ 4,625	$ 3,575
Labor and Management @ $500/mo[a]	$ 7,000	$ 6,500
% of total capital, labor & mgt.	77	75
Annual Contributions of Partner B		
12 months of labor & mgt. @ $500/mo	$ 6,000	$ 6,000
% of total capital, labor & mgt.	23	25
Net farm income	$ 38,200	$ 18,400
Partner A's share of net income	$ 29,414	$ 13,800
Partner B's share of net income	$ 8,786	$ 4,600

Source: Indiana Farm Account Summaries.

[a] Partner A furnishes all needed labor on the farm except the 12 months provided by Partner B.

example it is assumed that Partner B furnishes 12 months of labor and contributes management in proportion to labor inputs. Partner A furnishes all other inputs.

Other variations of this agreement might be:

1. Partner A might assume the role of a landlord, or the land might be rented from a third party. Partners A and B would then share only the renters' net income on the basis of labor, management, and capital contributions of the joint renters.

2. Partner B might contribute capital in any amount and would be compensated at the agreed-upon rate of interest as was true for Partner A.

3. The farm business might be incorporated and Partner B given an opportunity to buy stock in the business. Partners A and B might rent the farm from the corporation and operate as joint renters, or the corporation might simply hire both A and B to manage and operate the business.

21

Labor Relations Problems in the Meat Packing Industry*

HAROLD W. DAVEY

FEW INDUSTRIES illustrate better the range and diversity of union-management relationships than does the meat packing industry. If one elects to accentuate the positive, the industry affords some of the best examples of durable, constructive collective bargaining relationships that can be found in the U.S. economy. If one chooses to stress the negative, the packing industry can still come up with some graphic examples of labor relations at its worst. Some illuminating examples of progress from bitter conflict to a contemporary pattern of mutually satisfactory accommodation can also be noted.

UNION-MANAGEMENT RELATIONS TODAY

The packing industry has something for everyone. Yet in retrospect there can be little doubt that labor relations in meat packing generally have become more stable, constructive, and peaceful than was the case before and immediately following World War II.

Labor relations patterns are still in an evolutionary state in response to the force of technological change, decentralization and deconcentration of the industry, and the balance of forces between the two major unions representing workers in the industry.

This chapter reflects mainly the perspective of one who has had considerable experience since 1950 as a grievance arbitrator in the industry.[1] Thus the emphasis is more on labor relations problems than on the economics of collective bargaining as such. However, as a labor

---

* This chapter also appeared as "Present and Future Labor Relations Problems in the Meat Packing Industry," *Labor Law Journal*, Dec. 1967, 18:739–51.

[1] The writer has served as arbitrator on a considerable number of cases involving Rath and UPWA. Other companies with UPWA contracts under which he has served as arbitrator include Hormel, Needham, and Glaser. The only Amalgamated cases he has arbitrated were under contracts with Safeway Stores, Inc. He has also arbitrated cases involving independent unions holding contracts with Farm Best and Iowa Beef Packers, Inc.

economist I would be remiss if I failed to note some economic aspects of the industry that have clearly conditioned the thinking of both management and union representatives in their approach to the bargaining table.

In observing the variety of union-management relationships in the industry, and keeping in mind that the audience for this chapter is management-oriented, I am choosing as a theme a dictum enunciated many years ago by the late Clinton Golden and Harold Ruttenberg.[2] Writing as union leaders, these two steelworker officials generalized that management gets the type of union it deserves. As a detached observer, I am tempted to add the qualifying phrase "in the long run." One can always think of specific cases where their formula did not work out in the short run. However, I have satisfied myself empirically that Golden and Ruttenberg are pretty close to the mark.

MANAGEMENT ATTITUDES LARGELY DETERMINE UNION RESPONSES

When management chooses to fight against the right of workers to form and join unions, and when management refuses to bargain collectively in good faith, the invariable consequence is a bitter and highly aggressive union response. The carryover effects sometimes linger for years after management has grudgingly decided to change its spots and come to accept the union as an integral part of the industrial relations framework.

On the other hand, where management has accepted the union as exclusive bargaining agent for its production and maintenance employees, has bargained in good faith to an ageement, and has then administered the resultant contract in terms of its intent, spirit, and letter, the approach has generally produced an affirmative and constructive response from the union in question. If the union leaders and members do not feel threatened by management, if they believe that management understands the import of Father Purcell's research findings on dual loyalty,[3] and if they are convinced that management intends to live with the contractual relationship and make it work, the response will usually be a positive one. The union leadership that emerges will be of a more stable and responsible nature.

SOME SPECIFIC ILLUSTRATIONS

The basic validity of these generalizations can be illustrated in the history of the meat packing industry as well as in many other industries The two major unions involved are the constants and management is

---

[2] Clinton S. Golden and Harold J. Ruttenberg, *The Dynamics of Industrial Democracy*, New York: Harper & Brothers, 1942.

[3] Father Purcell has demonstrated convincingly in two empirical studies, based on extensive interviews with packinghouse employees, that the worker carries a dual allegiance—to the company for which he works and to the union of which he is a member. See Theodore V. Purcell, *The Worker Speaks His Mind*, Cambridge, Mass.: Harvard University Press, 1953; and *Blue Collar Man*, Cambridge, Mass.: Harvard University Press, 1960. Management representatives in any industry can benefit greatly from the insights into the worker's mind revealed in Father Purcell's studies.

the determining variable. The United Packinghouse, Food, and Allied Workers of America (hereafter referred to as UPWA) and the Amalgamated Meat Cutters and Butcher Workmen of North America (hereafter referred to as the Amalgamated) can be shown to have shaped and changed their goals and strategies in accordance with the type of management they encountered. The illustrations here are from UPWA relationships, since the writer's firsthand knowledge of this union is more extensive.

Not too many years ago Armour, Swift, and Wilson had elected to fight the UPWA. In so doing they encountered a high degree of leadership and rank-and-file militancy. The continuous conflict situation built up a tremendous reservoir of worker suspicion as to management motivations and intentions that carried over long after basic changes in management thinking had occurred. Gradually, however, relationships began to improve until we arrive at 1967 with the new Armour contract being successfully and peacefully negotiated jointly with UPWA and the Amalgamated some months ahead of the expiration deadline and setting a pattern for similar peaceful accommodation elsewhere in the industry.

The 1967 Armour contract provides for a continuation of the highly publicized Automation Fund arrangement first instituted in 1959. Whatever the operational "bugs" may have been over the years since the Automation Fund and committee were first conceived,[4] the fact remains that it constitutes a responsible joint effort on the part of management and union leadership to face up to the industry's most serious problem from an employee standpoint, i.e., how to maintain job security without impeding technological advances and locational shifts as the industry deconcentrates and as firms decentralize their operations.

The darker side of the coin is seen in the recent efforts of some independent packers to thwart unionization by methods reminiscent of the unreconstructed 1930's. The importation of strikebreakers from California and the refusal to bargain in good faith on the part of Western Iowa Pork Company in Harlan, Iowa, produced a regrettably violent reaction on the part of UPWA members in a normally peaceful Iowa community. A potentially explosive strike situation at Fort Dodge, Iowa, in 1966, involving Iowa Beef Packers and UPWA, was cooled down only by the strong mediation of Governor Harold E. Hughes.[5]

In short, the industry in some sectors is still not far removed from the open labor warfare stage that used to be the norm in the early

---

[4] A readable account, based on extensive personal interviews, of the early trials and tribulations of the Armour Automation Committee will be found in James J. Healy, ed., *Creative Collective Bargaining*, Englewood Cliffs, N.J.: Prentice-Hall, Inc., 1965, pp. 137–65.

[5] Both the Harlan and Fort Dodge situations are described in some detail in a recent study by Donald Eugene Whistler. See his *The Involvement of Governor Harold E. Hughes in Three Labor Disputes*, unpublished M.S. thesis, Iowa State University, Ames, 1967.

years of UPWA.[6] Fortunately the 1967 evidence appears to be generally encouraging from the standpoint of one who firmly believes that management-union conflict is sometimes necessary but not inevitable. It has already been demonstrated in meat packing as well as in many other industries that collective bargaining remains a viable process for determining the terms and conditions of employment.[7] It has been further demonstrated that mutually satisfactory agreements can be reached without resorting to economic force either at contract expiration time or in the form of wildcat strikes during the life of existing contracts.

In contrasting the development of stable bargaining relationships with those that remain in a state of continuous conflict, the thesis is maintained here that the crucial variable is management's posture, policies, and goals in particular situations. This is the kind of hypothesis that is hard to test or prove in the usual sense. However, it should provide a stimulating analytical framework for examining current and future labor relations problems in the meat packing industry.

UNIONS IN MEAT PACKING INDUSTRY

The latest available membership figures from the Bureau of Labor Statistics show the UPWA reporting 135,000 members and the Amalgamated 353,059.[8] No membership data are available for the National Brotherhood of Packinghouse and Dairy Workers, an independent labor organization not affiliated with the AFL-CIO. An informal estimate indicates that the Brotherhood currently has somewhere between five and six thousand members.[9]

The Amalgamated's jurisdictional range is much more extensive than that of UPWA. The latter's membership is concentrated in the major packing plants and some of the principal independents. The Amalgamated does not have great membership strength in meat packing as such, but the union has continued to grow in recent years by virtue of

---

[6] The writer served as chairman of a three-man arbitration board in a case involving Needham Packing Company of Sioux City and UPWA. The initial dispute derived from the firing of a union steward for shutting down the line and the subsequent wildcat walkout of all bargaining unit employees. The case raises a number of legal questions. Space and propriety preclude commenting here on the merits. However, the text of the arbitration board's decision can be read with profit and interest as a case history of a union-management relations conflict situation. See *In re Needham Packing Co., Inc., and Local No. 721, UPWA,* Vol. 44, *Labor Arbitration Reports,* 1057–1101, Washington, D.C.: The Bureau of National Affairs, Inc., 1966. The events involved in the Needham case occurred in 1961.

[7] For evidence supporting this generalization see Harold W. Davey, "The Continuing Viability of Collective Bargaining," *Labor Law Journal,* Feb., 1965, 16:111–22. See also an excellent paper by Frederick Harbison, entitled "Collective Bargaining in Perspective," in John H. G. Crispo, ed., *Industrial Relations: Challenges and Responses,* Toronto, Canada: University of Toronto Press, 1966, pp. 60–72.

[8] *1965 Directory of National and International Labor Unions in the United States,* BLS Bull. No. 1493, U.S. Department of Labor, Washington, D.C.

[9] The Brotherhood's president, Don Mahon of Des Moines, Iowa, was present as a conferee during the delivery of this paper. Mr. Mahon would neither confirm nor deny the accuracy of the membership estimate given, indicating that membership figures were available only to dues-paying members of his organization.

extensive organizational activity.[10] As far back as 1936 the Amalgamated, whose hard-core strength has always been with the retail meat cutters, decided to organize poultry, egg, and creamery workers as well as wholesale and retail fish workers.[11] In 1940 the Amalgamated decided to unionize sheep shearers and stockyard employees and spread out also to include canneries, fishing and oystering, and a miscellany of food processing firms. In some of these cases the Amalgamated ran into AFL opposition to its jurisdictional expansionism, but it has continued to grow in the retail food field and a variety of others.

The UPWA has not been able to diversify its membership base appreciably, although it has opened the door to doing so by changing its name to embrace "food and allied workers." From the beginning UPWA has been essentially a packinghouse organization. Over the thirty years of its life, UPWA generally has had all it could do to organize and maintain its collective bargaining relationships in the packing industry. It has had little money, time, or energy for new organizational conquests.

Relationships between UPWA and the Amalgamated have run the gamut from bitter hostility and mutual suspicion to highly effective joint bargaining efforts with the major packers. The merger negotiations that nearly succeeded and the reasons for their last-minute failure constitute a story in themselves.[12] In the years since the organic merger failed to materialize the two unions have continued to recognize the need for functional cooperation in bargaining and on other matters. The 1967 Armour pact carries on each page of the negotiated modifications and additions to the 1964–67 contract the initials of both Ralph Helstein, president of UPWA, and Patrick E. Gorman, long-time leader of the Amalgamated.

The present analysis is limited to meat packing as such and thus more concerned with UPWA than the Amalgamated. The Amalgamated is much the stronger of the two unions both financially and in membership. It has continued to grow and to expand in the retail and food processing fields. The UPWA, on the other hand, has had to undergo the traumatic experience of adaptation to fundamental changes in the technology, structure, and location of the packing industry which is UPWA's organizational base.

From the standpoint of the union as an institution, the deconcentration and decentralization of the meat packing industry have posed serious problems of a financial and organizational nature. The UPWA started out as one of the CIO's brand new organization ventures, the Packing-

[10] In recent years several excellent biographies of American unions have appeared. One of these deals with the Amalgamated. See David Brody, *The Butcher Workmen: A Study of Unionization,* Cambridge, Mass.: Harvard University Press, 1964. Regrettably, no scholar has yet attempted a biography of UPWA.

[11] *Ibid.,* p. 247.

[12] For an informative and illuminating account of the history of efforts at organic merger and the reasons for their failure, see Joel Seidman, "Unity in Meat Packing: Problems and Prospects," in Harold W. Davey, Howard S. Kaltenborn and Stanley H. Ruttenberg, eds., *New Dimensions in Collective Bargaining,* New York: Harper & Row, 1959, pp. 29–43.

house Workers Organizing Committee (PWOC). In the 1930's the new union could operate effectively with a high degree of centralization from Chicago as its base. Chicago still fitted Carl Sandburg's graphic phrase, "hog butcher to the world," although the deconcentration and decentralization process had already begun.

Technology and cost considerations have now changed the entire face of the industry. Serious labor relations problems are thus posed both for management and UPWA. The dramatic changes in the structure and composition of the industry can be illustrated in many ways. The story is a familiar one and therefore will be summarily treated here.

A few notes from a recent study by Richard J. Arnould should suffice to underscore the structural and locational changes that have led to worker problems of technological displacement and job security.[13]

Arnould cites the greatly increased use of truck transportation and plant technology changes as principal factors causing deconcentration of the industry. His study indicates that rail shipments in 1935 accounted for 75 percent of all shipments. This percentage had declined to 25 percent by 1958. Presumably the percentage of rail shipments has continued to decline since 1958.

Developments in refrigeration equipment have made the decentralized slaughterhouse operation both efficient and profitable. Other factors promoting deconcentration (cited by Arnould) included lower wages in nonmetropolitan areas, increased information, increased specialization, changes in wholesale distribution methods reducing the need for branch house systems, raw material procurement changes, federal grading systems, and reduced barriers to entry.

Arnould's study shows that the percentage of total cattle slaughter by the four largest firms in the industry declined from 51.5 percent to 29.5 percent between 1950 and 1962. However, the market share for the next four firms increased slightly over the same period. Thus for the ten largest firms in the industry the percentage change of market share between 1950 and 1962 went from 60.2 to 39.9 percent.[14]

The most significant changes in technology contributing to both deconcentration and decentralization (with accompanying job attrition) include refrigeration improvements both within the plant and for transit operations, electric cutting knives, mechanical kill lines and on-the-rail systems. Taken together, these developments make for a new optimal size slaughterhouse and packing plant, accompanied by marked changes in job mix and related factors crucial to collective bargaining.

Arnould's comments on labor cost differentials between the national packers and the smaller independents are based on a Bureau of Labor Statistics survey published in November, 1963.[15] In Arnould's view, "union pressure on the national packers is sufficiently stronger than on

[13] Richard J. Arnould, *Changing Patterns of Concentration in the Meat Packing Industry,* unpublished M.S. thesis, Iowa State University, Ames, 1965.

[14] *Ibid.,* pp. 47–48.

[15] BLS Bull. No. 1415, *Industry Wage Survey: Meat Products,* Washington, D.C.: U.S. Government Printing Office, 1963.

independent packers to cause considerable differences in wages as reflected in labor costs."[16]

Arnould continues:

> The data are sufficient to support a wage differential between small and large firms. In each region except the Pacific, earnings of workers in multi-plant companies are higher than those of workers in single plant companies. Taken nationally, the average divergence between multi-plant and single plant firms is 75 cents per hour. In the Midwest the difference is 60 cents per hour. In federally inspected plants the average hourly earnings are reported to be $1.02 higher than in nonfederally inspected plants. In metropolitan areas the average hourly wage is 24 cents higher than nonmetropolitan plants. The average hourly wage is 68 cents higher in plants with 500 or more workers than in smaller plants. There is a $1.15 difference between those plants where the majority of the workers are under union contract and those having none or a minority of union employees. It is interesting to note that only in the Middle West is the non-metropolitan wage higher than the metropolitan wage. This is caused by the major decentralization of the leading companies centered in Chicago, Omaha, and other Midwest cities. The majority of their new plants have remained in the area but at nonmetropolitan areas.[17]

The labor cost differential continues to be a problem for the national packers, although the writer would judge that more recent data would show less of a gap than the figures cited by Arnould.

CURRENT PROBLEMS RELATING TO JOB SECURITY

Nearly all economists as well as management leaders subscribe to the proposition that the only true route to higher material standards of living is through increasing productivity per man-hour. Arbitrators, whether lawyers or labor economists, also appear dedicated to the American way of regarding increases in productive efficiency as the ultimate goal of our economy. A recent study by James Gross of Cornell University[18] appears to verify empirically the foregoing generalization. Professor Gross has studied published arbitration decisions on issues relating to subcontracting and out-of-unit transfers of work. He concludes as follows:

> This analysis has considered standards of judgment or value orientations and their influence in the decision-making process of labor arbitration. Examination of arbitral opinion on management rights, subcontracting, and out-of-unit transfers of work has borne witness to the existence of a dominant value theme—efficiency, as the *summum bonum*.[19]

Professor Gross perhaps has not made enough allowance for a crucial consideration for experienced arbitrators. This is the constraint

---

[16] Arnould, *op. cit.*, p. 62. The labor cost problem posed for the national packers by the independents will be commented on again later in this paper.

[17] *Ibid.*, pp. 62–63.

[18] James A. Gross, "Value Judgments in the Decisions of Labor Arbitrators," *Industrial and Labor Relations Review*, Oct., 1967, 21:55–72.

[19] *Ibid.*, p. 70.

that requires deciding contract interpretation disputes in terms of how the contract is actually written rather than in terms of what might now be the desire of one party or the other or in terms of the value judgments of the arbitrator.[20] On subcontracting, for example, many contracts are silent. If the contract is silent on a particular subject, many arbitrators hold that management retains full discretion to act unless the union can prove that such management action conflicts with a specific provision of the agreement.[21]

It is essential to forego further comment on Professor Gross's intriguing empirical demonstration that arbitrators, just like everyone else, worship at the altar of efficiency. The main reason for introducing such evidence at this point is to stress that recent changes in industrial structure, technology, and location have provided the major labor relations challenge to both management and union leaders in the meat packing industry. Illustrations can be found of both constructive and destructive responses to this challenge.

The present analysis is predicated on two basic propositions that pose a source of potential union-management conflict at least in the short run, both in contract negotiation and in contract administration. These propositions may be stated as follows:

1. Management must retain freedom to innovate in terms of technology, structure of industrial operations, and location of plants, involving the shutting down of obsolete installations and the construction of optimal size units.

2. Employees are entitled to contractual protection of bargaining unit work opportunities to the maximum extent consistent with point 1 above and to negotiated provisions for cushioning the impact upon them of either technological displacement or loss of work occasioned by plant closures and/or removal to a different location.

UNION EMPHASIS ON JOB SECURITY

Neither the UPWA nor the Amalgamated would last very long if they did not supply convincing evidence to their members that they were doing everything in their power to protect job rights and improve wages and fringe benefits at the same time. The worst sin in the labor movement is that of bargaining backwards. At the same time, union leaders are cognizant of economic reality. The economics of the packing industry require the kind of structural, technological, and locational changes that have occurred in recent years and which are still in progress. Yet, whatever the long run beneficial economic effects may be, the blunt

---

[20] Many references can be cited to substantiate that the overwhelming majority of management practitioners, union representatives, and arbitrators adhere to the so-called "judicial school" of contract interpretation rather than the so-called "problem-solving school." That is, in most contractual relationships the parties make clear that they jointly desire the arbitrator to interpret the contract as it is written and to decide the dispute in this frame of reference. They do not want him to mediate a solution nor to innovate. See, for example, Harold W. Davey, "The Arbitrator Views the Agreement," *Labor Law Journal*, Dec., 1961, 12:1161–76.

[21] Some arbitrators, however, are fond of the "implied limitations" theory and will apply the "good faith" test in reviewing the employer's discretionary action. For full discussion see the article by Gross, cited *supra,* note 18, and references cited therein.

fact is that unions bargain for employees who are displaced in the short
run by technological change or locational shifts. The displaced worker
takes no comfort from the economist's bland assurance that in the long
run there may be no such thing as technological or structural unemployment. The displaced worker in meat packing expects, needs, and deserves an answer to his problem in the short run.

Unemployment for the packinghouse worker is made even more
serious by two factors: (1) Meat packing work is sufficiently distinctive
in nature that it is difficult to find suitable alternative employment opportunities for those who have been permanently displaced.[22] (2) Many
displaced packinghouse workers are Negroes who regrettably encounter
more than usual difficulties in obtaining alternative employment because
of the discrimination factor. Still another factor that complicates the
reemployment problem for former packinghouse workers is that they
have been accustomed to earning fairly good money not easily matched
by the firms that may have employment to offer.

These in brief are some of the reasons job security has been of paramount importance in recent meat packing negotiations.

SUMMARY OF 1967 ARMOUR CONTRACT CHANGES[23]

The preceding analysis supports UPWA's preoccupation with
strengthening severance pay provisions or technological adjustment pay
(TAP), as it is called at Armour. It explains the stress on liberalizing
transfer rights to new or relocated plants and lengthening the official
notification period of intent to close an existing facility. The 1967
agreements with the major packers, led off by the Armour contract, reflect all these considerations. For example, plant closing notification was
extended in the Armour contract to six months instead of the former
90 days.

The two unions did not allow their concern about protecting job
security to divert them from pressuring management for substantial wage
increases. The 1967–70 Armour contract provided for a 12-cent per hour
increase following ratification and 11-cent per hour increases effective
September 1, 1968, and September 1, 1969. The so-called "float" from
prior cost-of-living adjustments is also incorporated in the basic wage
rate schedules effective under the new agreement. The escalator clause is
continued under the 1967–70 contract.

Conventional fringes were by no means ignored in the 1967 bargaining. Pension benefits were increased from $3.25 per month per year
of service to $5.00 per month, effective January 1, 1968. Furthermore,
the new agreement provides for a linkage between pension rights and
severance pay. In plant or department closing, a displaced worker who
has not yet qualified for a full unreduced pension may receive his separation pay and retain his right to a full vested pension when he reaches

[22] Several studies authorized by the Armour Automation Committee conclusively
support this generalization.
[23] References to the 1967–70 Armour contract provisions are based on a summary
furnished by the Chicago law firm of Cotton, Watt, Jones and King, which represents
UPWA.

age 65. Those employees eligible under the age 55-twenty years of service pension combination arrangement may elect to take separation pay and defer their pension to age 62 at which time they will be eligible for nonactuarially reduced pensions. Prior to the 1967 agreement, a displaced worker had to make a difficult choice between separation pay *or* a heavily reduced early retirement pension; he could not collect both.

The 1967 agreement provides for early retirement with full pension benefits at age 62 for any worker with ten or more years of service. Full vesting is now provided for any Armour worker with ten or more years of service who leaves Armour's service for any reason at all. When he reaches age 65 he will receive a pension in accordance with his previous years of service with Armour.

Improvements in health and welfare features, paid vacations, and paid holidays were also negotiated in 1967.

The 1967 package of wage and fringe gains appears to be a good one from the worker's standpoint. However, it does not seem to be an unreasonable one in terms of fulfilling management's obligations to incumbent employees. The labor cost of this package is sufficient, however, to be a source of concern to the major packers who are "threatened" by the tough competition of "small" independent packers, many of whom are nonunion and some of whom are militantly anti-union.

ECONOMIC PROBLEM POSED BY INDEPENDENT PACKERS

The Armour pattern appears to have been substantially followed in peaceful negotiations to date with Wilson, Rath, Morrell, Cudahy, and Swift.[24] The labor cost burdens of the 1967 Armour package have thus been assumed by the major packers and some of the larger "nonmajors" such as Rath and Cudahy. Somewhat ironically, this development should give rise to common cause between the principal firms in the industry and the two major unions in the industry. Both the national packers and the unions are doubtless concerned about the competition from a considerable number of independent packers who are either nonunion or are dealing with unaffiliated (independent) labor organizations that may be willing to settle for considerably less than the 1967 pattern just summarized. Considering the fact that labor cost is still a fairly substantial element of total cost in the packing industry, the major packers and the unions have a mutual concern over the threat to current standards from what both would *now* regard as "substandard" wage and fringe benefit levels.

The specifics of this intra-industry conflict are difficult to discuss briefly. Profit margins have historically been fairly slim in meat packing as an industry.[25] The technological and marketing changes that have induced the big packers to decentralize and abandon large plants in

---

[24] Personal communication from Irving M. King, Esq., of Cotton, Watt, Jones and King, dated Sept. 26, 1967. Morrell signed with UPWA subsequent to the receipt of Mr. King's letter.

[25] Arnould observes that the meat packing industry "shows a much lower rate of return on net worth, total assets, and sales than most other industries." Richard J. Arnould, *op. cit.*, p. 69.

favor of modern smaller plants close to the source of livestock are still
going on. It may not be an exaggeration to state that industrial peace
in major meat packing contracts in 1967 is directly, though not openly,
related to the fear on the part of the major packers that the independent
firms in the industry would gain too much ground if economic conflict
developed during the 1967 negotiation. Now those who are signed up
have three years of industrial peace in which to stay ahead of or at least
to keep pace with their competitors. The major packers at this point
should have a staunch ally in the major unions. Both UPWA and the
Amalgamated, wherever they represent workers of newer and smaller
plants, may be expected to work hard to keep the wage and fringe package as close to the standards already established by the negotiations with
Armour, Swift, Wilson, *et al.* as they possibly can.

We are accustomed to hearing that politics makes strange bedfellows. In the present fluid and dynamic state of the meat packing
industry, it can be said that labor relations appears to be making strange
bedfellows. The UPWA, for example, although accustomed over many
years to bitter conflict relationships with the major packers, now finds
itself negotiating on a reasonably satisfactory basis with its former "ene-
mies." At the the same time it is carrying on the fight for unionization
and higher economic standards among the proliferating number of small
slaughtering and packing establishments in Iowa and other midwestern
states. In this effort, I am confident that UPWA enjoys at least the tacit
approval of the major packers.

UNIONIZATION AMONG NEW FIRMS

How effective UPWA's drive will be among the new entries in the
packing industry is still problematical. Successes to date have been approximately matched by failures. In some cases, employees of the newer,
smaller plants have elected to be represented by an independent local
union rather than to join either UPWA or the Amalgamated. The two
affiliated unions regard the local independent unions as company-dom-
inated, "dummy" organizations. However, they have not always been
able to prove this to the satisfaction of the National Labor Relations
Board.

One of the main difficulties faced in unionizing employees of the
newer entries in the slaughtering and packing fields is that most of the
new firms are located in small towns in rural areas. Typically these
towns have very few job opportunities of an industrial nature. Also
many in the labor force possess the traditional suspicion of unions.

Another difficulty is the high cost of organizing these small establishments. Unions must operate on a budget. They have to consider
the cost of organizing new groups of employees. Their primary financial
commitment must be the amount necessary to maintain bargaining
relationships for employees with firms already unionized. In the case
of UPWA in particular this means precious little money or staff is
available for new organizing ventures. The difficulty is especially

troublesome when the membership base is being whittled down steadily by the continuing impact of technology.

The organizing task facing the unions is, of course, exacerbated when the new firms choose to resort to violations of the National Labor Relations Act as a means of defeating organization efforts. This brings us back to the theme that management gets the kind of unionism it deserves. The UPWA has demonstrated during the 1967 negotiations with the major packers its willingness to bargain out a settlement peacefully. It has also recently shown a willingness to bend backward to save job opportunities in the case of the Hormel plant at Fort Dodge, Iowa.[26] Thus the UPWA can show a record of resonsible conduct when dealing with management representatives that accept unionism and collective bargaining. When pressed, however, UPWA will continue to fight fire with fire as it did in Harlan in 1966 and 1967 and as it was prepared to do in the confrontation with Iowa Beef Packers, Inc., at Fort Dodge in 1966. In the writer's judgment, violence was avoided in the latter dispute only because of the strong personal chemistry of Governor Harold E. Hughes who mediated this dispute with a heavy hand.[27]

Many of the newer firms have not attempted to influence their employees in the latter's decision as to whether they wished to be represented by a labor organization. Where management has kept its hands off (as it properly should, in my judgment) the employees have voted for union representation in some cases and in others they have voted the union down. This is as it should be. The choice is one for employees to make. I believe in the present national labor policy which declares it to be an unfair practice for either management or unions to interfere with or coerce employees when the latter are making their decision as to whether to form and join unions or to refrain from self-organization.

Management has been prohibited by law since 1935 from interfering with the right of workers to organize and to bargain collectively through representatives of their own choosing. Unions have been prohibited by law since 1947 from interfering with the right of workers to refrain from unionizing if that is their desire. It is easy to recognize the legitimacy of these twin rights in principle, but it is hard to guarantee both simultaneously in particular cases. Nevertheless, we should be sufficiently mature in labor relations to honor in practice the right of workers to make a free choice on this crucially important question. Once the choice has been made it should be respected. The meat packing industry has some of the most encouraging examples of constructive labor relations to be found in American industry today. Regrettably, it can also still

[26] Des Moines *Register,* Oct. 3, 1967. Hormel had served the required one-year notices to 150 employees. However, the company agreed to rescind the notices after UPWA agreed to incentive pay reductions.

[27] Whistler's study, cited *supra,* note 5, confirms the writer's personal impression as to the importance of the role played by Governor Hughes in effecting a settlement. Whistler interviewed key management and union representatives who were directly involved in the dispute.

furnish some distasteful examples of labor relations at its most primitive level.

FUTURE PROBLEMS

The pattern of decentralization and deconcentration is now firmly established in slaughtering and packing operations. It is equally clear that we have not yet reached the optimal point in technological advance. Thus the probability is that job attrition, changes in job mix, and unemployment due to locational shifts will continue to be the focal point of contract negotiation in the predictable future.

There appear to be some factors that might warrant pessimistic predictions on future labor relations in the industry. These include the following:

1. Union organizational conflict between affiliated and independent unions competing for the allegiance of workers in new plants.

2. The possibility of a serious cost squeeze resulting from increased labor costs combined with intensified competition that precludes rationalizing increased costs by increasing prices.

3. Some uncertainties as to the nature and quality of future union leadership in UPWA and the Amalgamated after Helstein and Gorman leave the scene.

In the writer's judgment, however, the grounds for an optimistic prognosis are more convincing than those arguing for a pessimistic outlook. The factors supporting such a conclusion include the following:

1. Visibly improving union-management relationships in a number of former trouble spots.

2. Continued effective functional cooperation between UPWA and the Amalgamated that may lead ultimately to an organic merger.

3. Increasingly effective use of joint study committees in long-range problems and joint willingness to negotiate in meaningful fashion well in advance of contract expiration deadlines.[28]

4. More intelligent use of informed neutrals in difficult bargaining situations and better factual information as a result of empirical research by university labor economists, principally those carried out pursuant to Armour Automation Committee requests.

5. Visibly improved contract administration, with apparently fewer wildcat stoppages and fewer cases going to arbitration, thus indicating a disposition by the parties to "live with" the agreements they have negotiated as they are written.

DETERMINANTS OF CONSTRUCTIVE LABOR RELATIONS

Whatever the industry or unions involved, there exist certain "first principles" of constructive labor relations. Some "first principles" that

---

[28] The 1967–70 Armour pact is an excellent illustration of this point. For a perceptive analysis by a leading participant in the Armour negotiations, see Fred Livingston's paper at the 20th Annual New York University Conference on Labor, delivered in New York City Apr. 19, 1967. Livingston is an attorney who represents Armour & Co. in contract negotiations. The NYU conference proceedings will be published by The Bureau of National Affairs, Inc.

are as relevant to meat packing as to any other field of union-management relations include the following:[29]

1. Effective collective bargaining requires an intelligent understanding by both management and union of the needs, aspirations, objectives, and problems of the other party.

2. Management must recognize the union as an integral part of the total industrial relations picture. Once management has done so, the union must respond in kind by working to utilize collective bargaining as a method of problem solving.

3. Both management and the union must have a healthy regard for the rights and responsibilities of the other party to the contract. Although collective bargaining is a process involving conflict, in a constructive relationship there must be a continuing effort to reach workable accommodations and compromises of conflicting basic interests.

4. Finally, in order to satisfy the points already made, there must be leadership of maturity and competence on both sides of the bargaining table.

The 1967–70 contracts between the major packers and the two affiliated unions show promise of constructive labor relations in the years immediately ahead. The picture is perhaps less encouraging among some of the independent packers who have been recently unionized or who are currently at the stage of fighting off unionization, by fair means or foul.

---

[29] This summary statement is adapted from a fuller exposition in Harold W. Davey, *Contemporary Collective Bargaining*, Englewood Cliffs, N.J.: Prentice-Hall, Inc., 2nd ed., 1959, p. 38. See also pp. 363–65 for the writer's conception of the key elements in "positive" collective bargaining.

Index